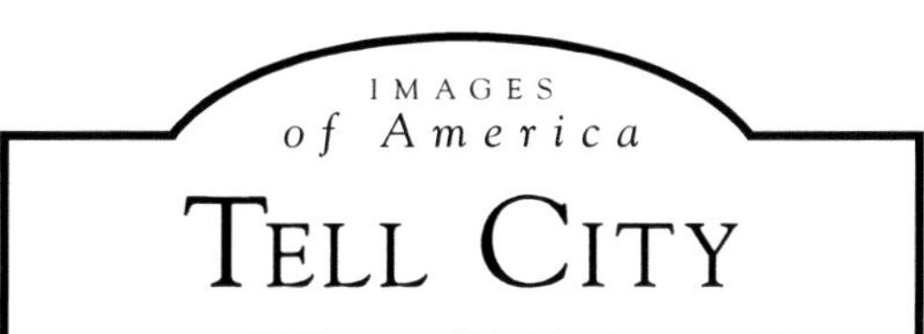
IMAGES
of America
TELL CITY

ON THE COVER: Shown on the cover is the 600 block of Main Street around 1900. Identified in the photograph are Johnson Peckenpaugh (left) and Claude Howell (11th from left). (Courtesy of Tell City Historical Society.)

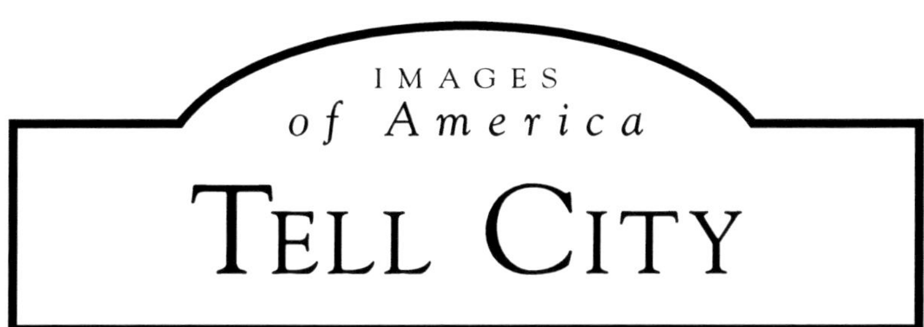

Chris Cail

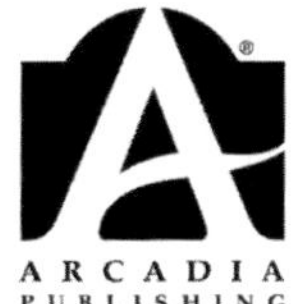

ISBN 978-1-4671-2653-3

Published by Arcadia Publishing
Charleston, South Carolina

Printed in the United States of America

Library of Congress Control Number: 2017931441

For all general information, please contact Arcadia Publishing:
Telephone 843-853-2070
Fax 843-853-0044
E-mail sales@arcadiapublishing.com
For customer service and orders:
Toll-Free 1-888-313-2665

Visit us on the Internet at www.arcadiapublishing.com

*I dedicate this book to the citizens of Tell City
and the Tell City Historical Society.*

Contents

ACKNOWLEDGMENTS

Tell City is fortunate to have so many people dedicated to preserving its history and willing to work hard at doing just that. A book like this would not be possible without the help of all those who are willing to give their time and energy to share the stories and photographs of city.

There are so many people to thank. First and foremost, I want to thank the Tell City Historical Society, which has contributed numerous photographs and history to make this book possible. Also someone who helped me that I could never thank is Charlie Schreiber. I never had the opportunity to meet him, but if he had not preserved and written down the history of Tell City, this book would have been lacking. His foresight to record the history of Tell City has allowed our citizens to relive the past through his words and images. I would also like to thank those who helped me throughout the process of writing this book—Joan Hess, Mark Ress, Mark Laflin, and the *Perry County News*.

The people of Tell City should be proud that their traditions and past are in such caring hands and help support the Tell City Historical Society.

Unless otherwise noted, all images are from the author's personal collection.

Introduction

Tell City is an unusual city. It was not the scene of a battle with Indians, and it did not grow from a campground of settlers going west. It was carefully planned by a group of Swiss people, immigrants from northern Switzerland who spoke and wrote in the German language, in Cincinnati, Ohio. They named their organization the Swiss Colonization Society and discussed making a city of their own. First, they would need a place for their ideal city, so committees of men were sent to find such a place. There were several requirements. One was that the city must be on a river. If industries were to develop, a means of transportation must be available. In a wilderness, the best transportation was by rivers. The city must also have space for straight, wide streets.

Several states were considered. Only after much discussion was this area in southern Indiana, on the Ohio River, selected. Land in Kentucky was more level, but people were held as slaves in that state. The Swiss believed in freedom for everyone; therefore, Kentucky was not acceptable. Then the Swiss noticed the beautiful southern Indiana hills that looked so much like parts of their homeland. When they found the land could be purchased, they decided that this was the place they wanted for their city. At some point, people from Germany joined with the Swiss in the society. Their aims and purposes were the same—to make a city where industries could develop and grow—and they spoke the same language.

Individuals purchased shares of ownership in the planned city. One share entitled a person to one lot for a dwelling and one garden plot. When each shareowner was given his land, he agreed to the following: He would build a brick or frame house on his lot. The house would have two rooms and be worth not less than $125. It would be built within one year after he settled here. The Swiss Colonization Society would provide the materials for the house, and he would repay the society within three years.

At first, they planned to name this city Helvetia. That was an early Latin name for the area where Switzerland is, and the Swiss still use that name for their homeland. It was the only name agreeable to the people who spoke German. Then it was decided that here in America this city should have an American-sounding name. Wanting to proclaim the Swiss origin and honor their hero William Tell, they chose Tell City.

It took much work and planning to build Tell City. A surveyor was hired to survey the three-square-mile area and plan city blocks and streets. In March 1858, the lots were distributed. By September 1858, the records show, "there were in the settlement 262 dwelling houses." The streets were laid out. Streets running north and south were given numbers. Streets running east and west were given names of famous people. One street was named for a composer, Mozart; another for a famous educator, Pestalozzi. Some streets were named for American statesmen such as Franklin, Washington, and Jefferson. Some were named for inventors such as Watt and Fulton, and, of course, one street was named for William Tell. Tell Street was planned to be one of the most important streets in the new city.

Where nice paved streets are today, in 1858 there were high hills or swampland. The Swiss and German people who came here were hardworking and patient. They had known they would have to work hard to build their city in the wilderness. The hills were leveled, and the swamp areas were filled in. After the houses were built, they constructed factories and, most importantly, schools. Education was very important.

The first school was built in 1859. It was just one large room (30 feet wide by 40 feet long), but it had a second story. Upstairs there was space where the schoolteacher could live. In the beginning, all classes were taught in German, but English was the language of the United States, and eventually classes were changed to English.

Music has always been important in Tell City. There have been bands, musical programs in the town, and choirs in all the churches with organs or pianos to accompany them. Parades with marching bands were held often—on the Fourth of July, at the beginning of the Christmas season, and on any other special occasion. Everyone turned out to see the parades.

The first church was a Catholic church, built in the 1000 block of Main Street. Later, St. Paul's built a twin-spired church that housed the town clock. That has been replaced by a modern building at the corner of Jefferson and Main Streets. The first Protestant church was the German Evangelical Church, established in 1861. The church was erected in 1863 at Tenth and Jefferson Streets, where its newer building stands today. The name evolved to Evangelical United Church of Christ. Other churches were soon established, and congregations had church buildings constructed. The Methodists organized their church in 1892. The first building was on Ninth Street. In 1923, the United Methodist Church building was erected at Tenth and Mozart Streets. Now, Tell City has over 10 denominations.

Boats played an important part in Tell City life. They provided the only way people and their possessions could travel in this area before roads were built. All of the original settlers came to Tell City by boat—some from the east, through Cincinnati, and some through New Orleans, up the Mississippi and Ohio Rivers. Supplies came by boat, and manufactured goods were literally shipped out of Tell City by boat. The river was Tell City's early lifeline.

The river provided recreation also. People have enjoyed the river in various ways. For many years, there were showboats that brought entertainment to Tell City. There were also moonlight excursion boats that took large groups of people for trips up and down the river. On those boats, music was provided for dancing. Those excursion boats were popular—they were the nightclubs of the old days.

Smaller boats also were used for entertainment. People would go by boat to a favorite sandbar or to Rock Island for a picnic. Rock Island, up the river from Cannelton, is now covered by the river. This happened when the locks and dam were constructed above Cannelton.

In the 1880s, Tell City was an important port. It was one of the biggest ports between Louisville, Kentucky, and Evansville, Indiana. In 1889, the Louisville and Evansville Mail Line named a new boat *Tell City*. But river transportation was declining. Soon, the railroad became an important means of transporting goods manufactured in Tell City, such as furniture. Rail transportation took much business from riverboat companies.

The Ohio River gave an advantage to Tell City by providing transportation. However, there were times when the river caused much trouble. Heavy rains added to melting snow in the mountains near the source of the river caused floods. Some floods were very bad. The flood in 1937 was the worst ever known by people in the city. People had not believed there could be such a flood. It covered much of Tell City. Upstate, other Indiana people heard of Tell City's tremendous problems, and they provided all kinds of supplies and medicine. The Red Cross worked to guide the citizens through the emergency. Some families, who could not stay in their houses because of the water, lived with friends who had houses on higher ground. Others were housed in churches. One church prepared meals, many meals, for those people who needed food.

After the floodwater subsided, the citizens of Tell City said, "This must not happen again." The city leaders worked long and hard to get the government to build a floodwall. Now when the river rises, the gates are put into the wall. This closes some streets, but it keeps the river out of Tell City.

There is no other town in the United States that is named Tell City—probably no other town in the world with that name. It was planned and built as only a few cities have been. Tell City people purchased their lots and garden plots, built their own houses, and set up their own businesses. The Swiss Colonization Society planned a city, bought land, and sold it to people who wanted to settle Tell City. The society that began in Cincinnati moved its headquarters to Tell City about 1859. It controlled Tell City until the new city could function independently. Then it gave the remaining land to Tell City schools and to the city; closed its books; and on April 17, 1879, the Swiss Colonization Society disbanded.

Today, Tell City has a lot of interesting things to offer. Tell City Chair Company furniture may no longer be in business, but its fame and recognition still stand strong. Tell City is a proud of its Swiss heritage, offering the Schweizer Fest, a festival that has continued annually since 1958, and has always been a community that lives by ideals. It is a beautiful, clean city where neighbors help each other and everyone. If you have the chance, take time to visit the city to see for yourself.

One

Building a City

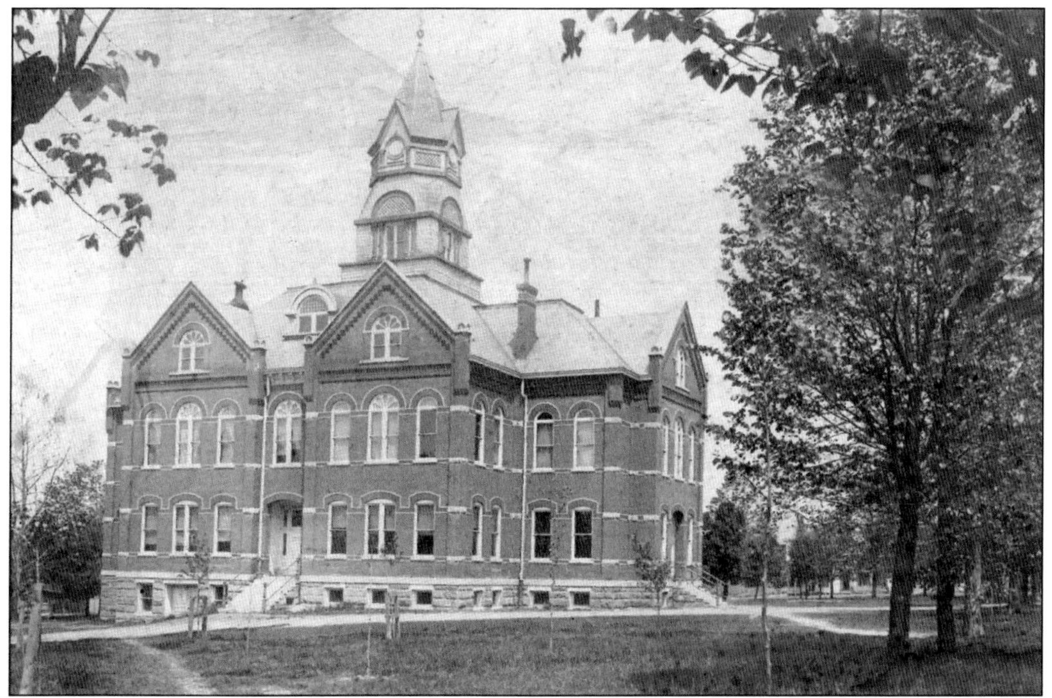

The Romanesque Revival city hall, with a central tower, was built in 1898. It is constructed of local bricks and limestone. Standing 133 feet tall atop a small rise in the center of City Park Square, the building is a focal point of the community. Note the tower—today this tower is all white, but in earlier days it appears to have been shaded a darker color.

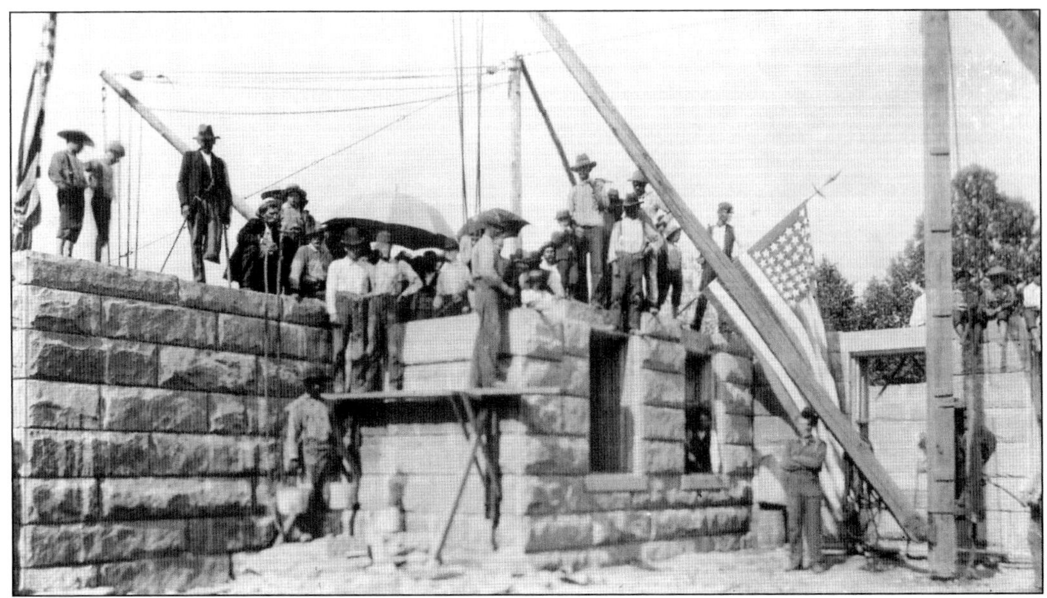

Depicted here on May 11, 1896, is foundation work and the laying of the cornerstone at city hall. The cornerstone reads: "A.P. Fenn Mayor, City Council M. Bettinger Jr., John B. Wichser, Theodore Kiefer, Chas. A. Meyenberg, Wm Schroder, Wm Kampschaefer A.D. 1896." Note the US flag with 44 stars and the gentleman missing part of his leg. (Courtesy of Tell City Historical Society.)

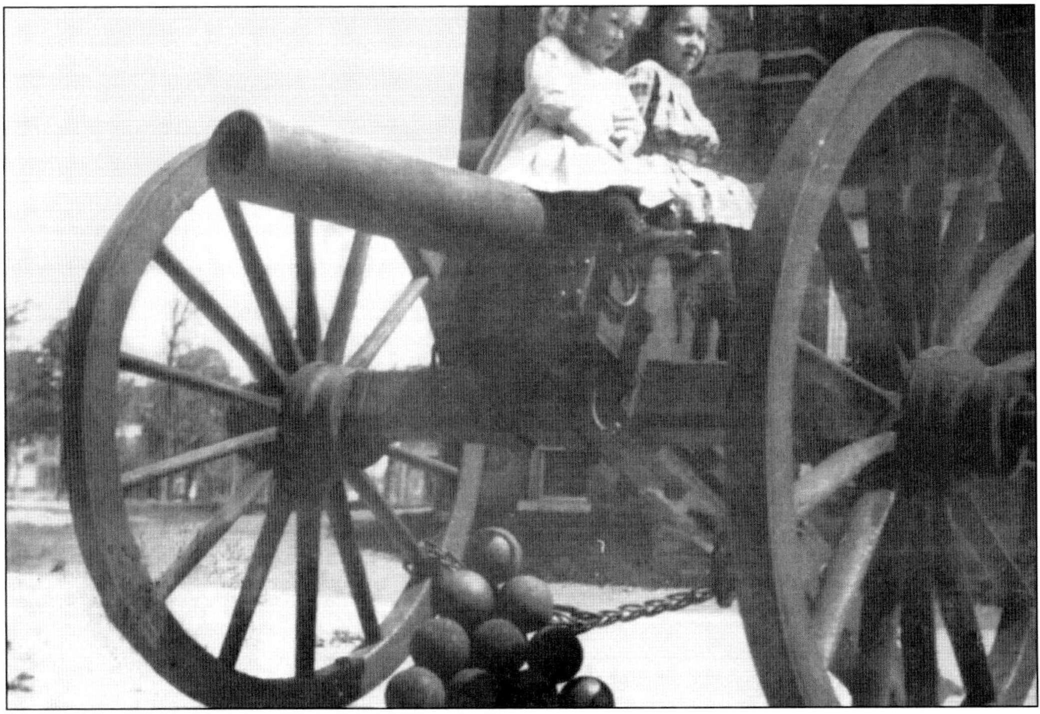

Pictured around 1916, this Civil War cannon was once in City Hall Park. It stood in front of city hall on the Main Street side. During World War II, the cannon was removed because the government had a shortage of metal. All available metal was utilized to help the war efforts. (Courtesy of Tell City Historical Society.)

There are two of these lions that were sculpted by local sculptor John Meyenberg (pictured). For many years, these lions stood on the river landing and later in the depot yard (right). They were moved to the site of Tell City's first swimming pool and later to City Hall Park. The lions are currently under restoration. (Courtesy of Mark Laflin.)

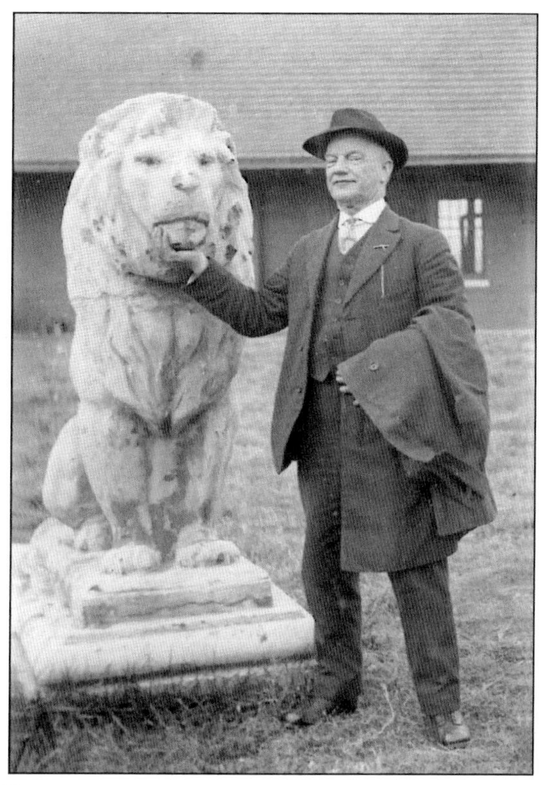

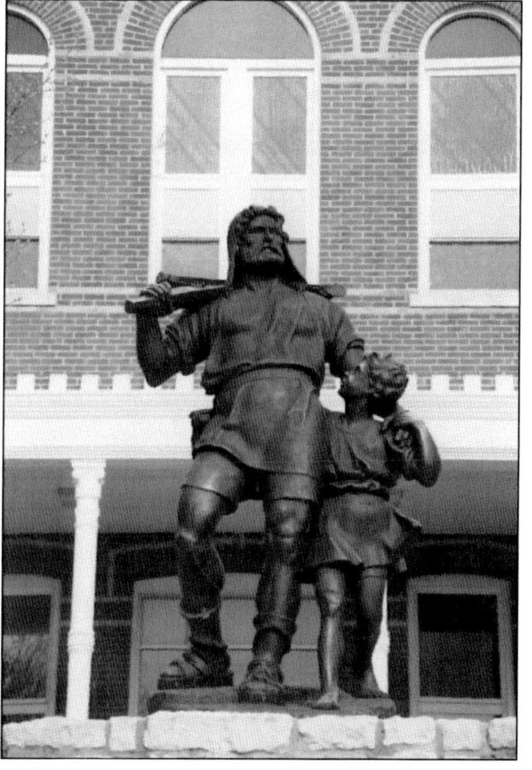

This statue of William Tell and son Walther, as well as the accompany fountain, is located in City Hall Park along Main Street. It was presented to the City of Tell City and dedicated to the people of Perry County. Before the statue was dedicated and installed, it became part of an FBI investigation; the statue was stolen while in transit to Tell City. The fountain, donated to the city by attorney Austin B. Corbin, was provided by Tell City National Bank to commemorate the bank's 100th anniversary. It was dedicated during the Schweizer Fest on August 9, 1974.

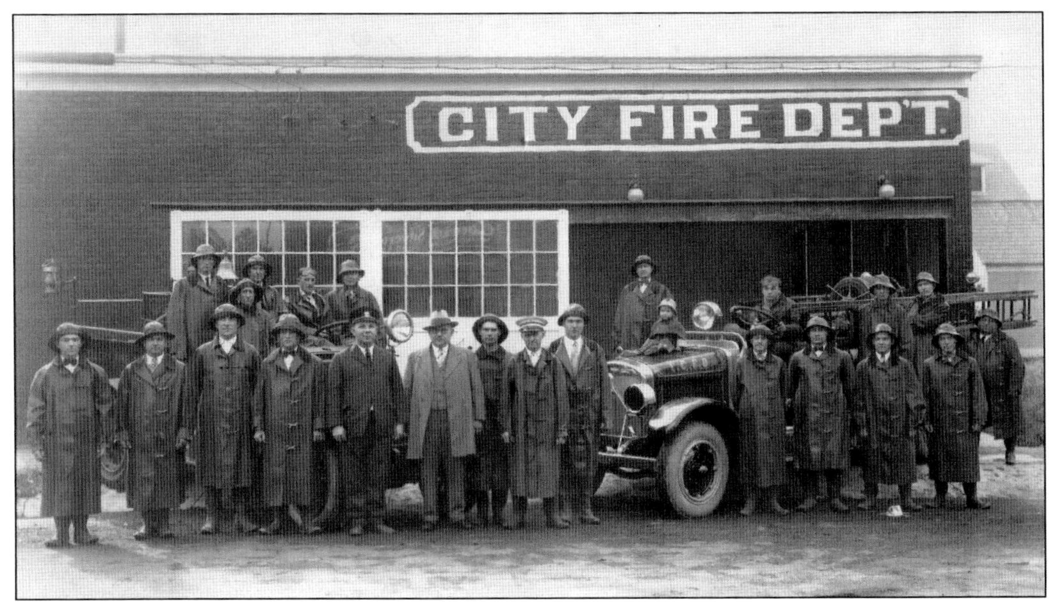

The Tell City Fire Department was located at 711 Humboldt Street. The Peter Pirsch fire truck is shown with a small child sitting atop the hood. Pictured around 1927 are, from left to right, (first row) Lee Hollander, Harry Hartz, Hobart Pyle, Lonnie Blake, Charles Hein, Mayor Jake Zoercher, Dewy Mitchell, William Hartz Sr., Jerome Richard, Ben Hartz, Roman Gaesser, Alvin Hollander, and William Logsdon; (second row) August Beumel, Andy Kallbrier, Sol Harpe, Tiny Bettinger, Louis Schertzer, Edward Hartz, Bill Bettinger, Tony Zuelly, Paul Kallbrier, Claud Dixon, and George Hess Jr.

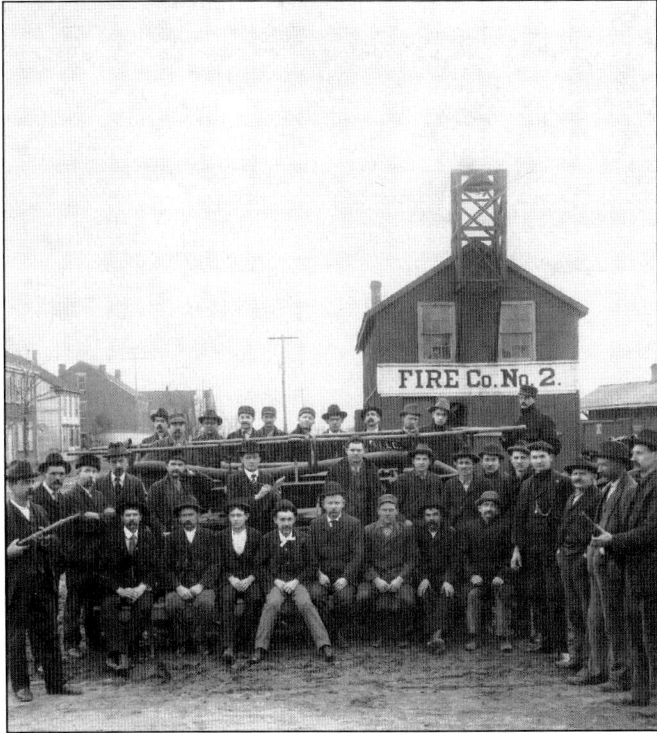

Shown is Tell City Fire Department No. 2, located at Main and Blum Streets, around 1887. Pictured are, from left to right, (seated, front row) Aleck Gass, Carl Herr, Fred Scheible, John Sheible, Fred Stettler, Lee Harr, John Rehsteiner, and Henry Krecker; (standing, middle row) William ?, Adolph Obrecht, Jacob Lipp, John Harr, John Deintzer, Ed Harrer, Leonard Herbert, John Herbert, Fred Steinauer, Henry Martin, Joe Knaebel, Louise Siebert, Louise Ziegelgruber, Sam Stettler, and William Boger; (standing, back row) Henry Truempy, Frank Ziegelgruber, Gus HerrJohn Meckert, Chas Meckert, William Stamp, Frank Schneider, Jacob Truempy, Al Herr, Ernest Stuehrk, and August Fricke.

Tell City policemen are pictured in front of the old opera house. Officer Philow Hickerson is pictured second from the left. This was Doc Hickerson's father. The rest are unidentified. (Courtesy of Tell City Historical Society.)

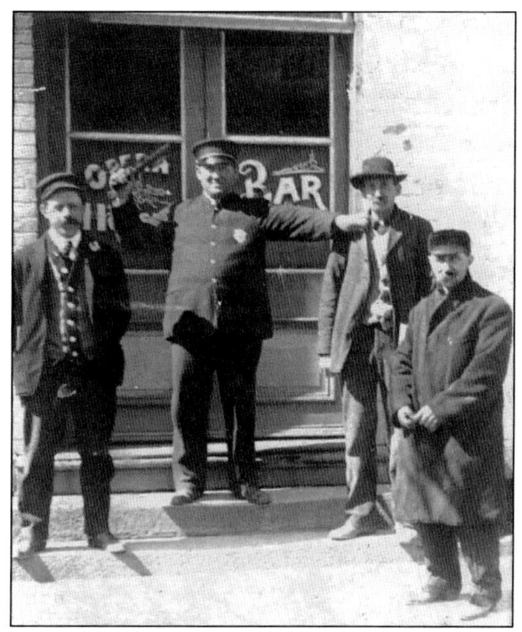

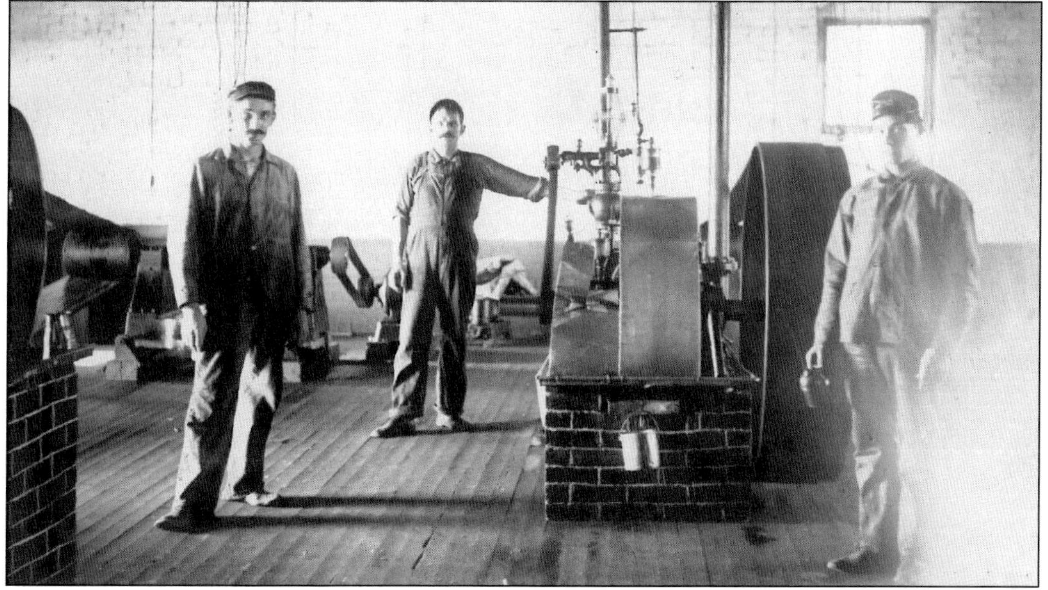

Tell City built a light plant around 1902 to provide electricity to the city. The workers pictured in this c. 1905 photograph are not identified. The plant was located on Fourth Street near the intersection of Fulton Street. In 1927, the city sold the electric utility to the Ohio River Power Company, which continued the plant operation. At one time, the plant generated all the electric energy used in Tell City, Cannelton, and Troy, as well as the Kentucky cities of Lewisport, Hawesville, Cloverport, and Irvington. During the 1937 flood, the plant was flooded and all generation temporary ceased. Because of financial problems, the Ohio River Power Company sold the plant and transmission lines back to the city in 1941. Due to the city's inability to produce enough power in a cost-efficient manner, the plant was shut down, and all power was purchased from Southern Indiana Gas and Electric. Today, Tell City's electric is provided by Indiana Municipal Power Agency (IMPA). (Courtesy of Tell City Historical Society.)

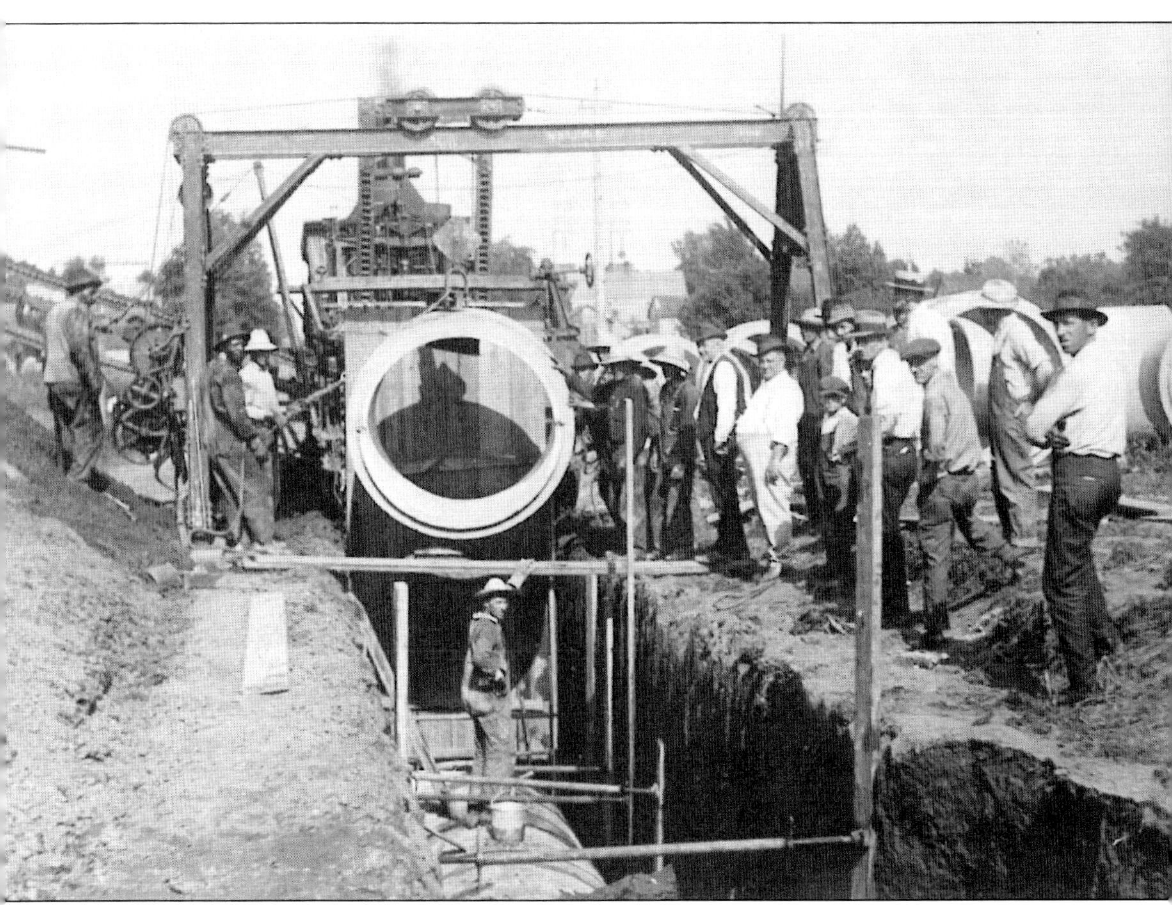

Pictured is the Twelfth Street sewer installation around 1922. The 48-inch-diameter sewer pipe was made at Cantex in the neighboring city of Cannelton. A steam shovel was used to dig the trench. Mayor John F. Hess is the gentleman in the white shirt standing in the center. (Courtesy of Tell City Historical Society.)

Morris Cail looks on as an unidentified street department employee installs the new street sign at the corner of Jefferson and Fifteenth Streets.

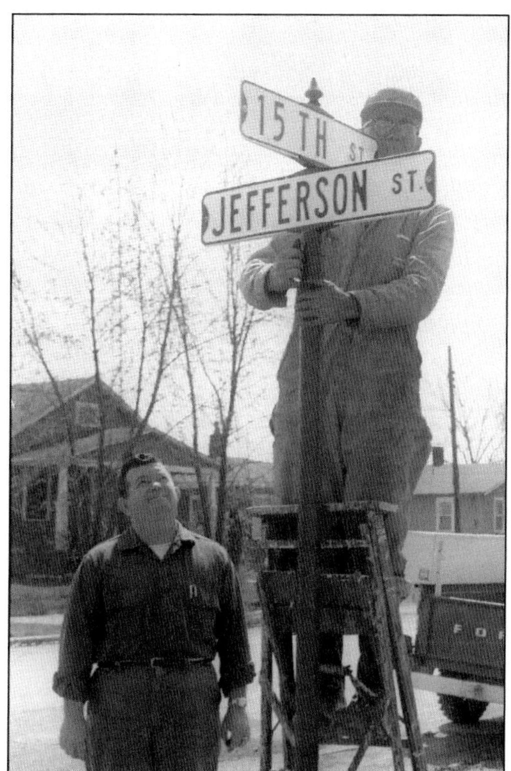

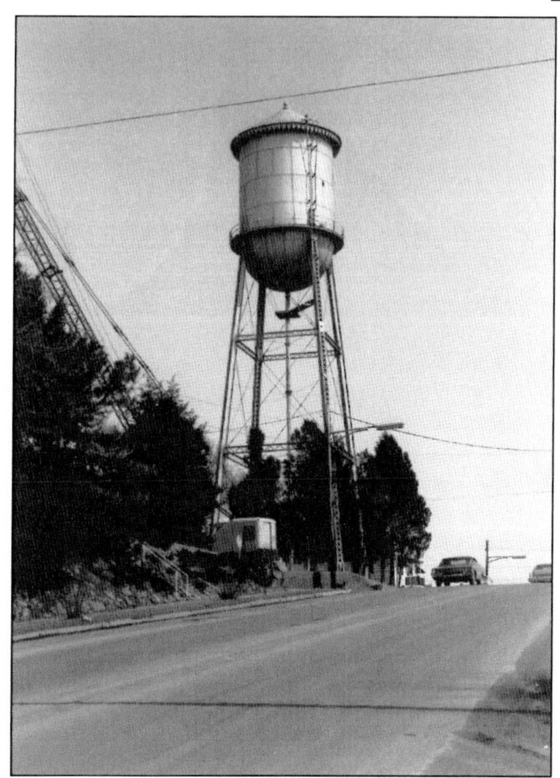

Tell City's oldest water tower was erected in 1901 and was located at Eleventh and Washington Streets. It was dismantled by Malone Construction Company in March 1978. (Courtesy of Tell City Historical Society.)

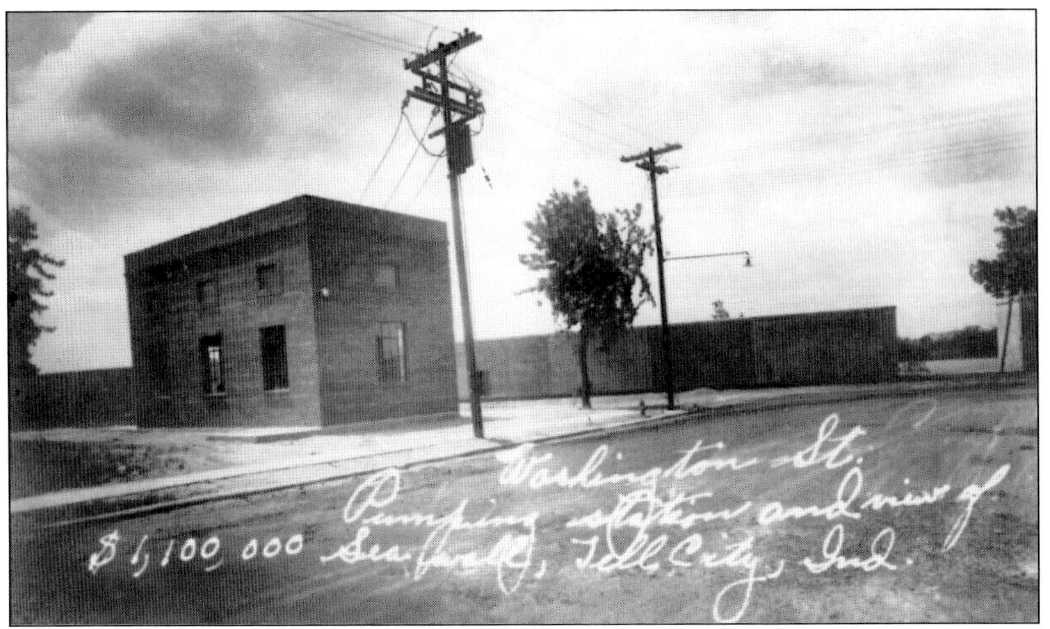

The pump house, located at the corner of Washington and Seventh Streets, is vital to the community. It was constructed when the floodwall was built. This pump house is still used today.

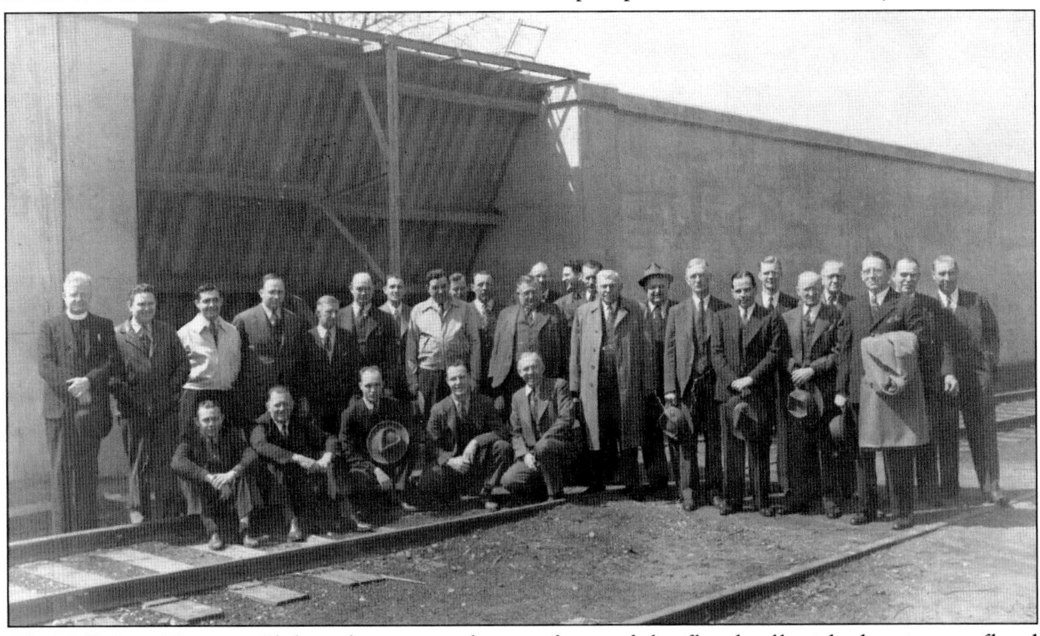

The Tell City Kiwanis Club is shown standing in front of the floodwall with the river at flood stage and the water on the other side for the first time, in March 1943. From left to right are (seated/kneeling on track) Karl Zoercher, Rev. H.H. Peters, Al G. Dauby, Tim Morris, and Emil Kroessman; (standing) Father Vollmer, Jim Meek, Anthony Oberhausen, Bill Ress, Cecil Powers, Napoleon Dixon, William Schergens, Eugene Huthsteiner, unidentified, Ralph Lipp, Chris Zoercher, Chris Fenn, Charles A. Schreiber, Al Goffinet, Jake Zoercher, Louis Zoercher, Dr. P.J. Coultas, Dr. L.C. Becker, Dr. Don Lashley, Sam Anderson, Winfield Partridge, Gene Schnock, Roy Fenn, and Jack O'Tool. (Courtesy of Tell City Historical Society.)

This image, taken at flood stage, shows that the floodwall is working and keeping the city dry. (Courtesy of Tell City Historical Society.)

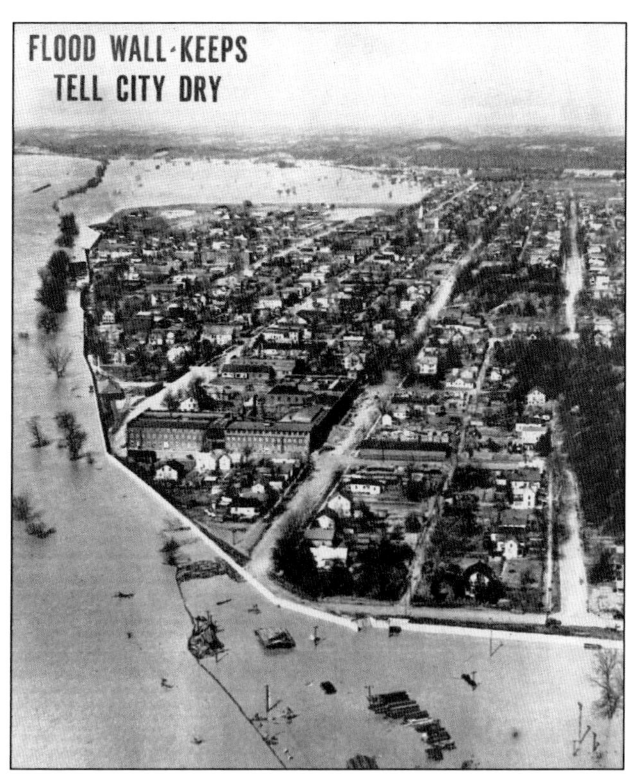

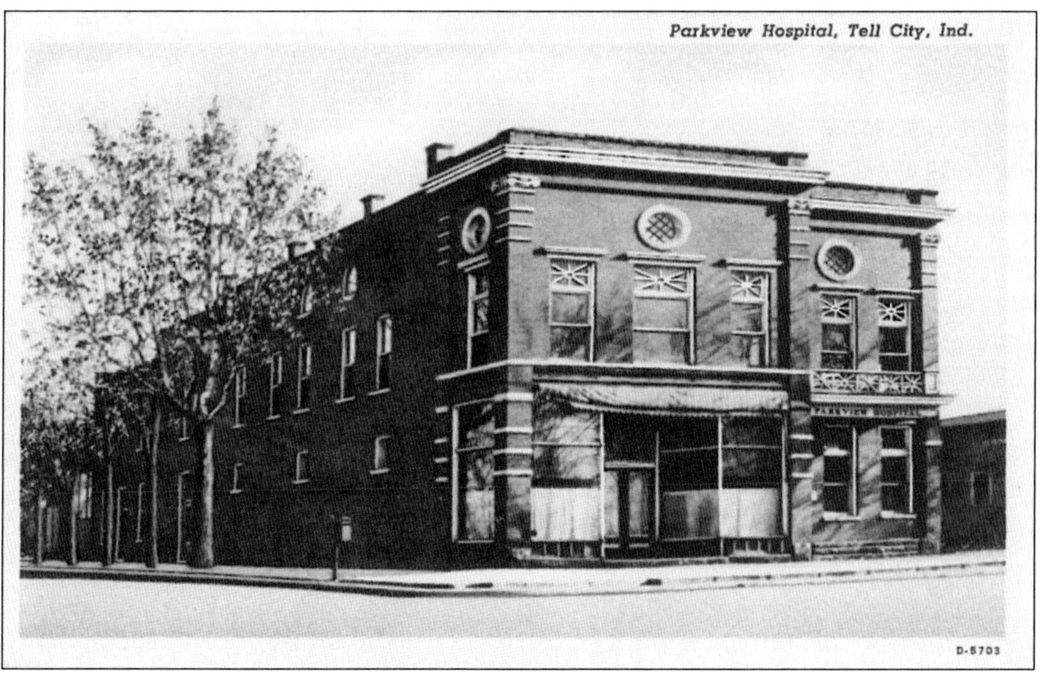

Before Parkview Hospital was located here, the building was Ferd Becker's store, where he sold groceries and dry goods. Dr. N.A. James established the Parkview Hospital. It closed after the Perry County Memorial Hospital was built in 1950. Since then, the building has been occupied by several different types of businesses.

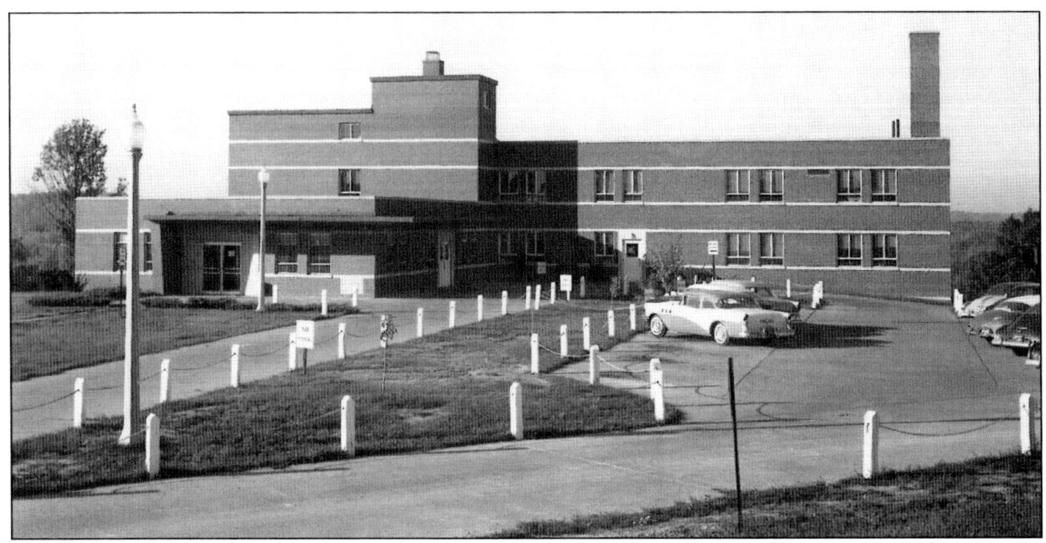

The Perry County Memorial Hospital opened for patients in October 1950. The facility was built of red brick and had 25 beds. The land on which the hospital was built was donated by Roy Fenn. Originally, the hospital was to be 50 beds but that was cut back to 25 to reduce the cost. There is an interesting story regarding the stairwells. The plan called for the walls to be covered with genuine ceramic tile. This was expensive and since these stairs would have little traffic, the hospital wanted to substitute with a much cheaper tile. However, the State Board of Health turned this idea down because the government required ceramic tile and nothing else. (Courtesy of Tell City Historical Society.)

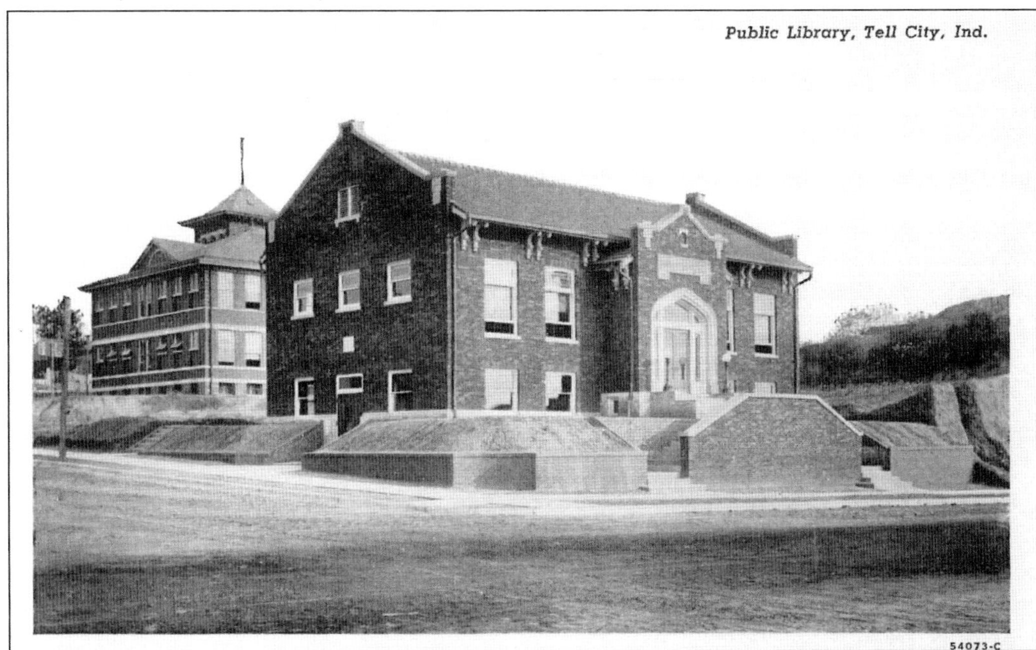

Tell City's Public Library was built in 1916 by George Hess Sr. It is located at Ninth and Franklin Streets and was one of the last Carnegie libraries built in Indiana. In 1967, an addition was built onto the back of the building. In 2002, the library moved to its new building on Tell Street. The Tell City Historical Society now occupies this structure.

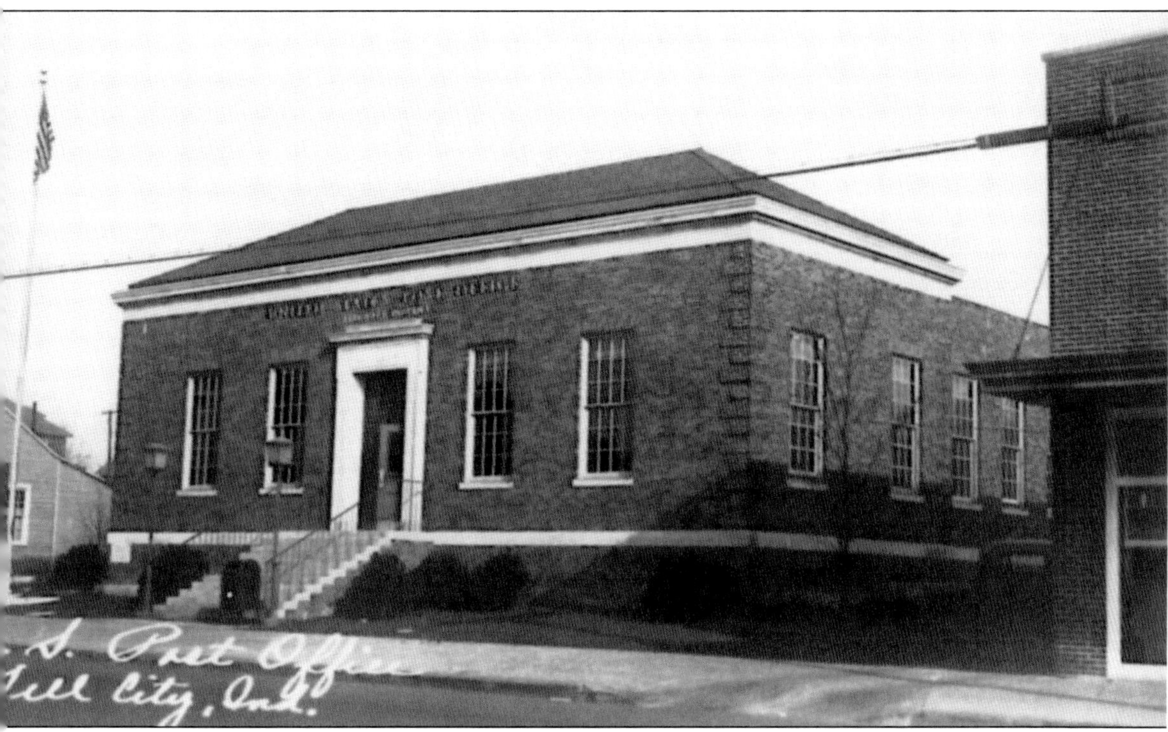

The Tell City Post Office, located at 516 Main Street, was built in 1937. During construction, the 1937 flood occurred and about a foot of water got in the building. After a new post office was built at the corner of Main and Humboldt Streets, the original post office closed in 1983. For years, the building sat empty before the Tell City Historical Society Museum was located in it. After the museum moved to its new location in the former public library in 2002, this structure became an Italian restaurant (Ryjo's) and later a sports bar (the Post).

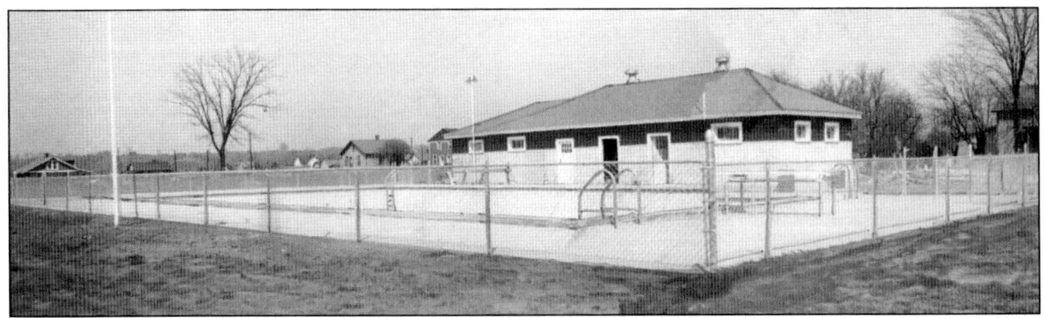

The Tell City Swimming Pool was officially dedicated in June 1937 and recorded over 20,000 entrances to the pool in the first swim season, which ended on Labor Day 1937. This pool was replaced by the present-day JFK Pool. Today, the former bathhouse is the William Tell Senior Citizens Center. The pool was filled in with the intention of it becoming an ice rink, but that never happened.

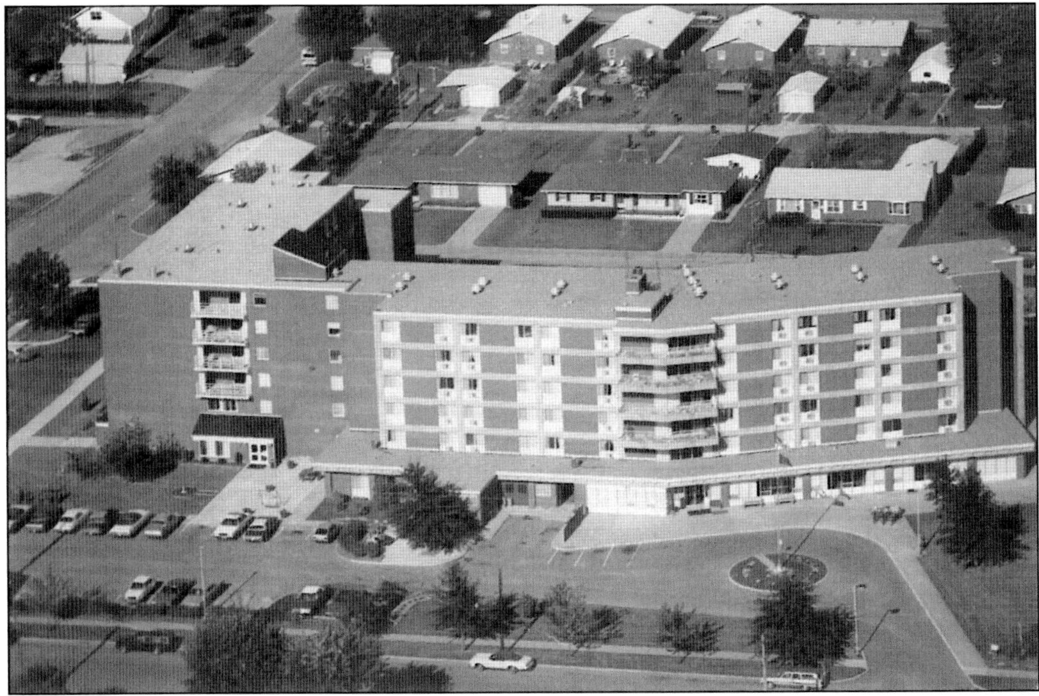

Twilight Towers (also known as High Rise), at 1648 Tenth Street, was originally constructed as a 79-unit apartment building. It was expanded to house 129 units. The apartment building is for the elderly and is managed by the Housing Authority of the City of Tell City.

Two

RIVER AND FLOODS

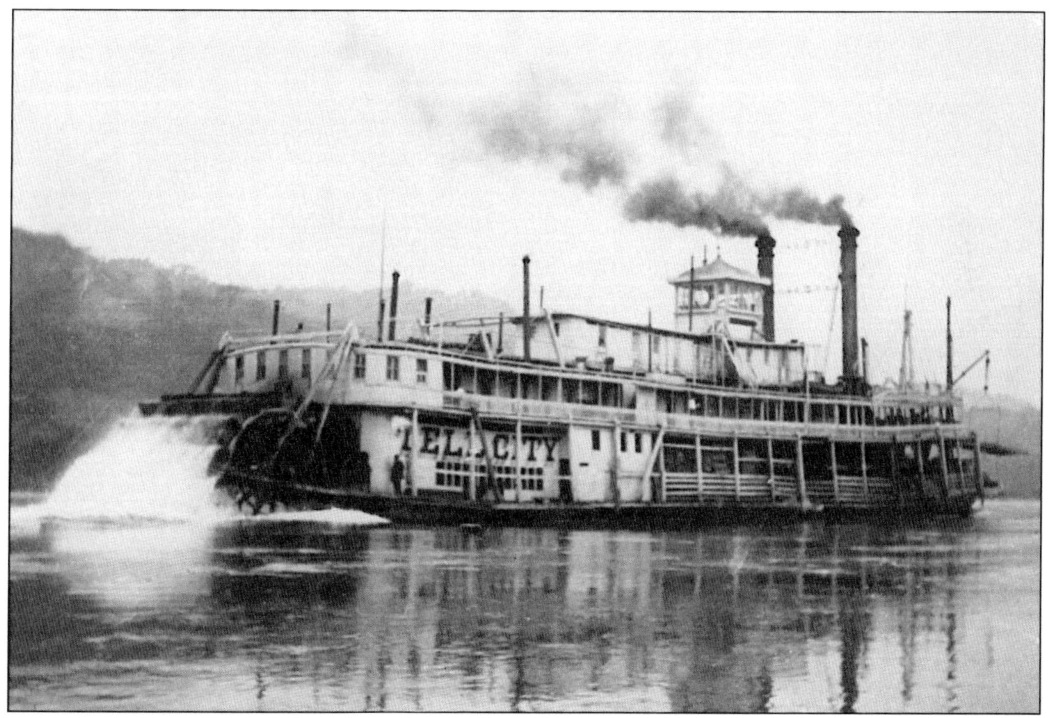

The *Tell City* steamboat made its maiden voyage in 1889. She was designed for the packet trade between Louisville and Evansville but spent time on many different parts of the Ohio River. The riverboat sank following an accident at Little Hocking, Ohio, on April 6, 1917. The pilothouse was salvaged and served as a summerhouse on the river for many years. The pilothouse is now at the Ohio River Museum in Marietta, Ohio. (Courtesy of Tell City Historical Society.)

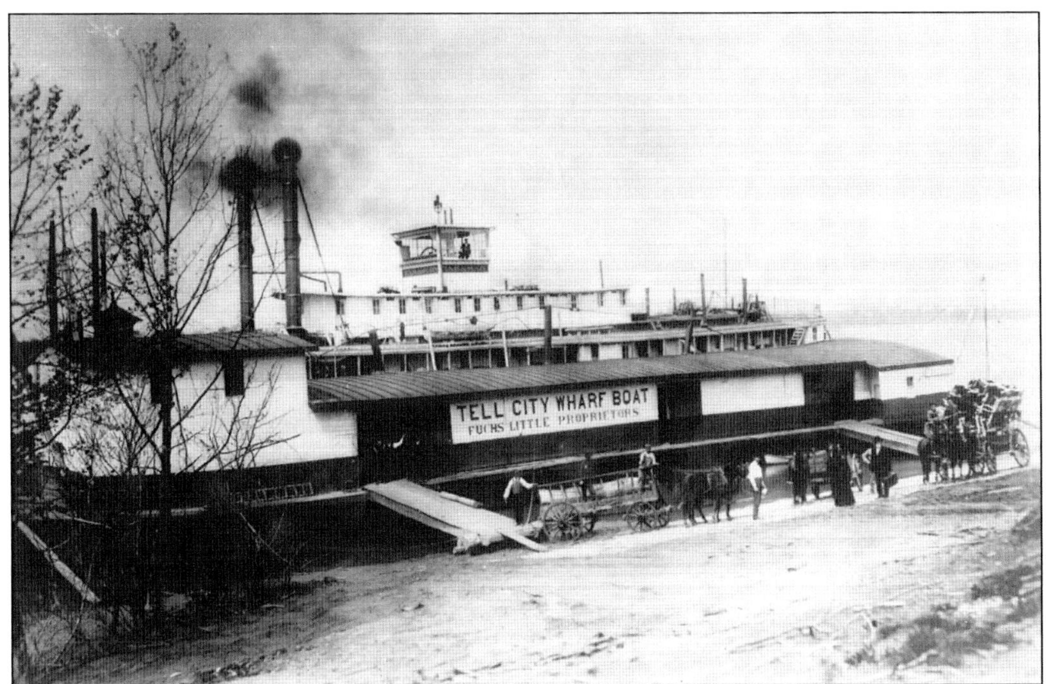

Tell City Wharf Boat was the hub of transportation in the early years of Tell City. Nearly all goods traveled to and from Tell City by the river. The riverboat behind the wharf boat is the *Tarascon*.

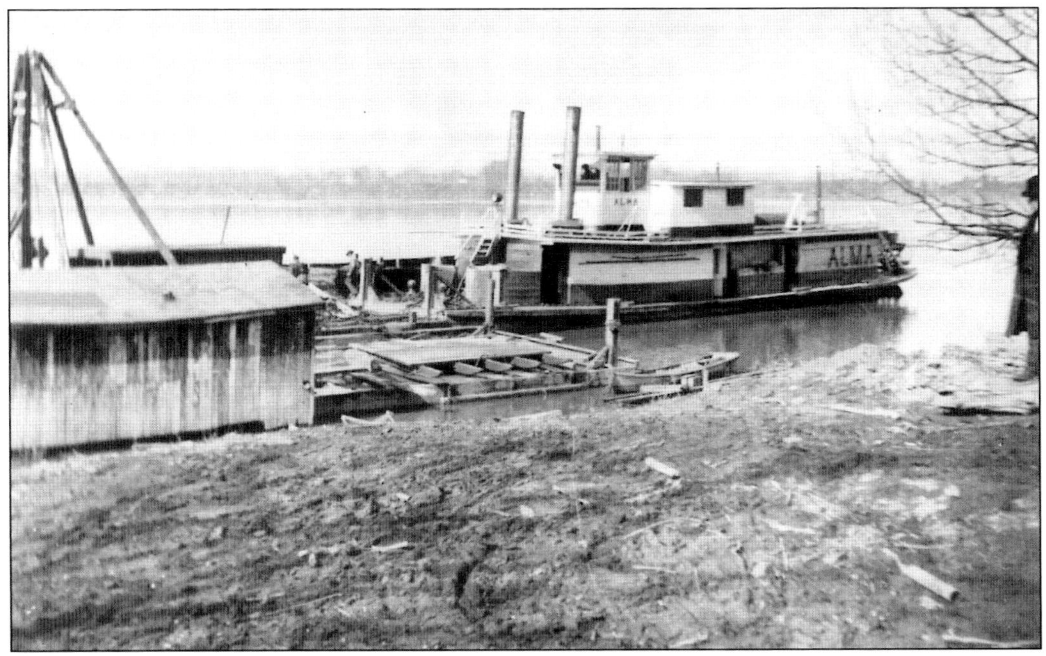

The *Alma* was owned by the Obrecht Manufacturing Company of Tell City from 1898 to 1927. The dock in the background is the Obrecht dock, which was located just north of the Tell City Wharf Boat between Blum and Washington Streets on the levee. This photograph was taken around 1925. (Courtesy of Tell City Historical Society.)

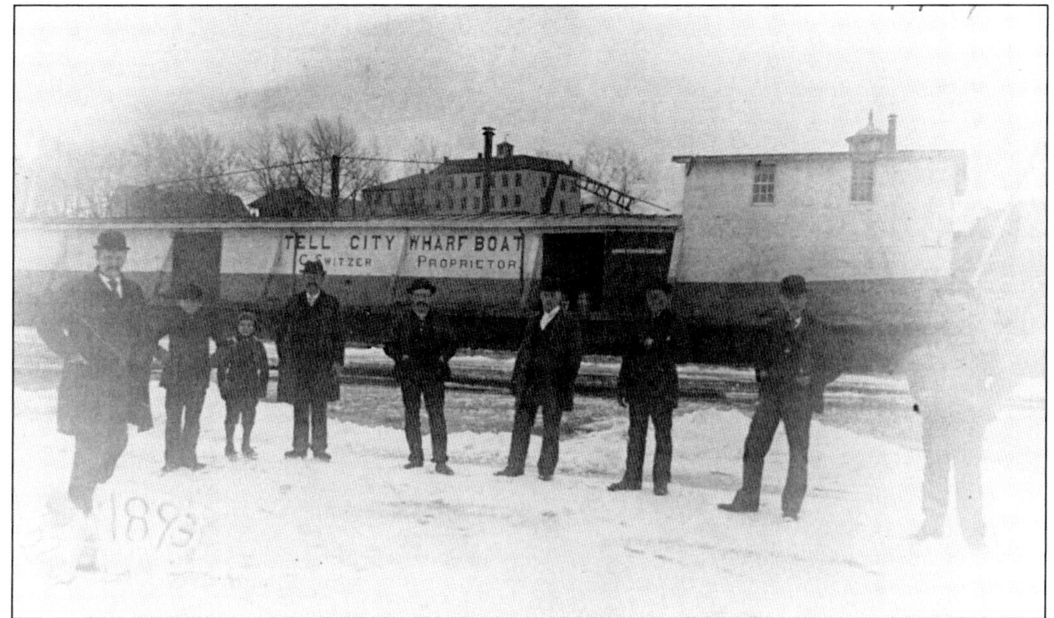

Floodwaters and ice can be seen at the Tell City Landing, located at Blum and Seventh Streets, in 1893. The Moraweck Hotel is in the background. Clay Switzer was the wharfmaster for Adams Express Company on the Tell City Wharf Boat. It appears that several of the people pictured here have ice skates on. Oftentimes, the Ohio River would freeze and people would ice-skate on the river. (Courtesy of Tell City Historical Society.)

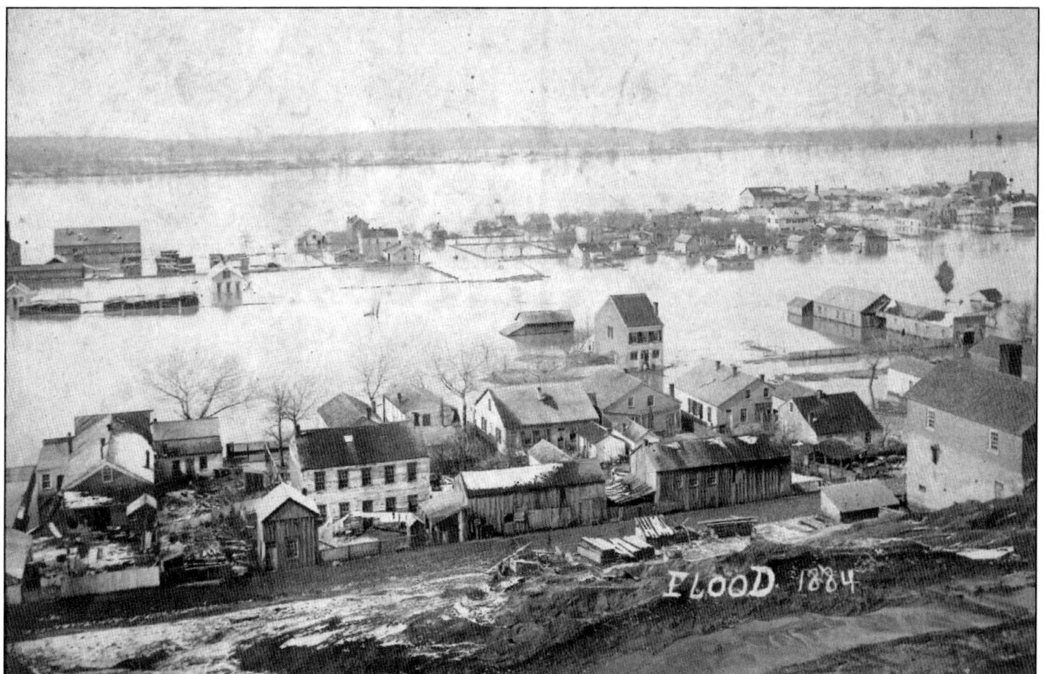

Tell City was only 26 years old when the first of many floods occurred in the city, in 1884. It was amazing how much the city had grown in those 26 years. (Courtesy of Tell City Historical Society.)

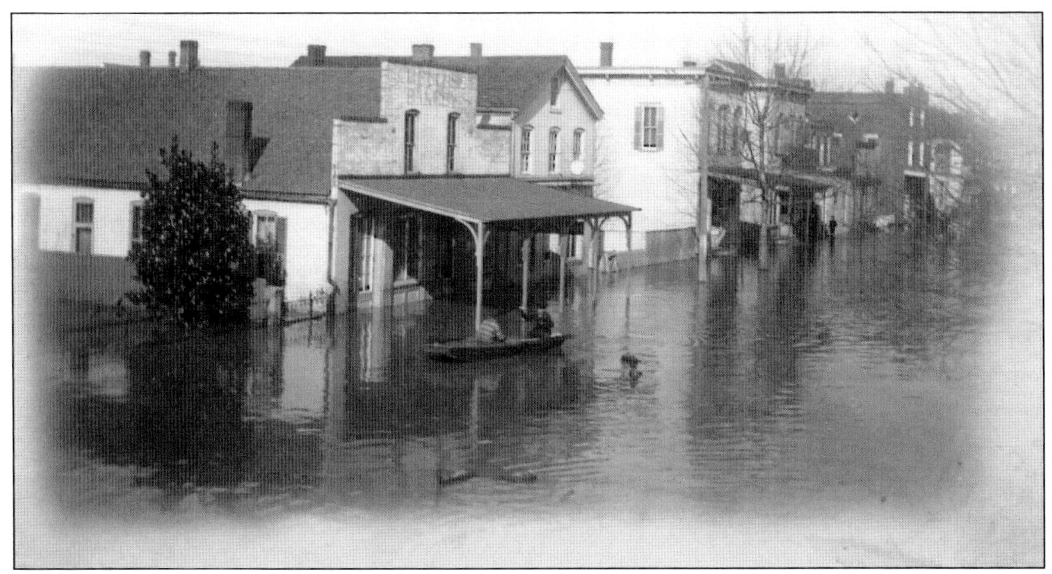

Two men float by H. Fuches Bakery and Heinzel Jewelry during the 1907 flood. The H. Fuches Bakery building still stands today. In the 1930s, the front of the building was redone and remains the same to this date.

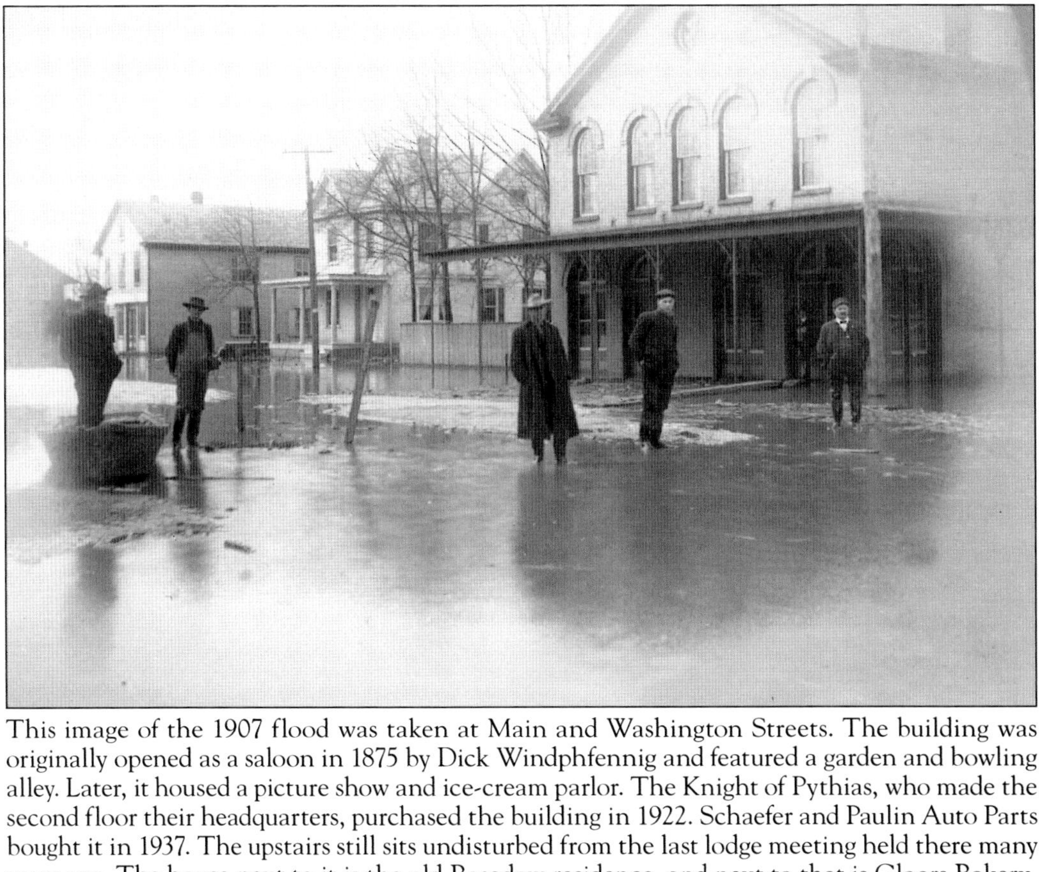

This image of the 1907 flood was taken at Main and Washington Streets. The building was originally opened as a saloon in 1875 by Dick Windphfennig and featured a garden and bowling alley. Later, it housed a picture show and ice-cream parlor. The Knight of Pythias, who made the second floor their headquarters, purchased the building in 1922. Schaefer and Paulin Auto Parts bought it in 1937. The upstairs still sits undisturbed from the last lodge meeting held there many years ago. The house next to it is the old Basedow residence, and next to that is Gloors Bakery.

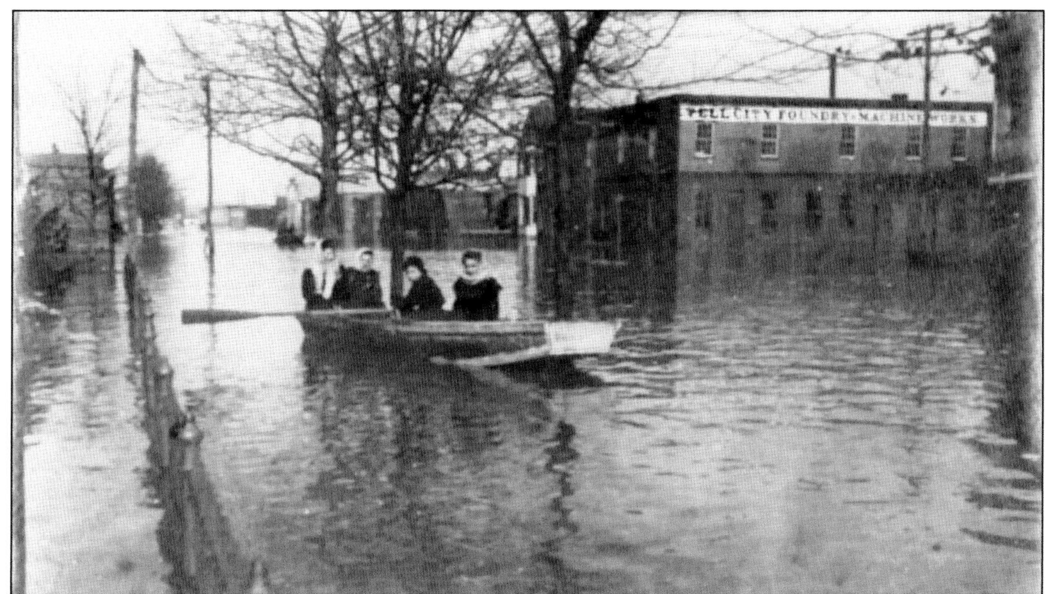

This image of the 1907 flood was taken at Seventh and Humboldt Streets. In the background is the Tell City Foundry and Machine Works. Note that the original building had two stories.

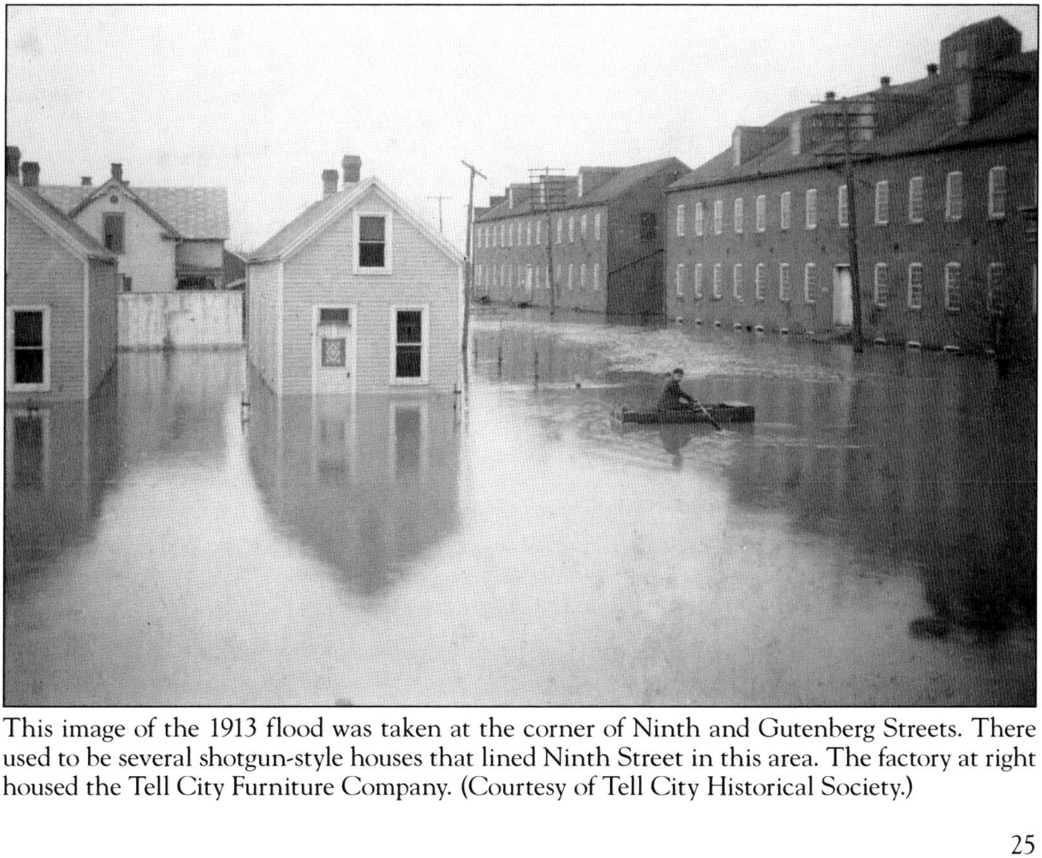

This image of the 1913 flood was taken at the corner of Ninth and Gutenberg Streets. There used to be several shotgun-style houses that lined Ninth Street in this area. The factory at right housed the Tell City Furniture Company. (Courtesy of Tell City Historical Society.)

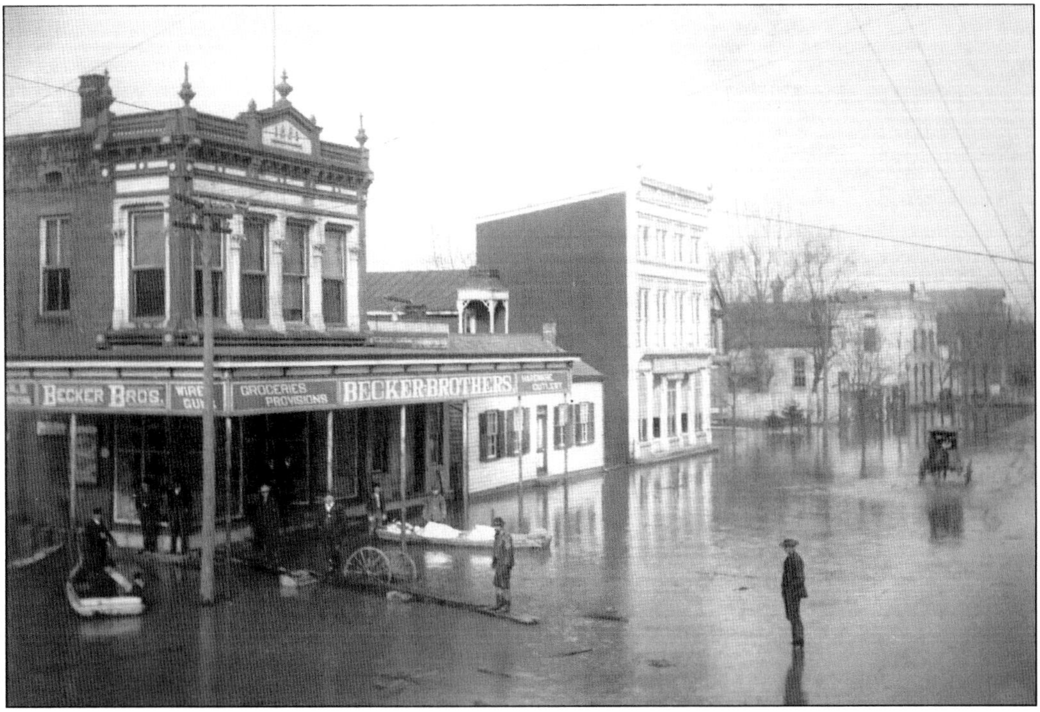

This image of the 1913 flood was taken at Main and Washington Streets. The Becker Bros. building was constructed in 1885. Around the 1950s, after it became the VFW, the building's top story was removed. Today, this building still stands but is covered with vinyl siding and looks nothing like the original. (Courtesy of Tell City Historical Society.)

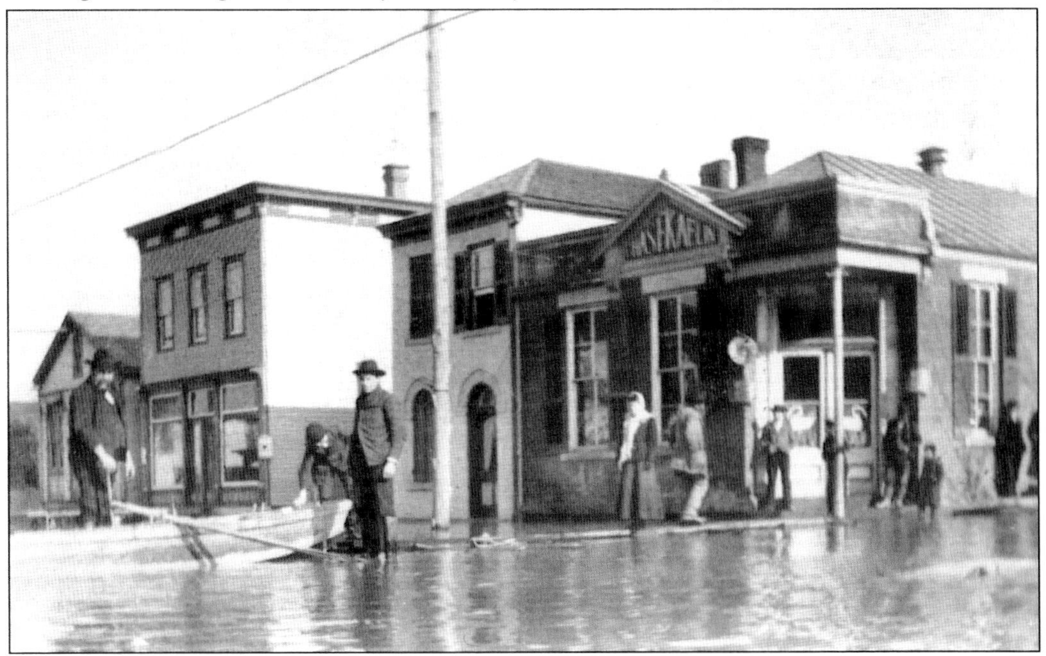

The White Swan Saloon was located at Main and Humboldt Streets. (Courtesy of Tell City Historical Society.)

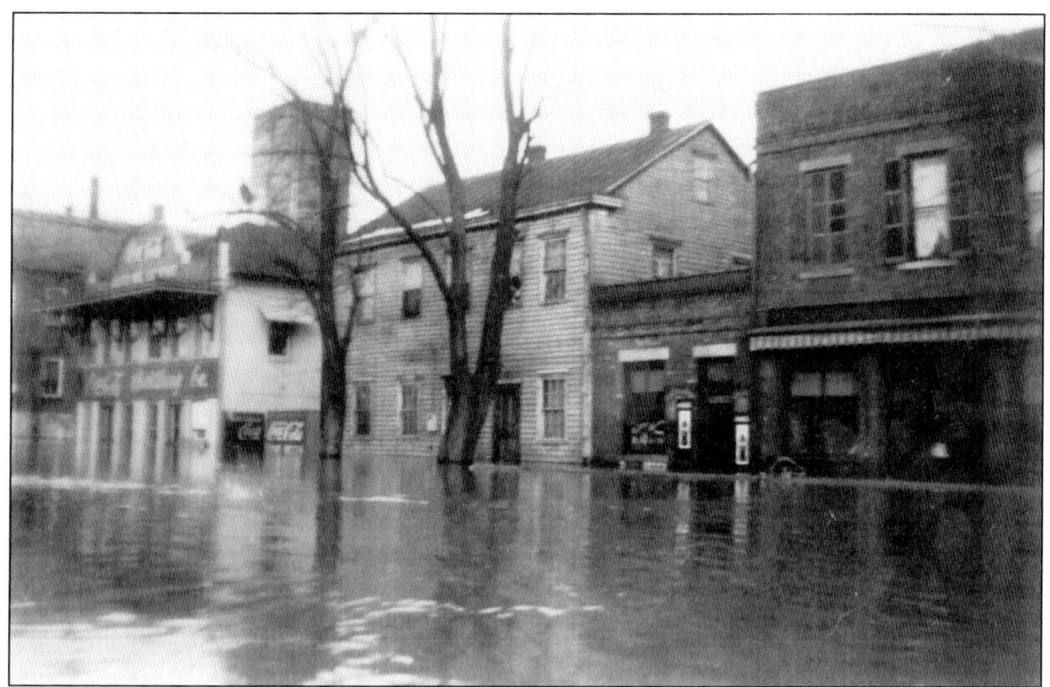

Pictured are the Coca-Cola Bottling Company plant (far left), a residence (center), and Basedow Bottling Works (far right). This photograph was taken at the corner of Ninth and Washington Streets during the 1937 flood.

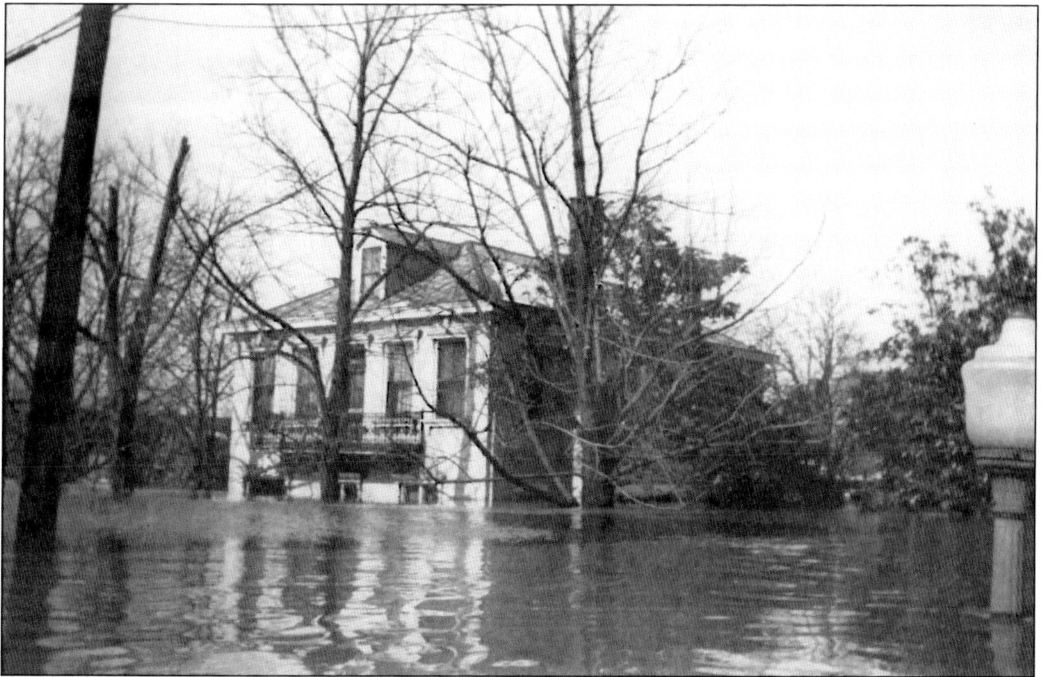

Pictured is the Mike Bettinger home at Main and Pestalozzi Streets during the 1937 flood. Note the height of river on the first-floor windows and on the lamppost. The floodwaters almost reached the second-story balcony.

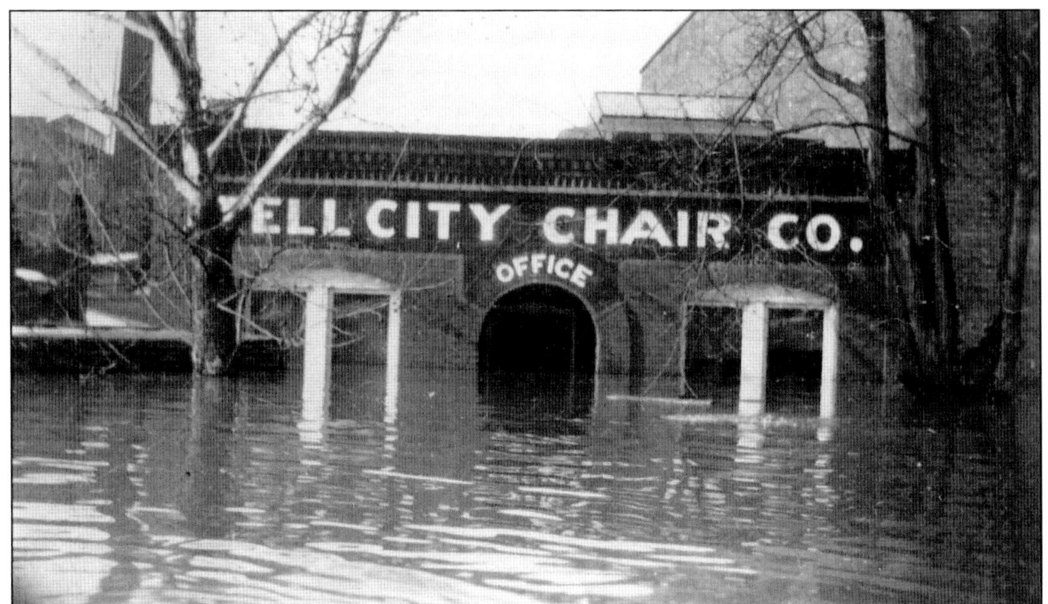

Tell City Chair Company's main office was located at 417 Seventh Street. Founded in 1865, the Chair Makers Union later became the Tell City Chair Company. The company made fine furniture, which still graces many homes throughout the world, including the White House. This building stopped being used as a general office in 1997.

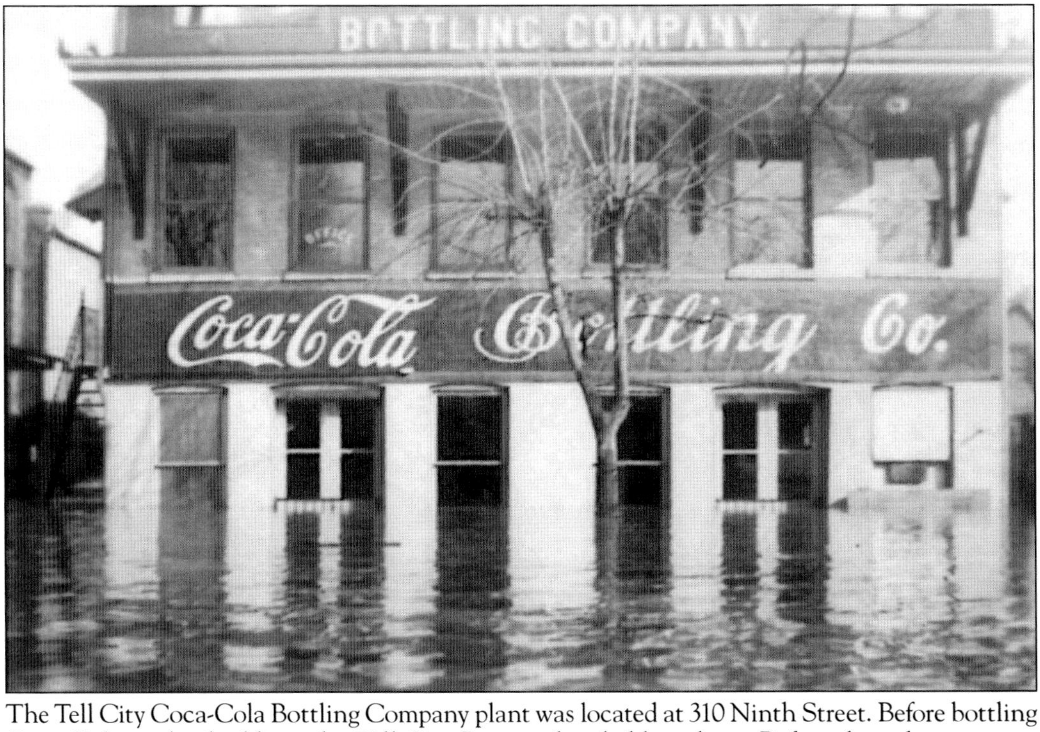

The Tell City Coca-Cola Bottling Company plant was located at 310 Ninth Street. Before bottling Coca-Cola in this building, the Tell City Brewery bottled beer here. Before that, the structure was used by the Swiss Colonization Society. This is one of the oldest commercial buildings still standing today in Tell City.

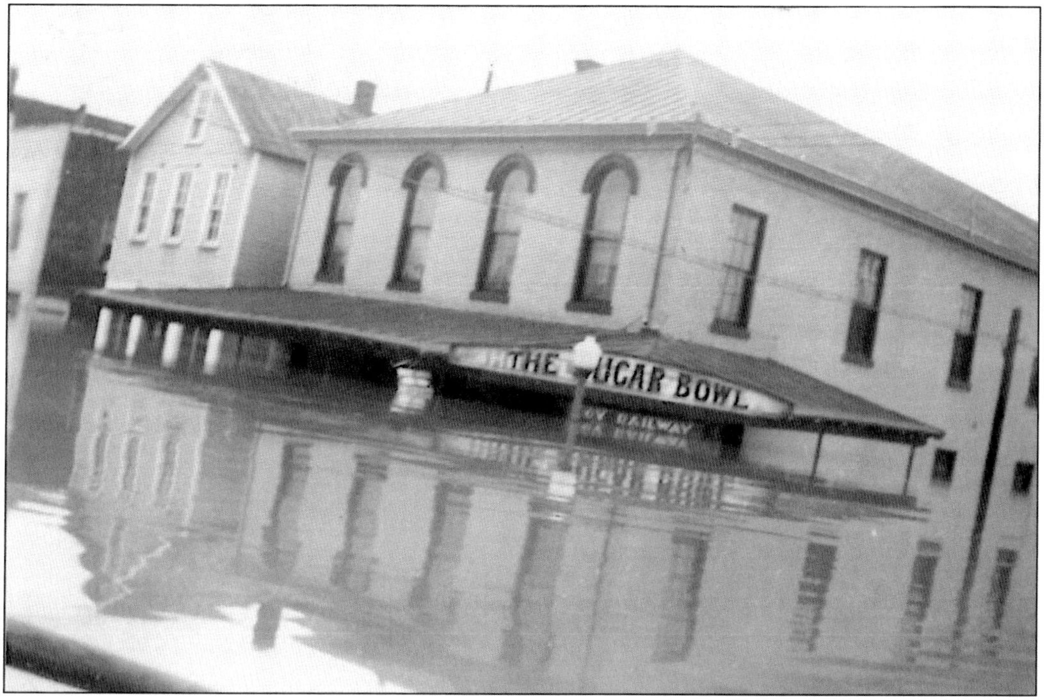

The 1937 flood encroaches upon the Sugar Bowl in the 400 block of Main Street.

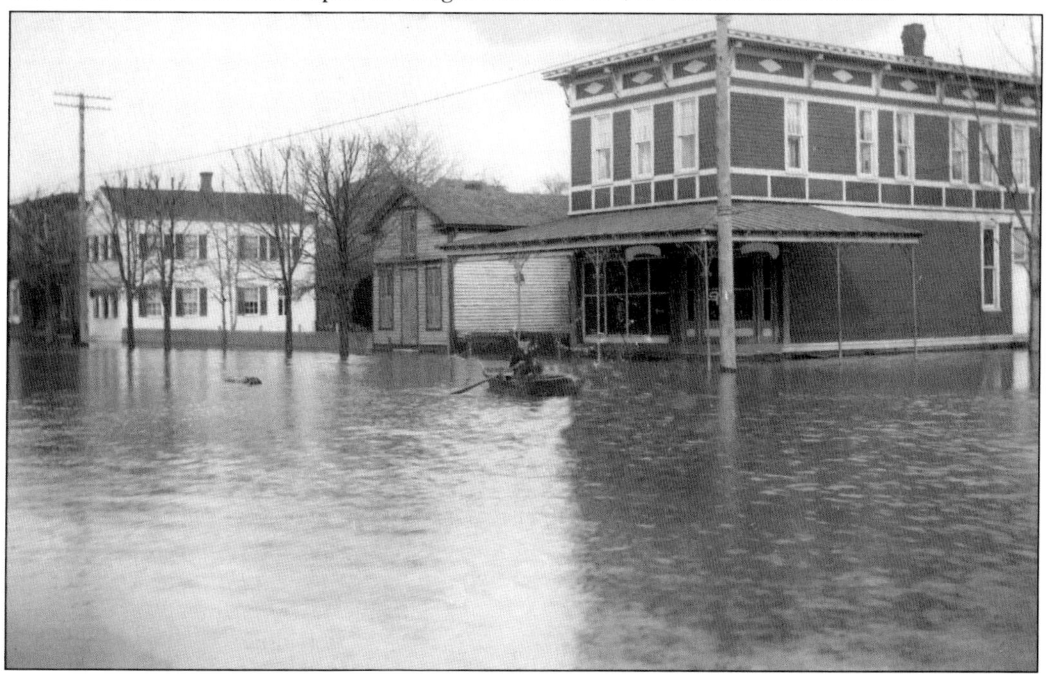

Dusch Drug Store was located at Pestalozzi and Main Streets. Dusch Drug Store began business in 1883. Gabriel S. and Mary Louise Dusch were the proprietors, and both were registered pharmacists. Mrs. Dusch was Tell City's only female pharmacist until 1957, when she passed away. Tell City's first bottle of Coca-Cola was sold in this store in 1903. (Courtesy of Tell City Historical Society.)

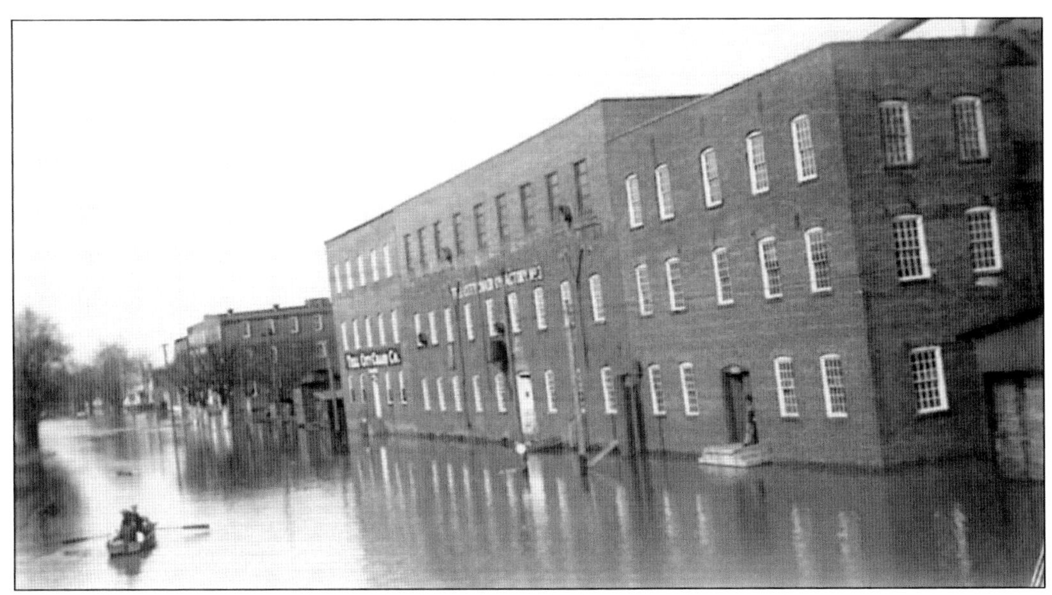

The flood threatens Tell City Chair Company's plant No. 3.

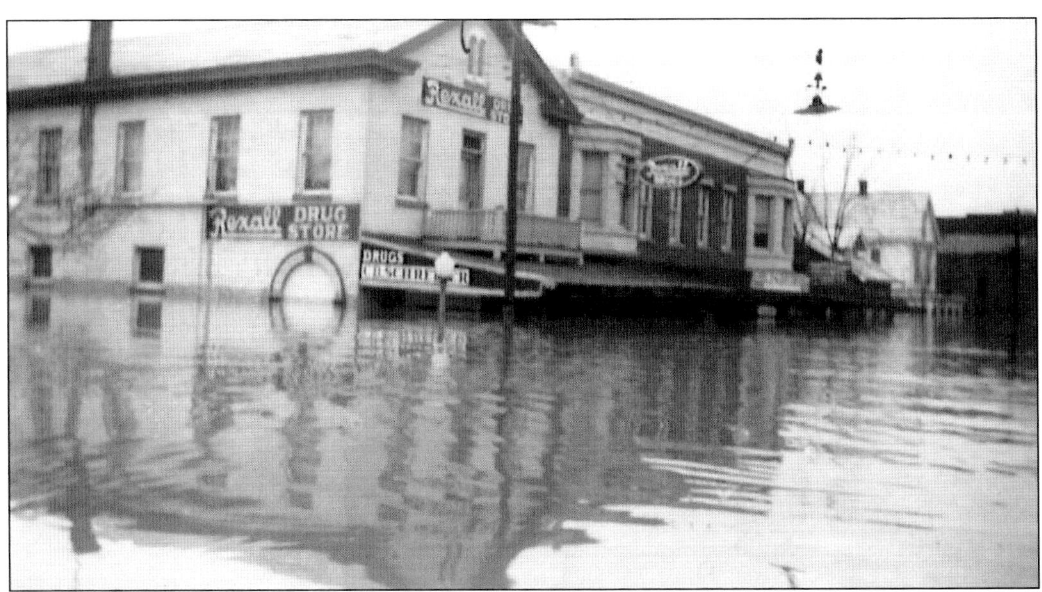

The 1937 flood laps up on Schreiber's Drug Store at Main and Humboldt Streets.

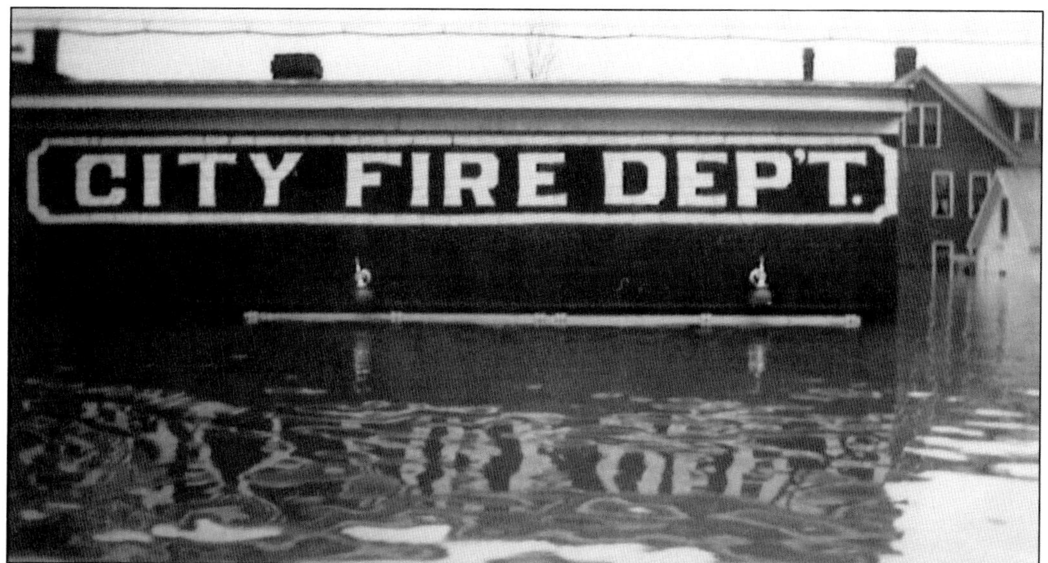

The Tell City Fire Department at 711 Humboldt Street is shown during the 1937 flood. Before this building was a fire department, it was a dry-cleaning business and later part of the power company. Today, it is Firehouse Printing.

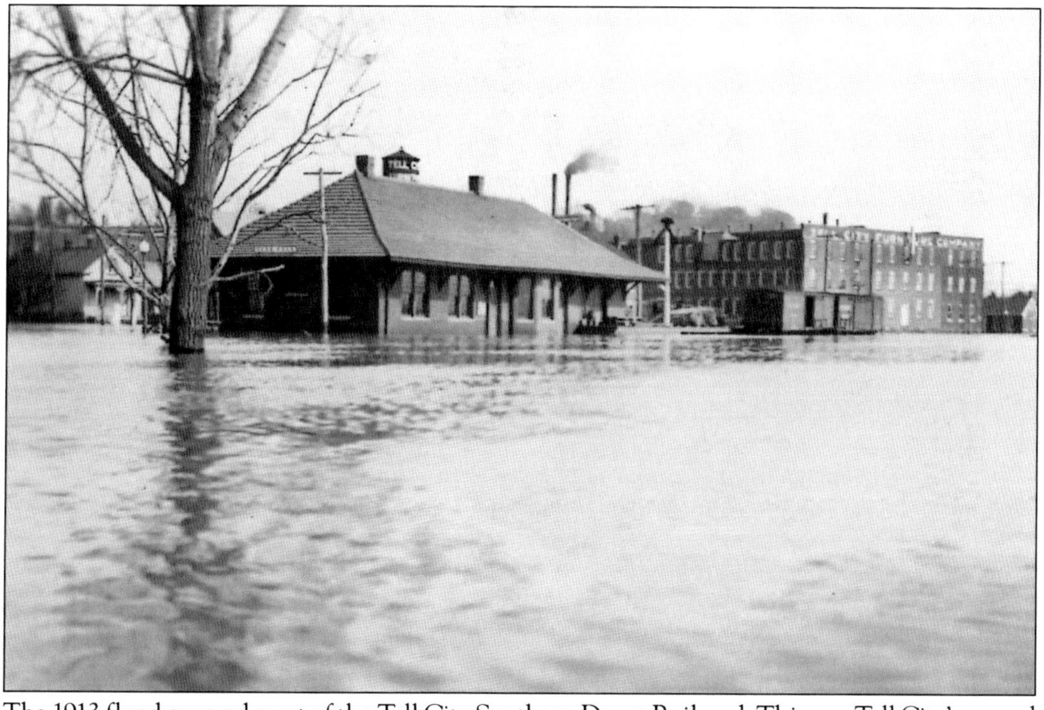

The 1913 flood covered most of the Tell City Southern Depot Railroad. This was Tell City's second depot; the first one was destroyed by fire. However, this depot met the same fate and burned in November 1989. The depot housed the Tell City Historical Society Museum at the time of the fire, and many of the artifacts were destroyed.

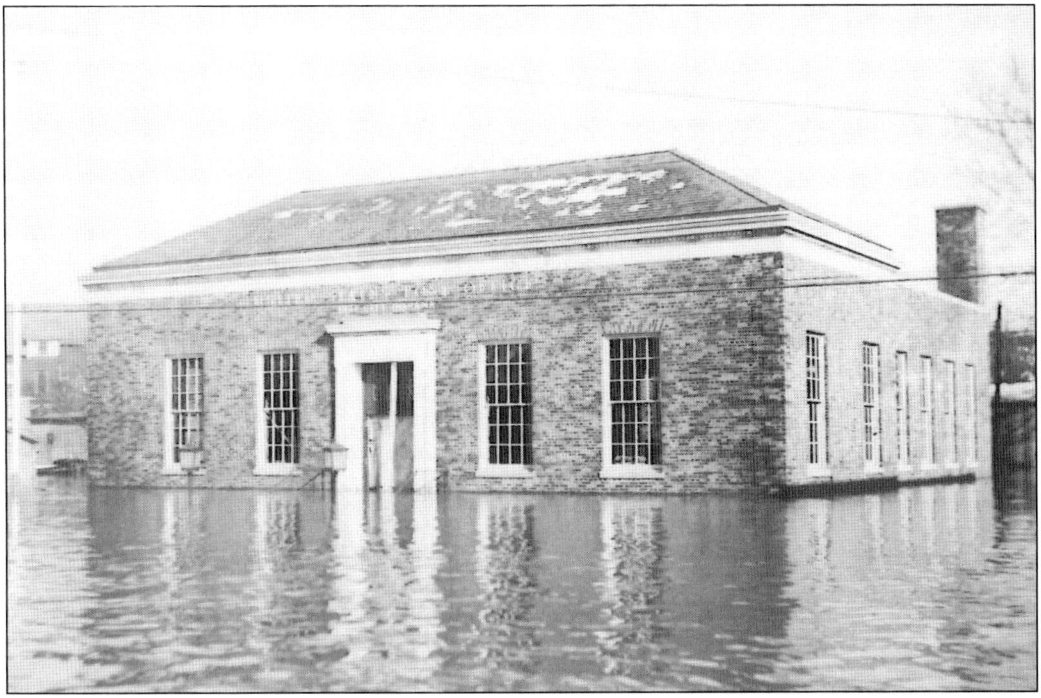

The post office at 516 Main Street was inundated during the 1937 flood. During the flood, this building was still under construction. It now houses a restaurant and sports bar. (Courtesy of Tell City Historical Society.)

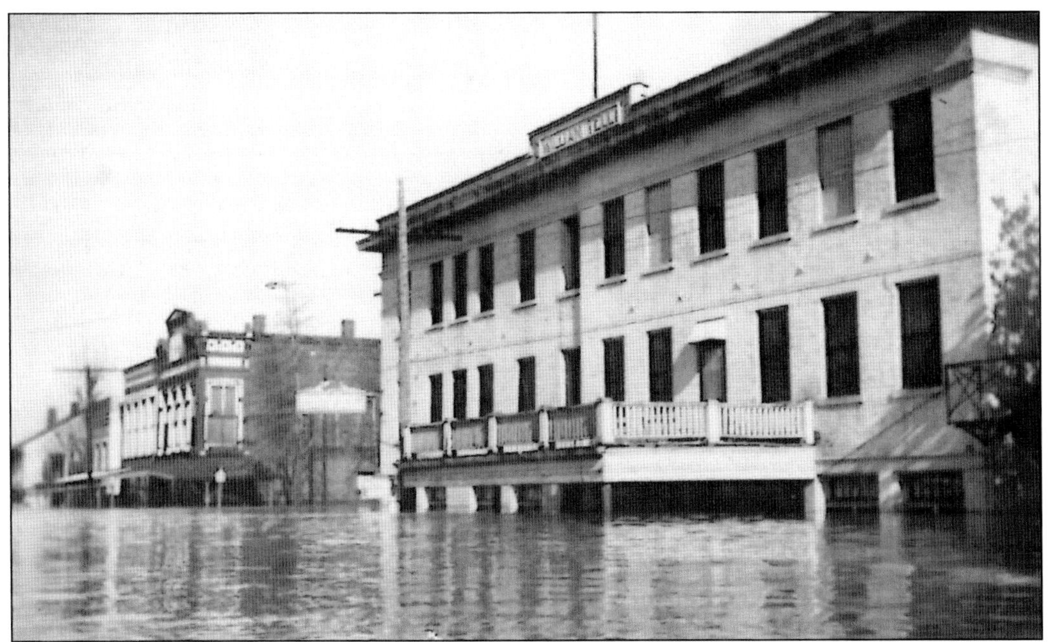

The 1937 flood and the William Tell Hotel are pictured in the 200 block of Main Street.

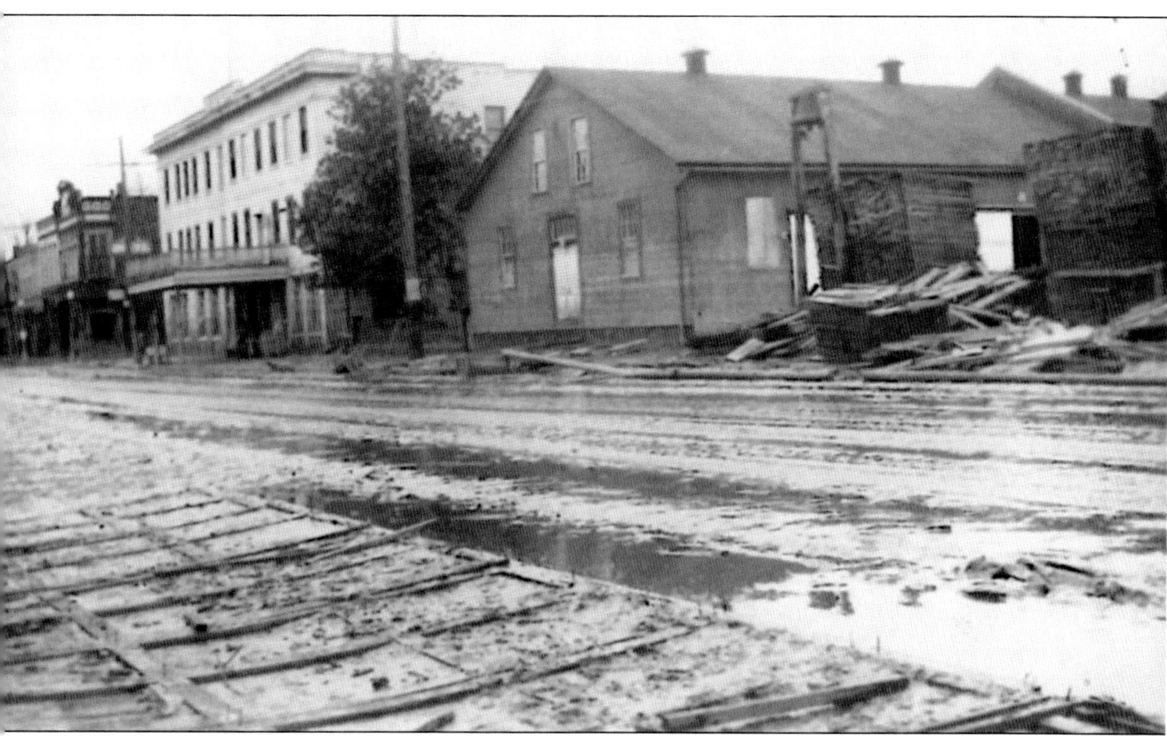

This photograph was taken after the water receded from the 1937 flood. The location is in the 200 block of Main Street. The structure at right is the Fischer Chair Company. Next to that is the William Tell Hotel.

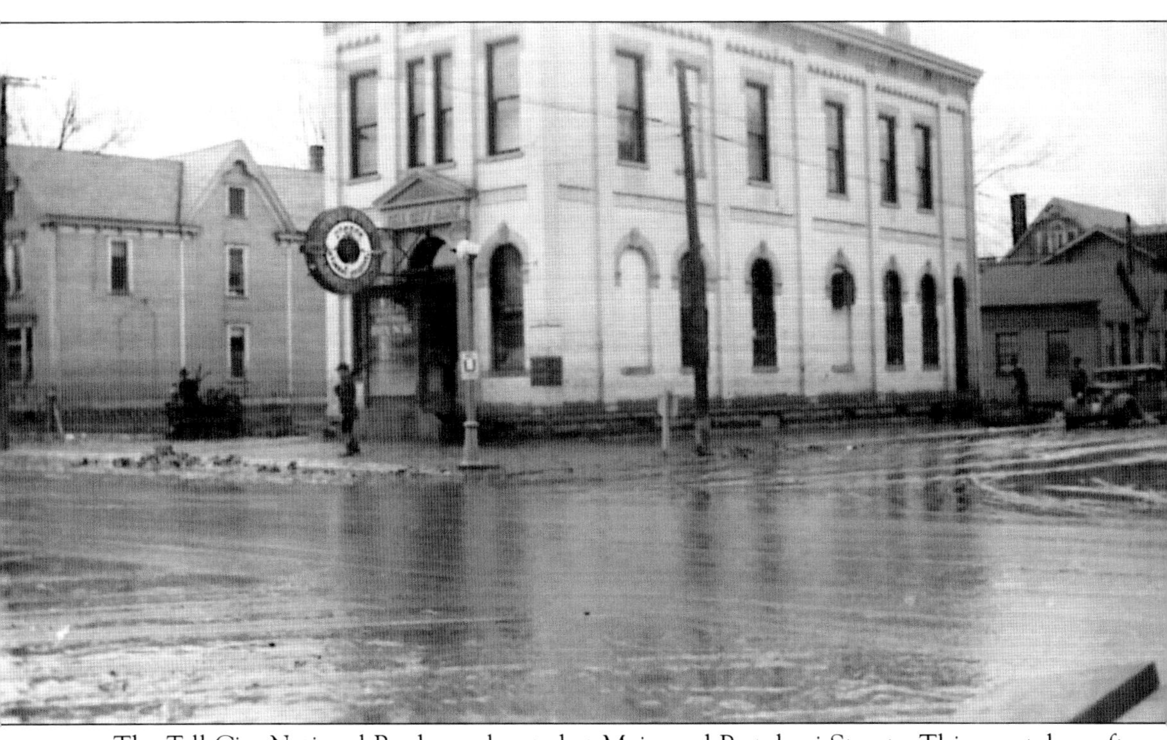

The Tell City National Bank was located at Main and Pestalozzi Streets. This was taken after the water had receded from the 1937 flood.

Three

We Made That

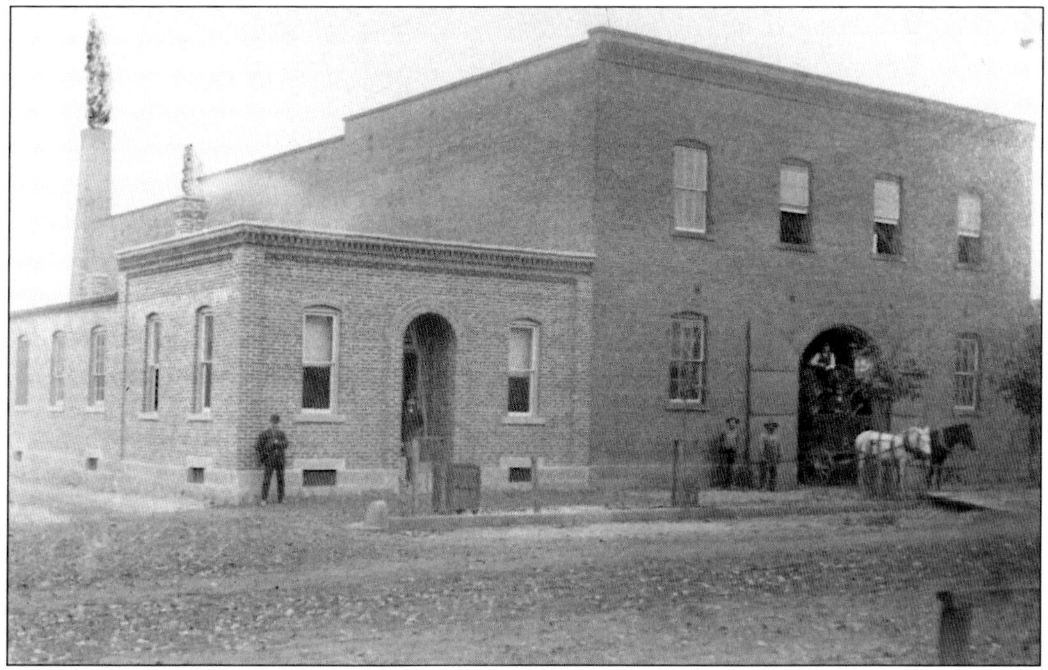

The Tell City Chair Company was founded in 1865 as the Chair Makers Union; later it became Tell City Chair Company. The factory was located along Seventh Street. The company made fine furniture, which has graced many homes throughout the world, including the White House. The Tell City Chair Company ceased operation in the late 1990s. The company did reopen for a short time, but it closed officially in 2011. (Courtesy of Tell City Historical Society.)

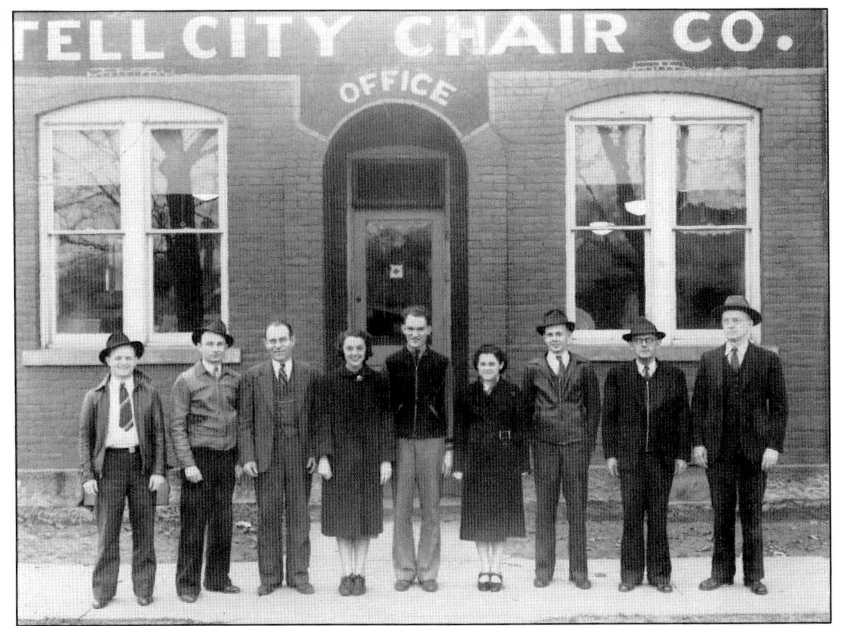

Pictured is Tell City Chair Company office staff. From the left to right are "Swat" Anderson, Walter Earl Becker, Roy Fenn, Marie Shroder, Bill Kreisle, Ruth Englebrecht, Louis Jarboe, unidentified, and Gus Ahlf.

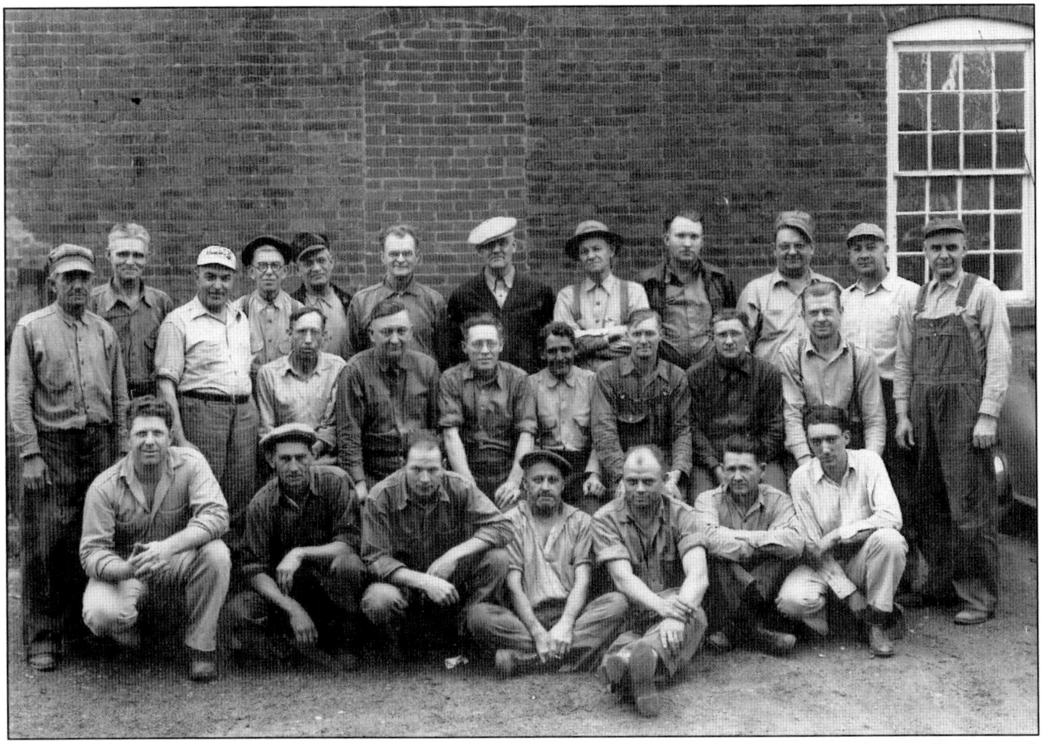

Tell City Chair Company employees are pictured here around 1930. From left to right are (kneeling) Russell "Red" Poehlein, Sam Bender, Peter Turner, Ike Bouile, "Ish" Biever, Chester Davis, and Fred Simpson; (sitting) Nelson Snyder, Albert Mehling, Bill Logsdon, Cat Miller, Leonard Oskins, Harry Powell, and Bob Waninger; (standing) William Ziegelgruber, Charles Schlachter, unidentified, Pete Kramer, Otto Fruewald, Fred Fruewald, Charlie Haaf, two unidentified, Ed Hurm, Romie Gaesser, and Edwin Schurterer. (Courtesy of Tell City Historical Society.)

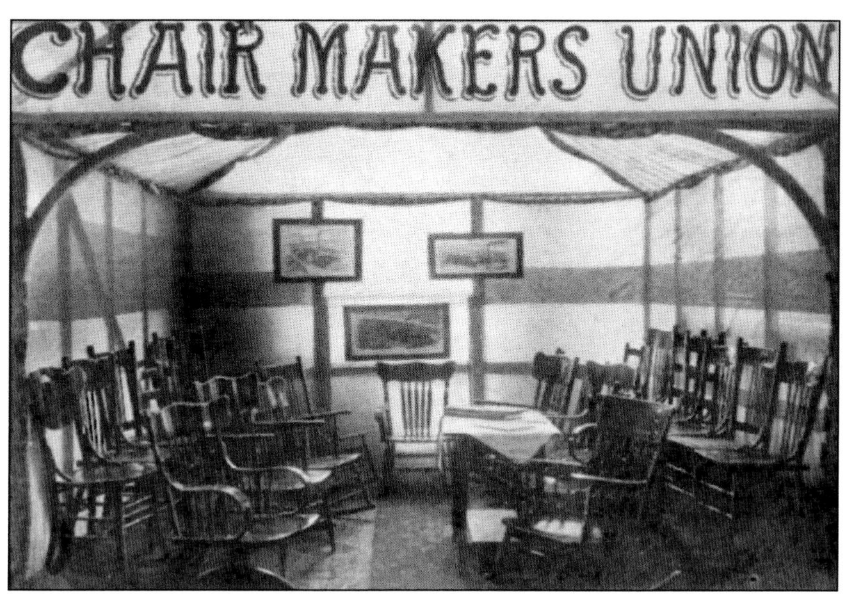

When Tell City staged a homecoming celebration in 1908, the Chair Makers Union (later the Tell City Chair Company) used the occasion to create an exhibit where it bragged a bit about its chairs.

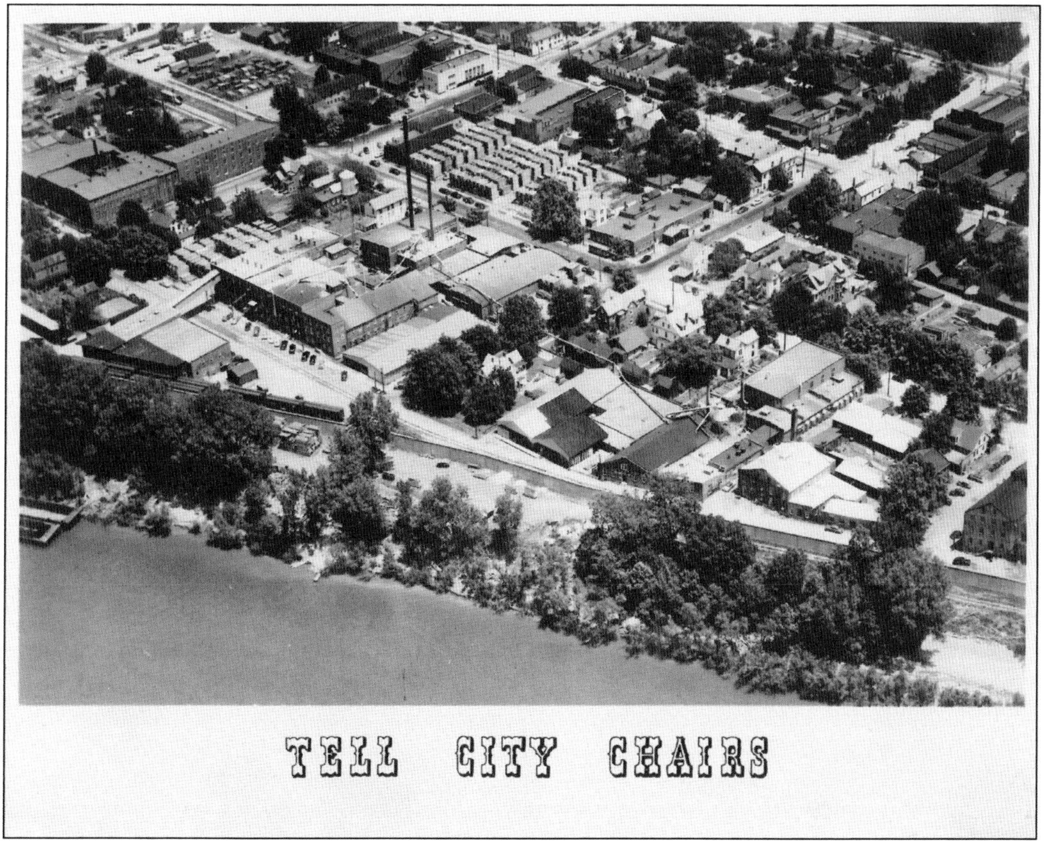

This aerial view shows the Tell City Chair Company plants—numbers 1, 3, and 2. Interestingly, the plants did not follow numerical order.

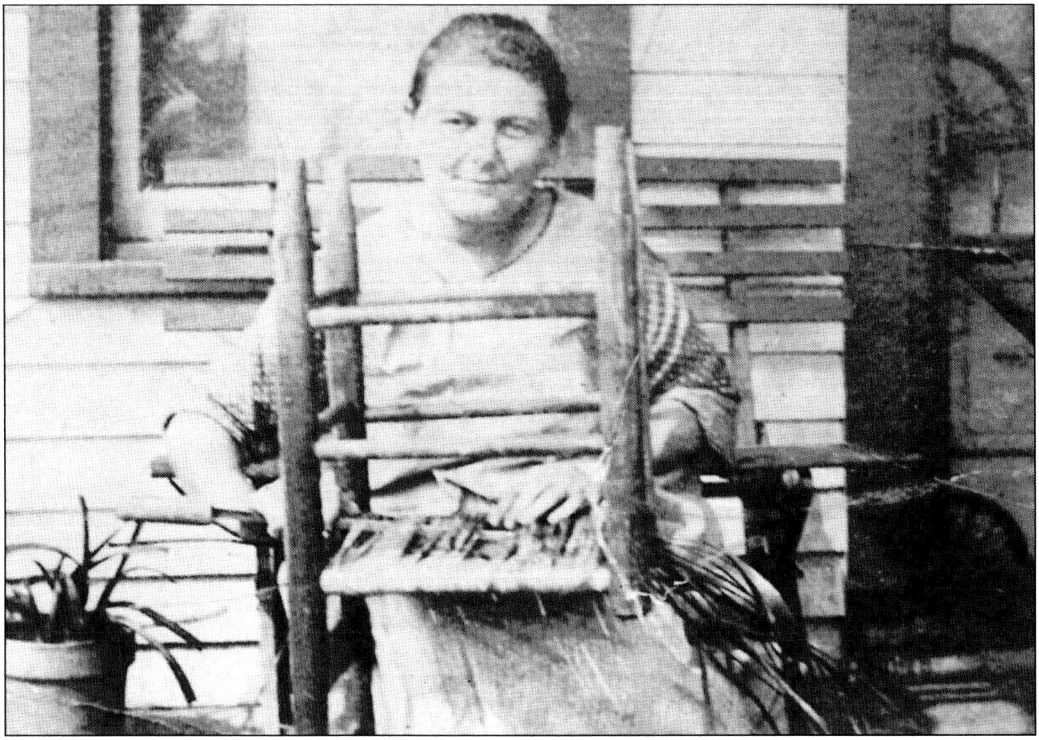

Rosa Jarboe is pictured weaving chair seats on the back porch of her home. Before labor laws were in existence, it was a common practice to do this at home.

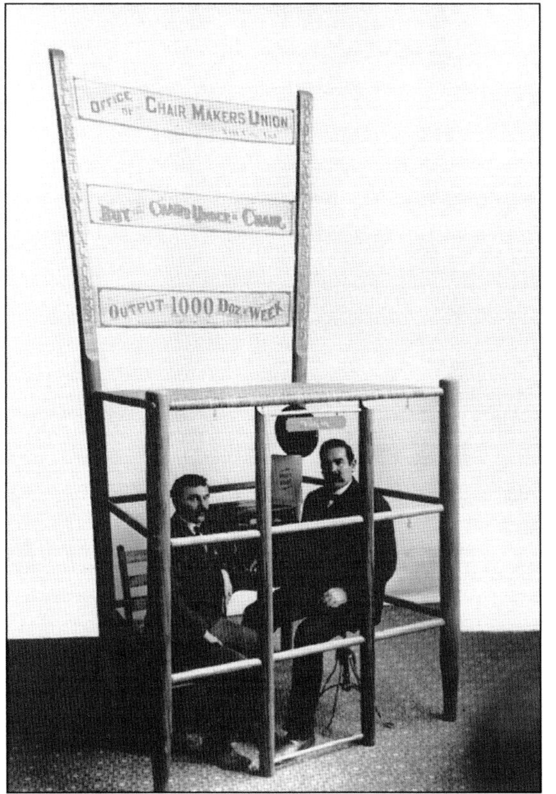

One of the wonders at the world's fair in St. Louis in 1904 was this chair built at the Chair Makers Union, predecessor to the Tell City Chair Company. The chair was 12 feet high, 6 feet across at the seat, and the seat was 6 feet from the floor. Seated in the office inside the big chair are Jacob Zoercher (left) and A.P. Fenn. These representatives of the company were all set up to receive orders from buyers.

The Tell City Chair Company's Giant Boston Rocker dates to 1958, when the company created the rocker for the city's centennial parade. It was made by George Connor, Norman Freeman, and Harry Powell, and it was designed to be double the size of the Boston Rocker. Approximately 93 board feet of lumber was used to build it. It stands 7 feet tall, has an overall width of 4 feet, and weighs 173 pounds. The seat is 40 inches wide and 38 inches deep. It is large enough to accommodate three men. Only three of these rockers were ever made. One was destroyed, one is housed at the Tell City Historical Society, and the other is owned by the author and currently is on display at the Tell City Depot.

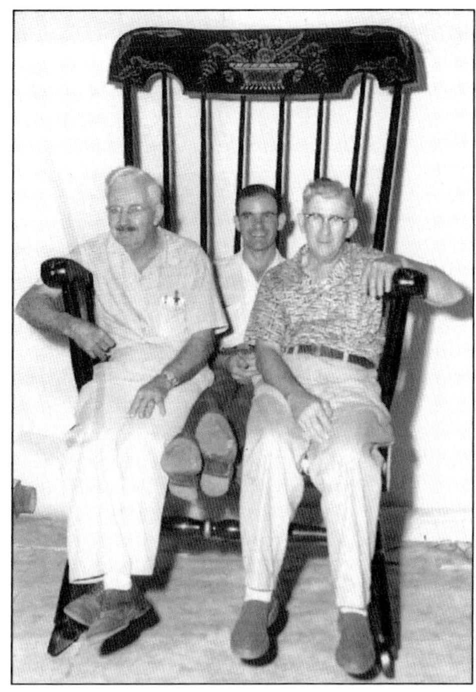

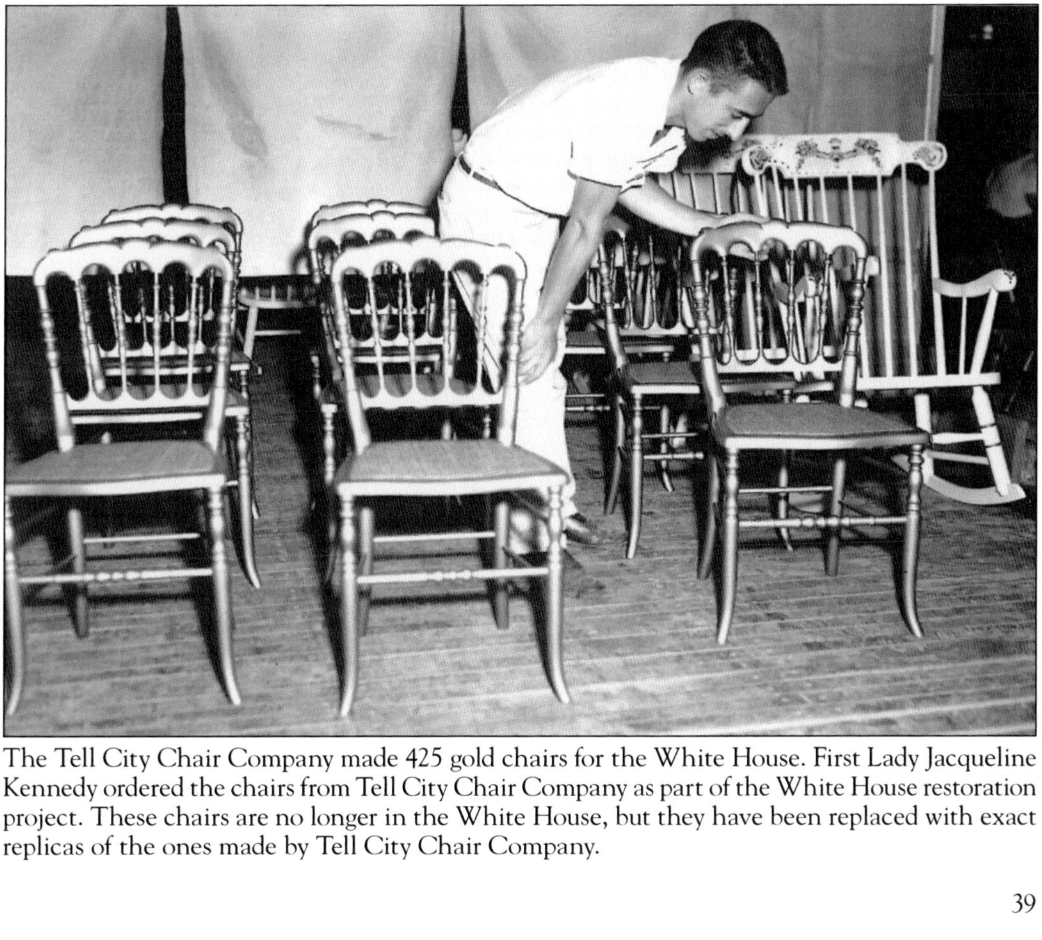

The Tell City Chair Company made 425 gold chairs for the White House. First Lady Jacqueline Kennedy ordered the chairs from Tell City Chair Company as part of the White House restoration project. These chairs are no longer in the White House, but they have been replaced with exact replicas of the ones made by Tell City Chair Company.

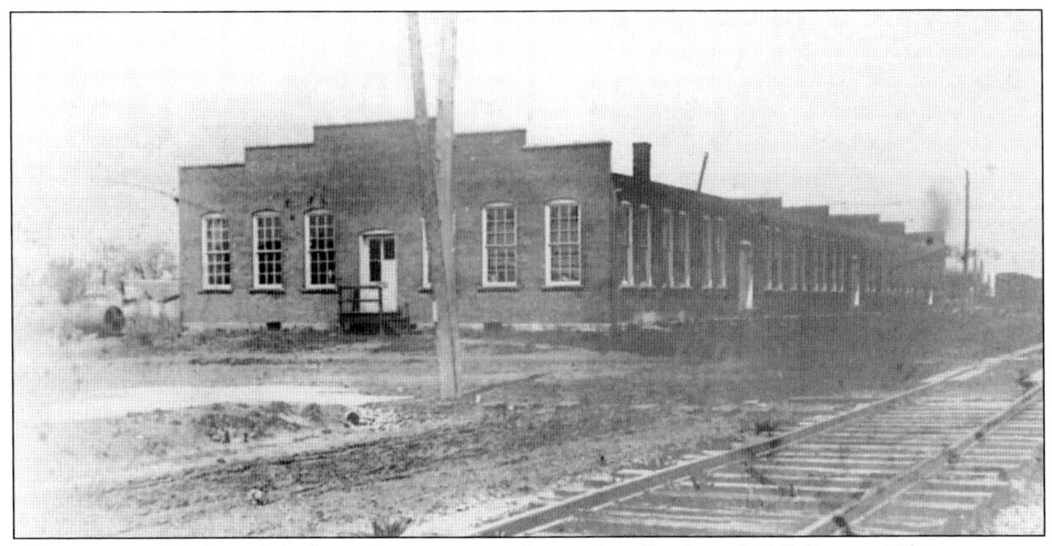

The Sanitary Washing Machine Company was located at Sixth and Tell Streets. This company was not in business very long because the washing machines actually tore up the clothing. Later, this was the site of the Knott Manufacturing Company, where they made wooden toilet seats. After that company closed, the Tell City Chair Company purchased the building and expanded its manufacturing facility. (Courtesy of Tell City Historical Society.)

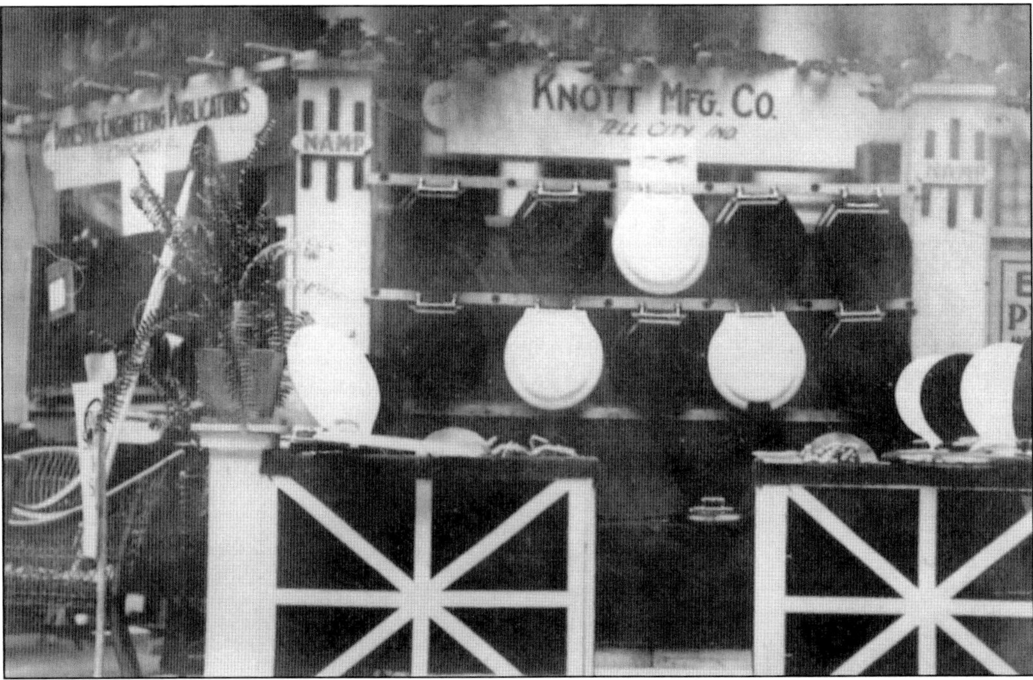

The Knott Manufacturing Company produced wooden toilet seats. It was located at Sixth and Tell Streets. Organized in Fort Wayne, Indiana, the company moved to Tell City under the supervision of J.T. Knott, who was manager and treasurer of the firm. Soon after, Knott sold his interest to Walter Huthsteiner. The company was then managed by Paul Bishop and later Charles Fournier and Alfred Goffinet (in 1931). This photograph shows a display by the firm at a Chicago trade show in 1920. (Courtesy of Tell City Historical Society.)

The Tell City Desk Company was located in the 600 block of Seventh Street. The company made desks for offices and mantels for residences. When the company closed, Tell City Chair Company purchased the property and machinery and expanded its facility. This was Tell City Plant No. 2.

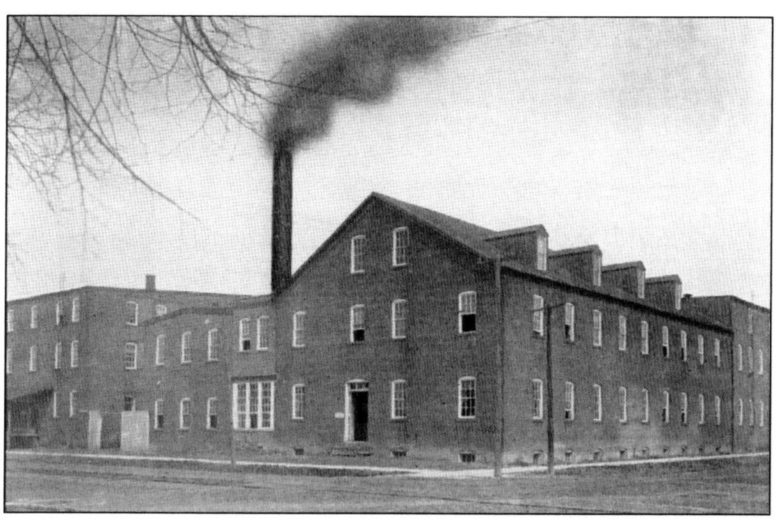

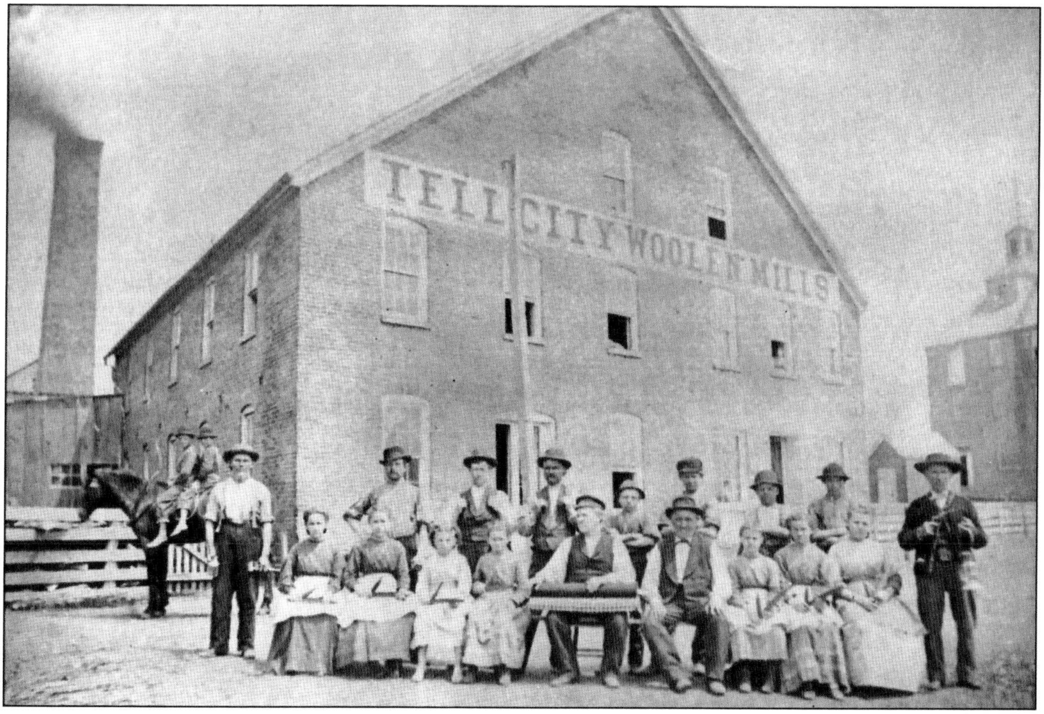

The Tell City Woolen Mills was one of the first industries established in Tell City. It was founded in 1864 by a Mr. Hauser and a Mr. Hartley. Michael Bettinger purchased the business in 1870. The mill was replaced with a larger structure in 1881 after a fire destroyed the original one. The mill closed in 1934, and the buildings became part of the Tell City Chair Company. (Courtesy of Tell City Historical Society.)

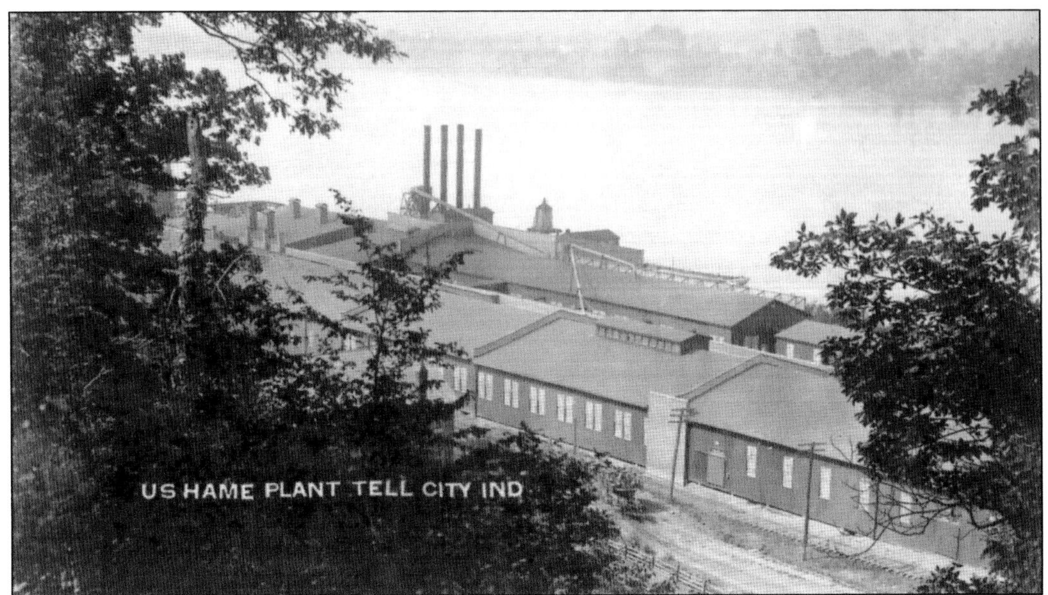

The US Hame Company plant was located on the south end of the city on land later occupied by the Maxon Construction Company. The US Hame Company came to Tell City in 1901, merging with the Herrmann Brothers factory at Ninth and Blum Streets. This plant was constructed around 1903. Along with hames (wooden pieces along the sides of horse collars to which the traces are attached), the factory produced packsaddles during World War I. In 1927, it began producing truck and station wagon bodies. After the 1937 flood, the plant was closed and operations moved to Frankfort, Indiana.

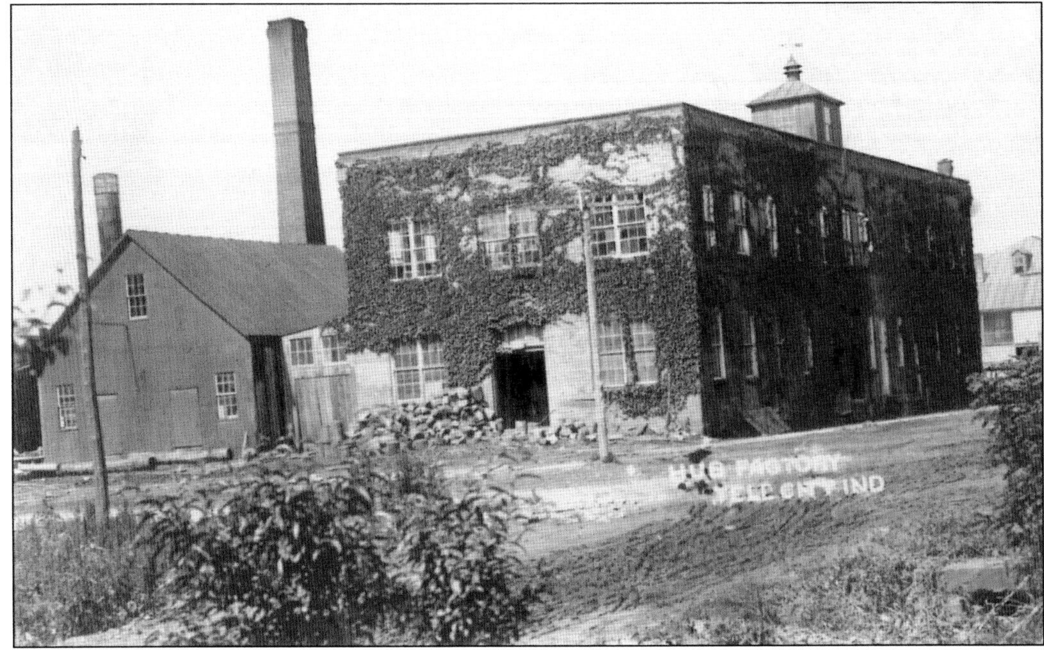

The Obrecht Hub Factory was built in the late 1890s and made wagon hubs for wheels. The company also made wooden swings and other porch furniture. This building later became part of Tell City Furniture Company and Swiss Plywood.

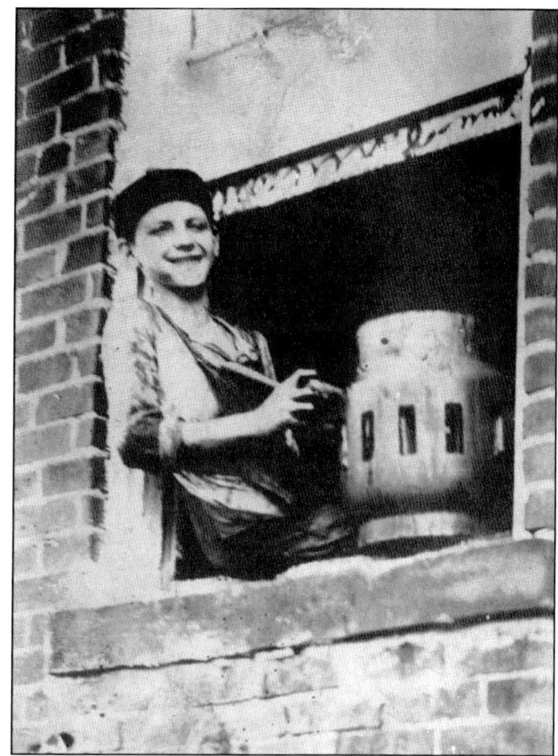

An unidentified boy sits in the widow of the Obrecht Hub Factory located at Ninth and Blum Streets. The Obrechts were a very prominent family in Tell City history. They were investors in many different businesses in the city. The Obrecht Hub Factory building still stands today and is part of the former Swiss Plywood. (Courtesy of Tell City Historical Society.)

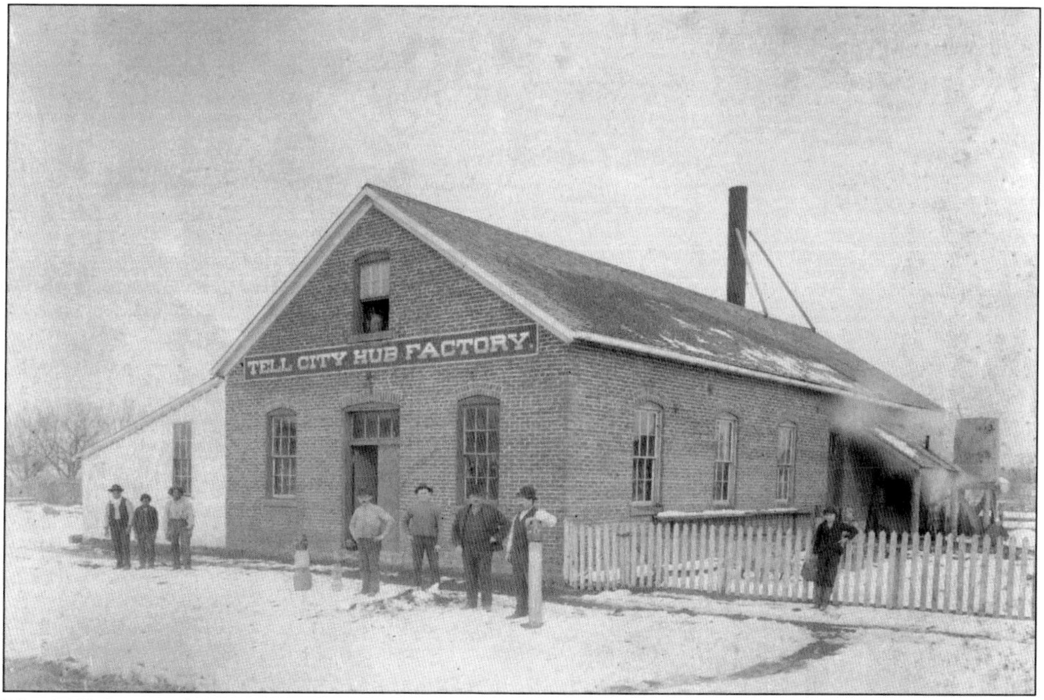

The Tell City Hub Factory was started in February 1882 by Joseph Adam at a cost of about $5,000. Six or eight hands were hired. About 150 hub sets, of four each, were manufactured, and each set retailed for about 65¢. (Courtesy of Tell City Historical Society.)

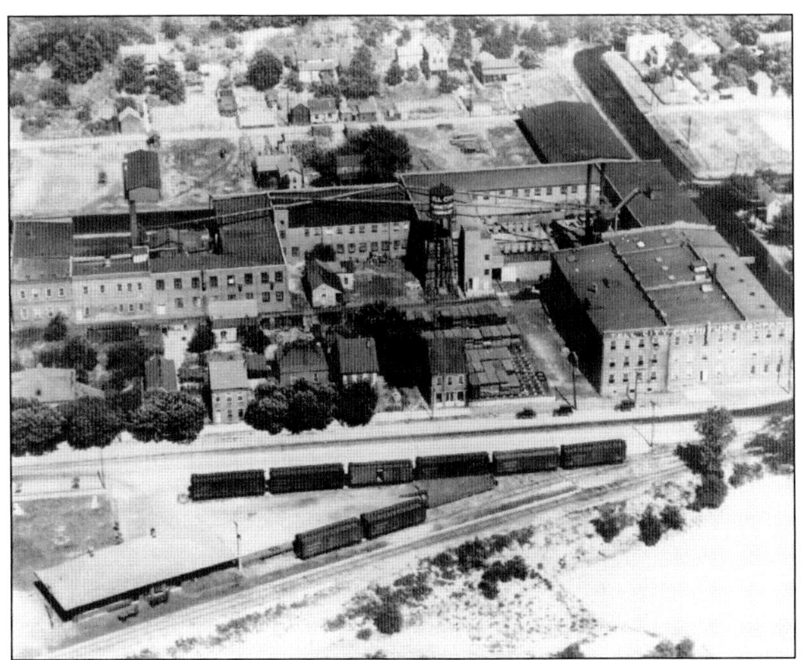

The Tell City Furniture Company was established in 1859. It was located between Guttenberg and Blum Streets and between Ninth and Main Streets. Swiss Plywood and William Tell Woodcrafters occupied the plant that was formerly the Tell City Furniture Company. Swiss Plywood closed on December 31, 2008. (Courtesy of Tell City Historical Society.)

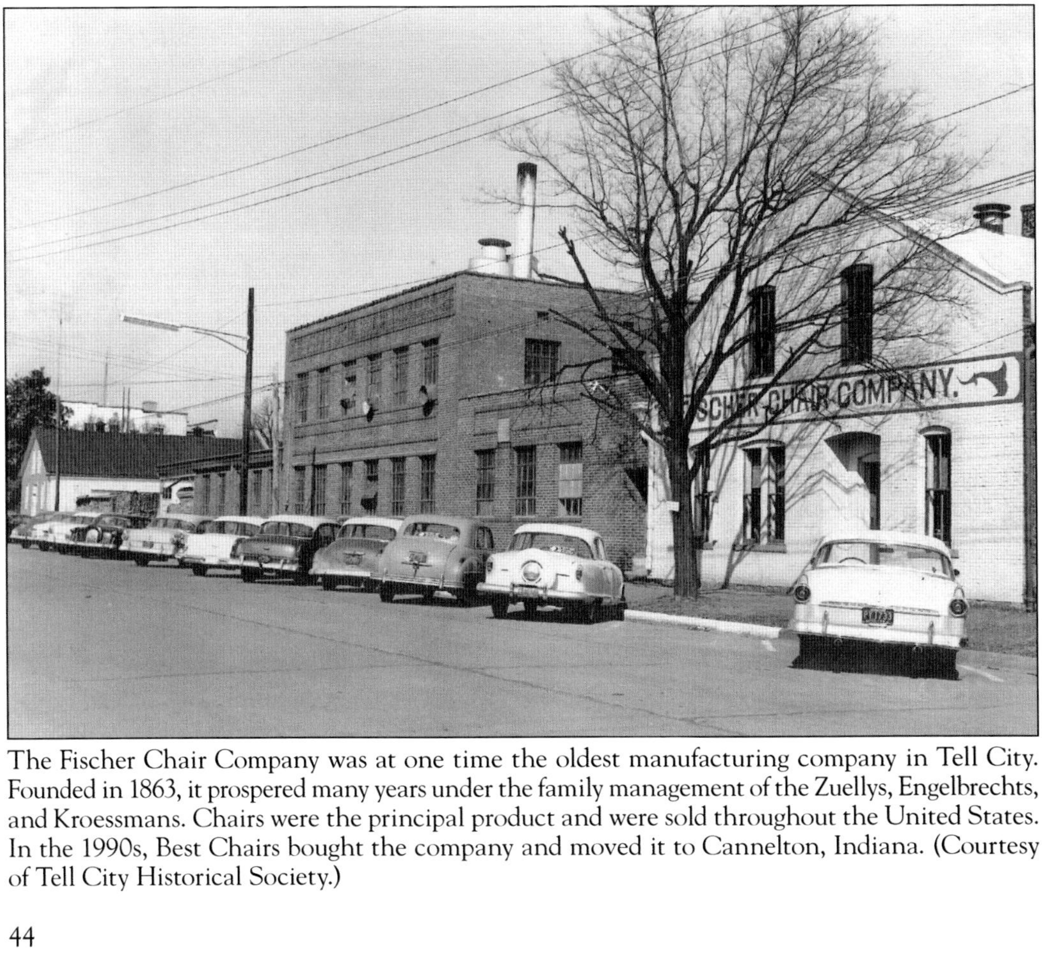

The Fischer Chair Company was at one time the oldest manufacturing company in Tell City. Founded in 1863, it prospered many years under the family management of the Zuellys, Engelbrechts, and Kroessmans. Chairs were the principal product and were sold throughout the United States. In the 1990s, Best Chairs bought the company and moved it to Cannelton, Indiana. (Courtesy of Tell City Historical Society.)

Pictured around 1875, Tell City Flour Mill employees are, from left to right, unidentified, Col Kaemmerling, Charles Steinauer, Andrew Steinauer, and August Steinauer. (Courtesy of Tell City Historical Society.)

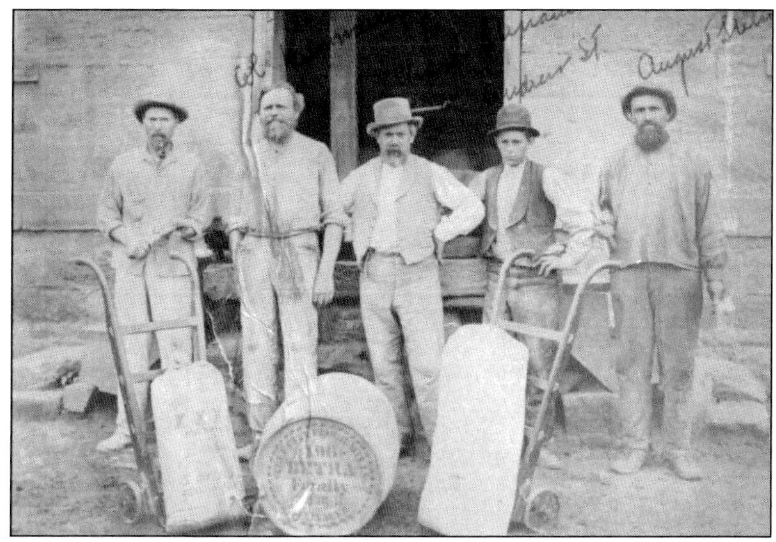

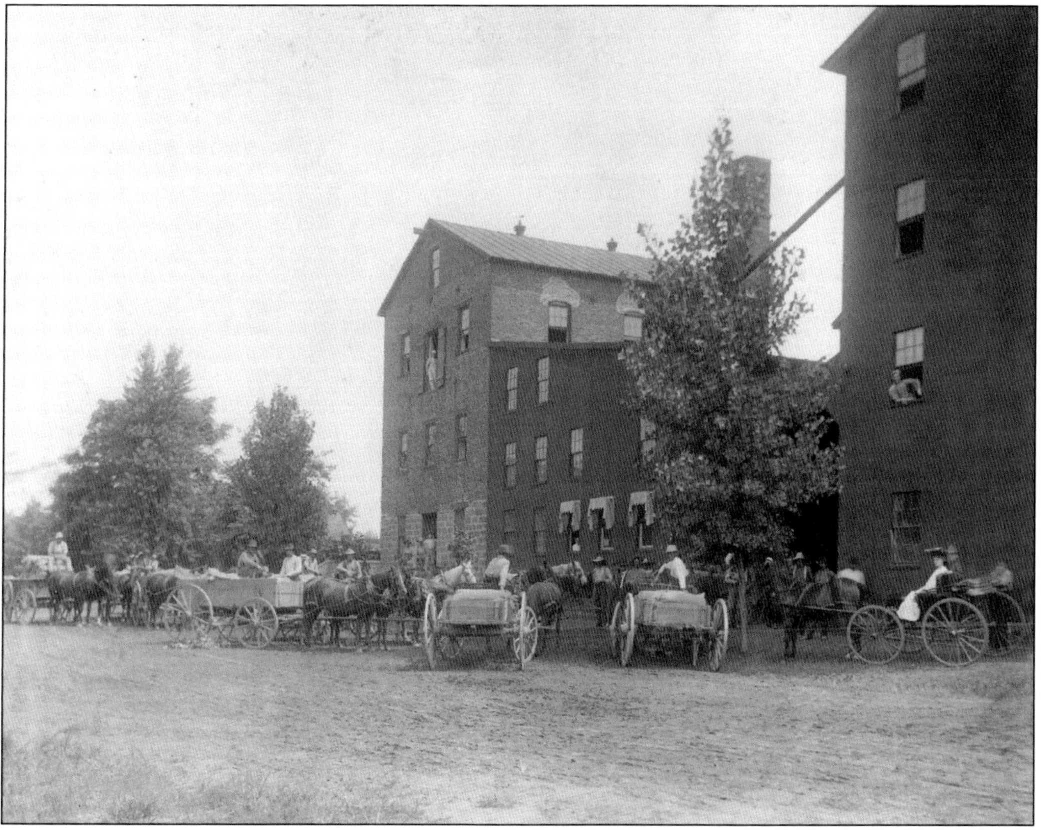

The Tell City Flour Mill was founded by Charles Steinauer in 1859. The flour mill went through several managers, owners, and buildings on this site. Most of the original building was destroyed by a fire in 1929. It was rebuilt and struck by a fire again in 1956. It was rebuilt once again in the area, this time serving agricultural needs for many years. (Courtesy of Tell City Historical Society.)

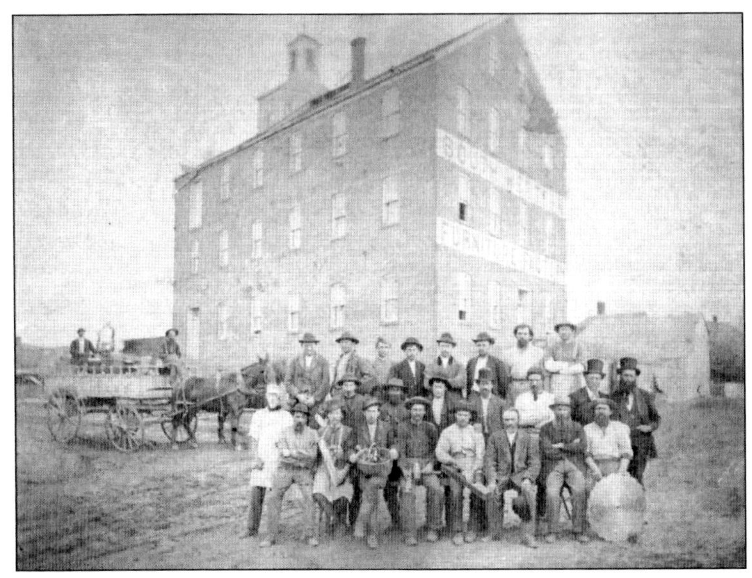

Southwestern Furniture Company, located in the 300 block of Seventh Street, started operations in 1873. This photograph was taken before the railroad came into existence; the tracks are now located just where the group was standing. Note the wagon and mules on the left. This is the type of wagon all local furniture plants used in the early days. The first railroad came into Tell City in 1887. (Courtesy of Tell City Historical Society.)

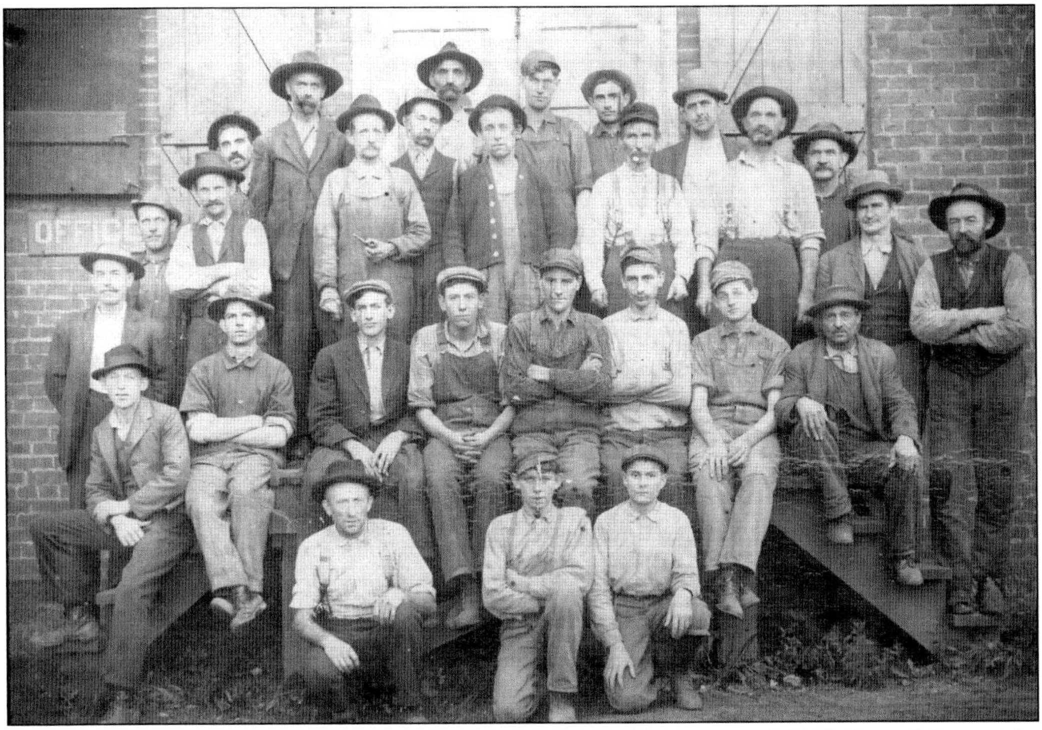

Southwestern Furniture Company employees are pictured here around 1910. From left to right are (first row) Bill Weiss, Sam Scott, and Al Baumgart; (second row) William Dreyling, George Scherzinger, Robert C. Schaerer, Sylvester Malone, Frank Wright, Victor Schneider, William Neutzel, and George Ludwig; (third row) Robert Huelsman, Ed Roehling, Mike Nuetzel, August Kaercher, Nenry Anson, Herman Wolf, Billy Stadler, Mike Kramer, John Scheible, Arnold Malone, Joe Bender, Gottlieb Heller, Harry Schergens, John Deinzer, Lawrence Fruehwald, Gus Meyenberg, and John Bettag.

The US Brick Company was located on the north end of Tell City. Bricks were made for several buildings and houses throughout Tell City and the surrounding area. (Courtesy of Tell City Historical Society.)

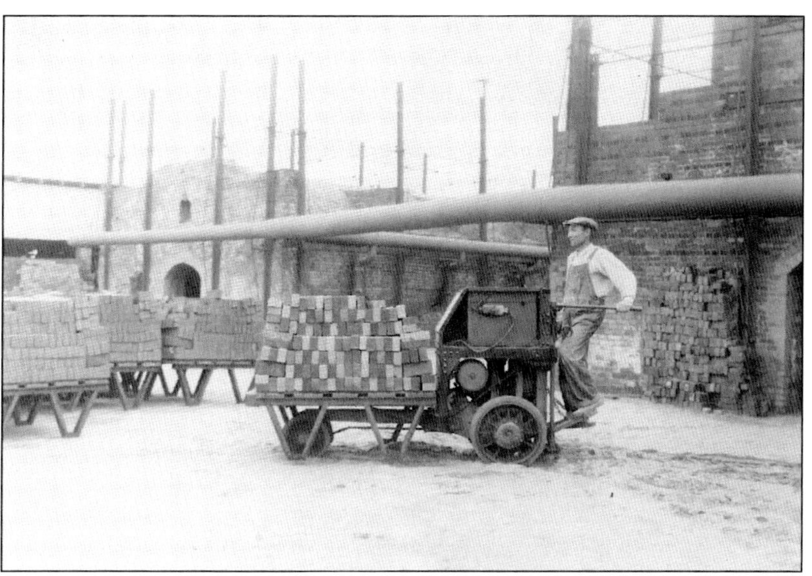

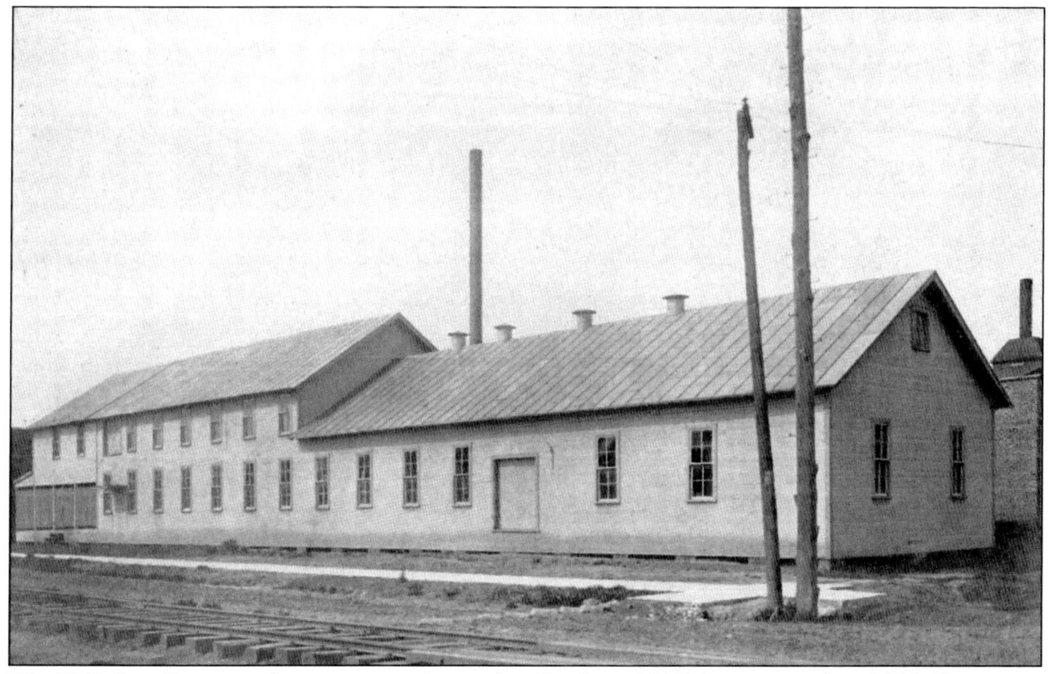

The Tell City Canning Company was located at Sixth and Tell Streets on the old Neff property that was bought by the company in 1905. Directors were Joseph Dodson, Jacob Hauser, Phillip Werner, Charles McCallister, Fred J. Herrmann, Henry Bader, and Walter Huthsteiner. In 1930, a total of $4,000 was raised and the American Packing Corporation took over the industry. Local farmers would bring their tomatoes to have them canned at this facility. An old story goes that the gentleman who invented V8 tomato juice started his career at this canning factory. In 1937, most of the machines were moved out and shipped to New York.

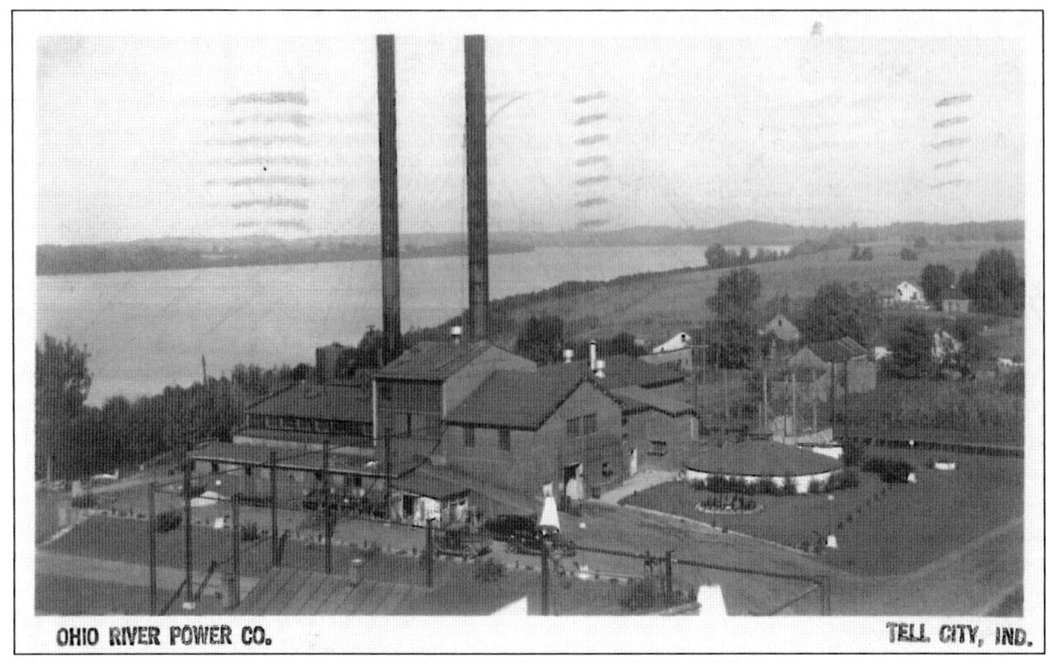

The Ohio River Power Company was located along Fourth and Fulton Streets.

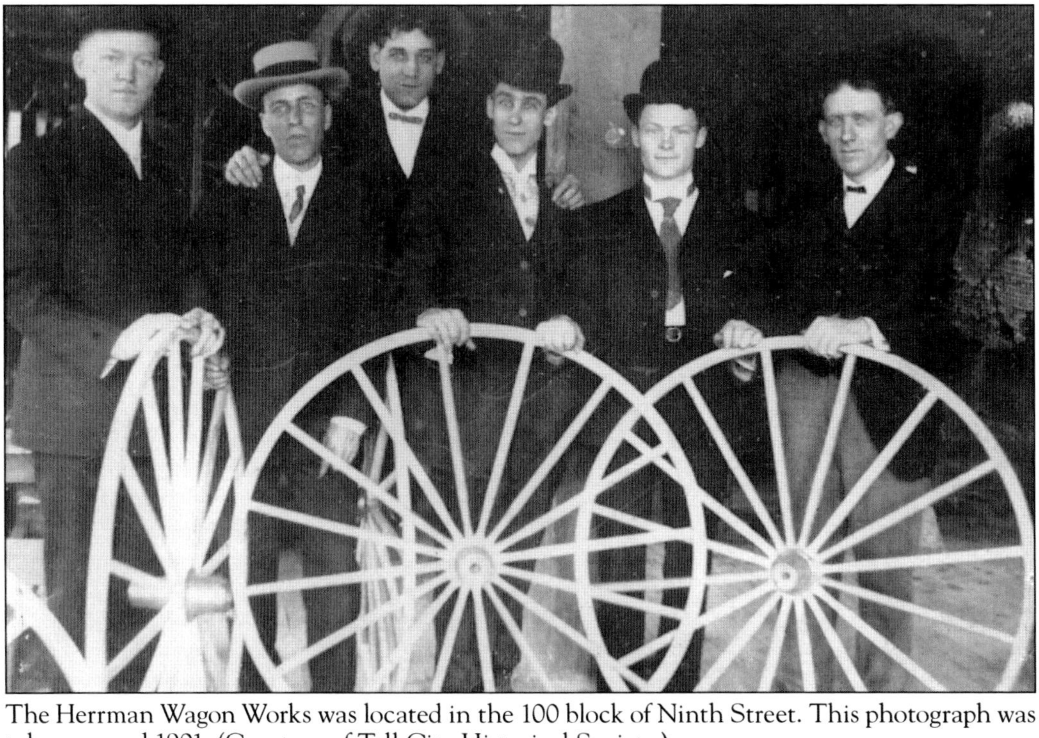

The Herrman Wagon Works was located in the 100 block of Ninth Street. This photograph was taken around 1901. (Courtesy of Tell City Historical Society.)

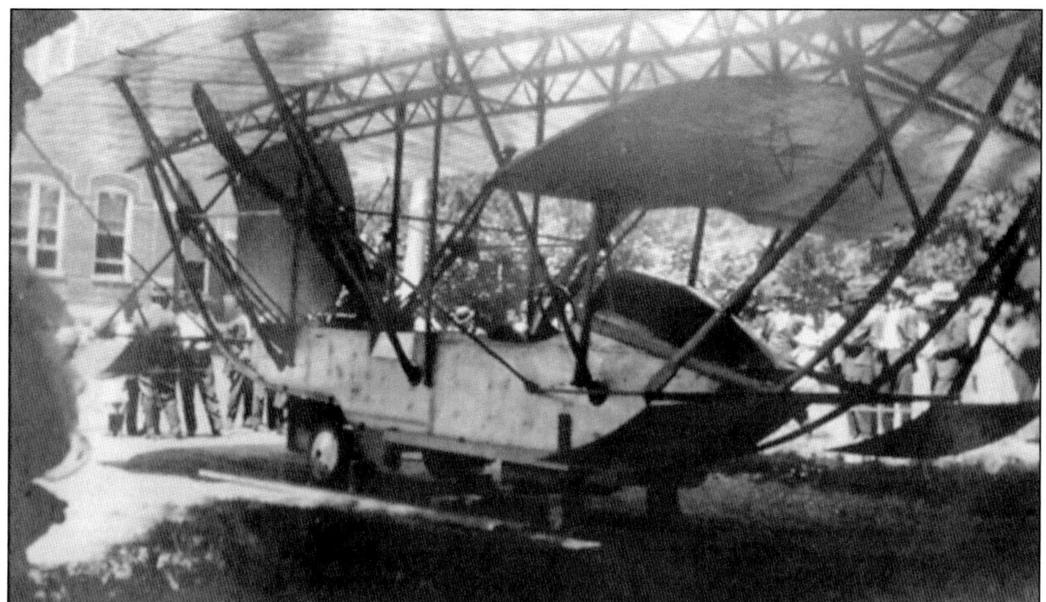

Shown here around 1915, Edwards Hydro Aeroplane, or Edward's Common Sense Aeroplane as it was called, was built in Tell City by R.C. Edwards. The plane was constructed at the Tell City Spoke Company (later Maxon Construction Company). The plane was on exhibit at City Hall Park. (Courtesy of Karen Marcroft.)

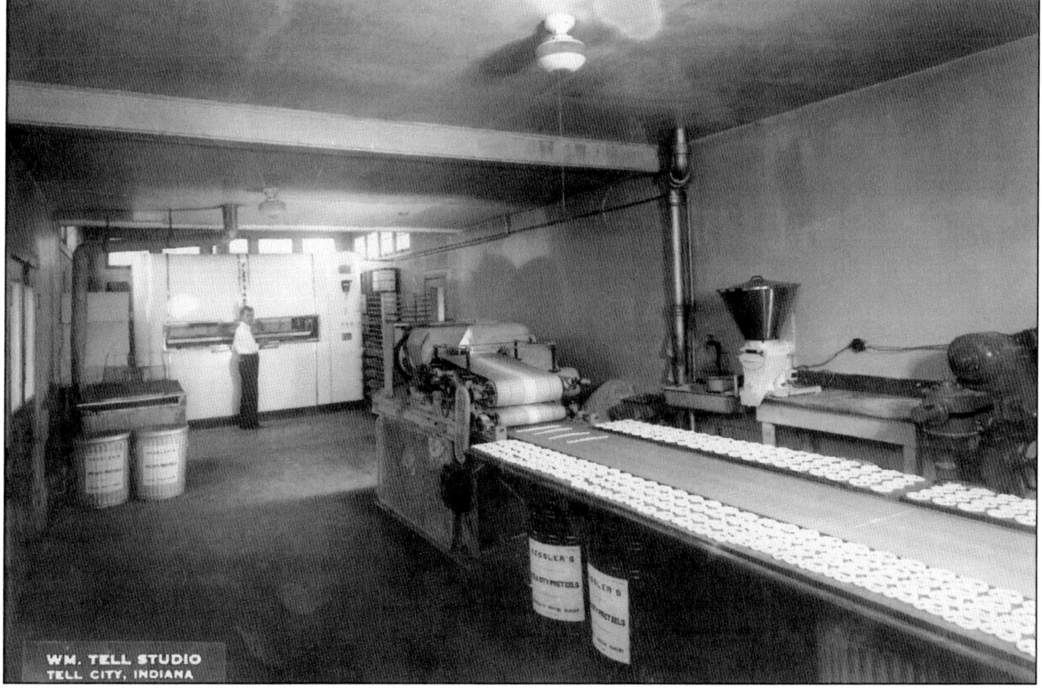

Kessler's Tell City Pretzels, pictured here around 1936, was located at Ninth and Fulton Streets. The recipe for these pretzels was passed down to Alex Kessler from Casper Gloor upon his death. Today, Tell City Pretzels is still in business and the pretzels are still made the old-fashioned way—by hand twisting. (Courtesy of Tell City Historical Society.)

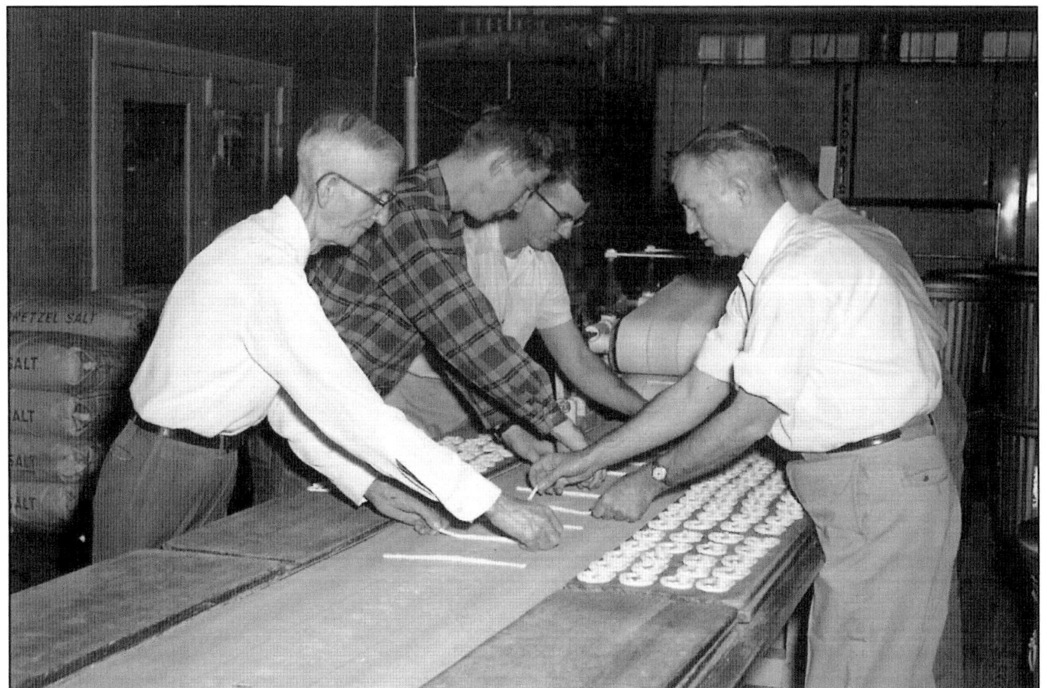

Pictured here around 1955, Kessler's Tell City Pretzels employees hand twist the pretzels. From left to right are Alex Kessler, unidentified, Russel Kessler, ? Kessler, and unidentified. (Courtesy of Tell City Historical Society.)

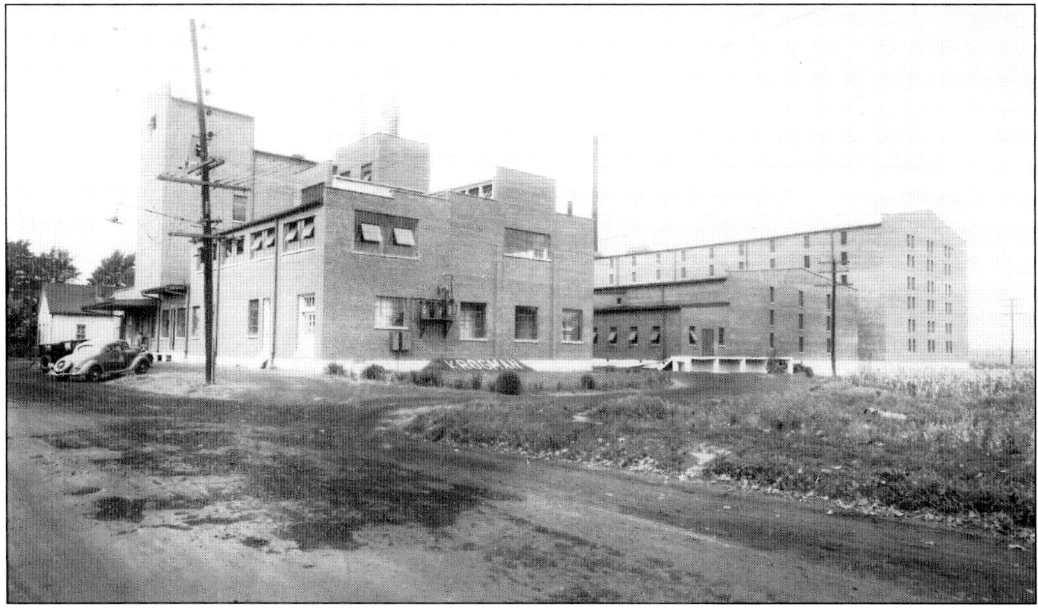

Krogman Distillery, located at Fifth and Jefferson Streets, was built in 1935. The buildings were constructed at a cost of $135,000. The plant had an operating capacity of 55 barrels daily. Another warehouse, with storage capacity of 15,000 barrels, was built next to the warehouse shown at the right, which had a capacity of 7,000 barrels. The warehouse was seven stories tall. Today, only part of these buildings still stand.

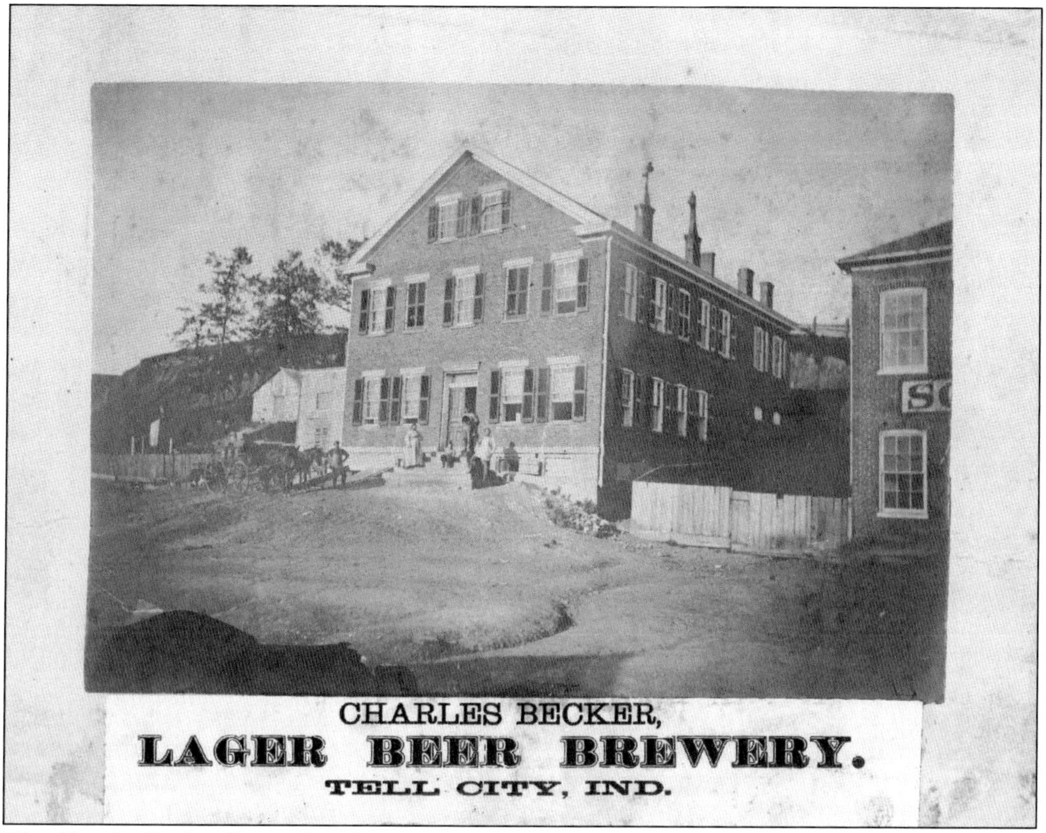

CHARLES BECKER,

LAGER BEER BREWERY.

TELL CITY, IND.

The Charles Becher Lager Beer Brewery was located on the east side of the 300 block of Ninth Street. This building was constructed in 1870 at a cost of $3,000. This photograph was taken before part of Ninth Street was cut down to its present level. The entrance seen here was still used after the street was cut down to grade and a higher stone step with railings was built, one going up from the south and one from the north. The offices of the Tell City Brewing Company were located in the front portion of this building, and this space was also used as offices by the Tell City Creamery. The building was razed in 1967. (Courtesy of Tell City Historical Society.)

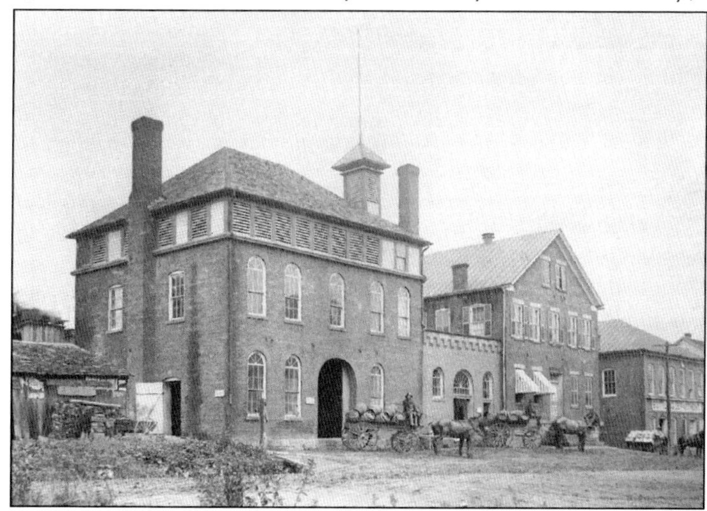

Originally the Tell City Brewery Company, this building has a long and colorful past as a brewery and the maker of Tell City's most famous beer, Edelweiss, named after the national flower of Switzerland. For many years, this was home to the Tell City Creamery. The center structure was where the beer was made, before being bottled next door in the building at far right. (Courtesy of Tell City Historical Society.)

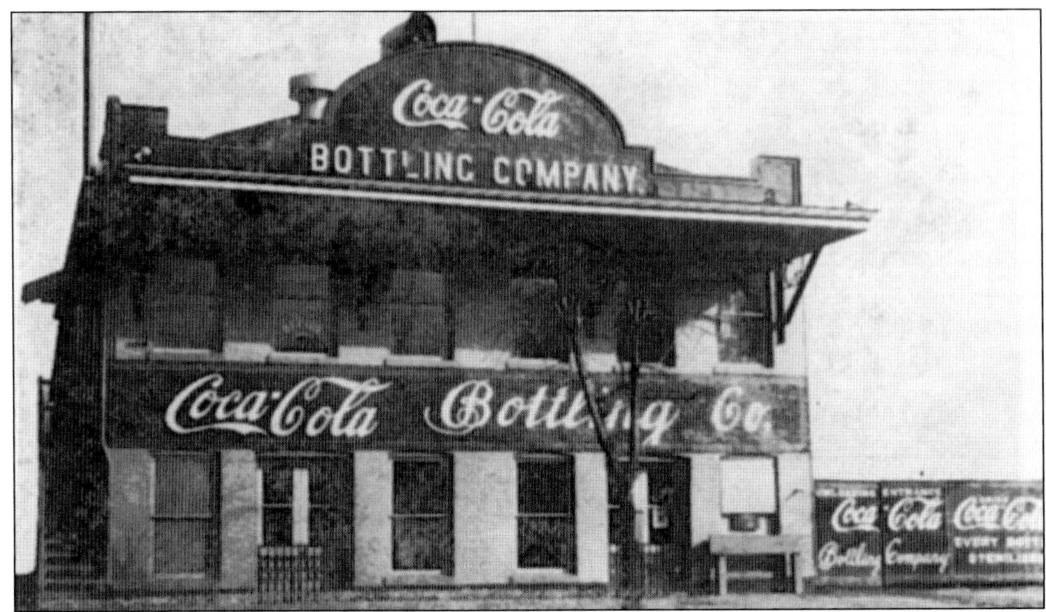

The Coca-Cola Bottling Company plant was originally known as Schweizer Hall. This building was owned by the Swiss Colonization Society and was used for meetings and gatherings during the first few years of the city's settlement. This hall was extensively used as temporary living quarters by arriving families until a permanent home could be built or purchased. In later years, it was occupied and used by the bottling plant for the Tell City Brewery Company. Later, it was used for Chero Cola bottling and then became a Coca-Cola Bottling Company plant after that. Currently, the building is being restored.

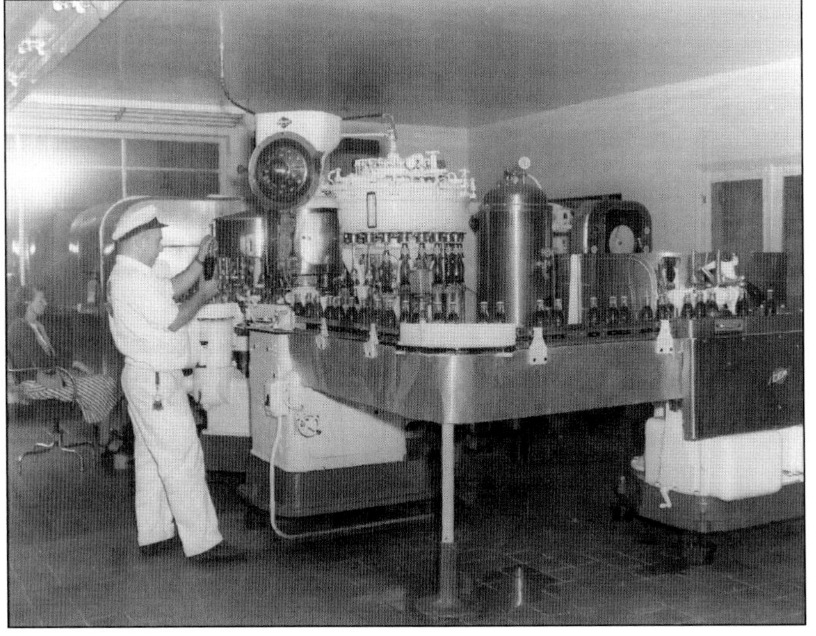

The Coca-Cola Bottling Company plant was located at 321 Ninth Street. Many citizens remember watching Coca-Cola being bottled as they passed the factory. Gabe Miller is the gentleman in the photograph inspecting the filled bottle. Bottling in the plant ceased in 1991. (Courtesy of Mary Emma Owen.)

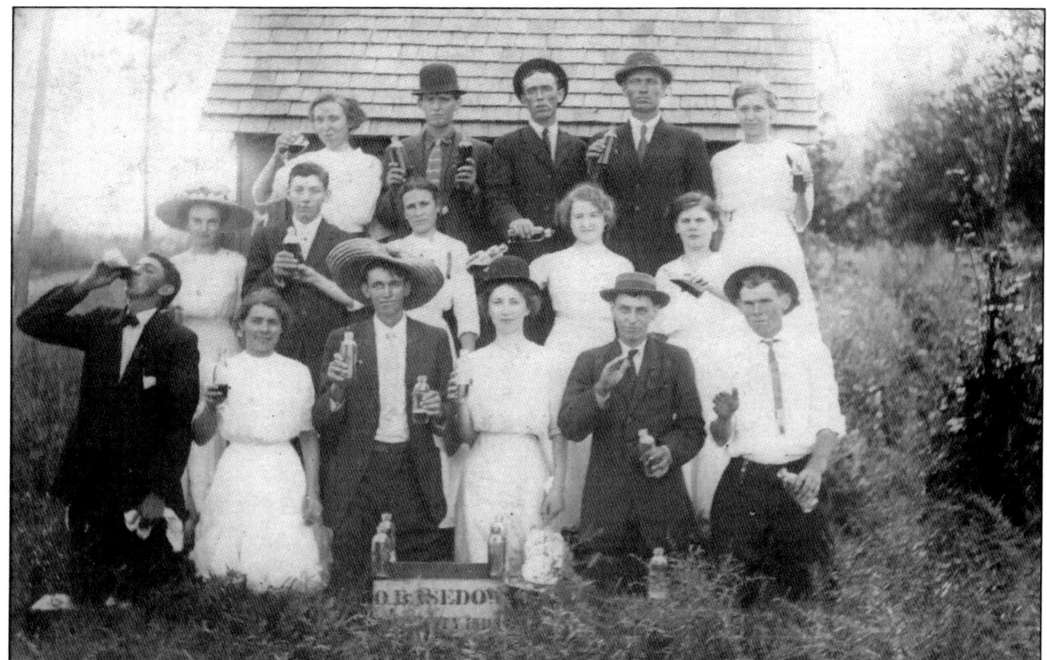

The Basedow Bottling Works was located at 302 Ninth Street. This picture, taken in 1911 in Gatchel, Indiana, depicts a group of individuals used for promotional advertisements displaying the bottles. From left to right are (first row) Henry Snyder (photographer), unidentified, John Snyder, two unidentified, and Carl Howell; (second row) Pearl Brown, unidentified, Rosa Smith, Zelda Walters, and Eulalia Howell; (third row) Emma Peckinpaw, unidentified, Grover Cleveland Miller, unidentified, and Evie Lawalin. (Courtesy of Al Hauenstein.)

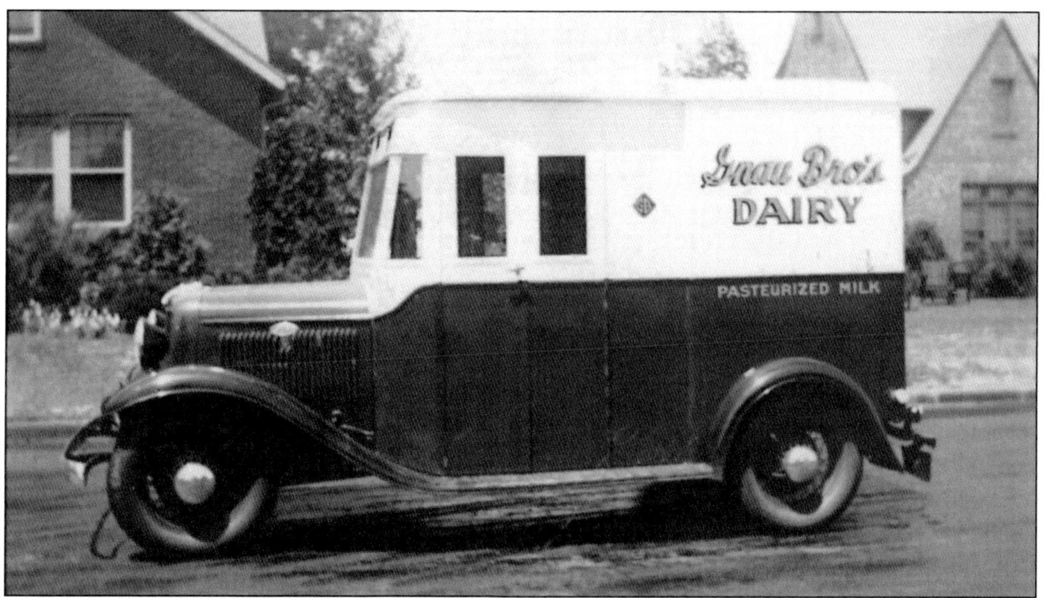

Many older citizens remember the days when milk was delivered to their homes. This delivery truck, pictured here around 1934, was used by Gnau Dairy to make home deliveries.

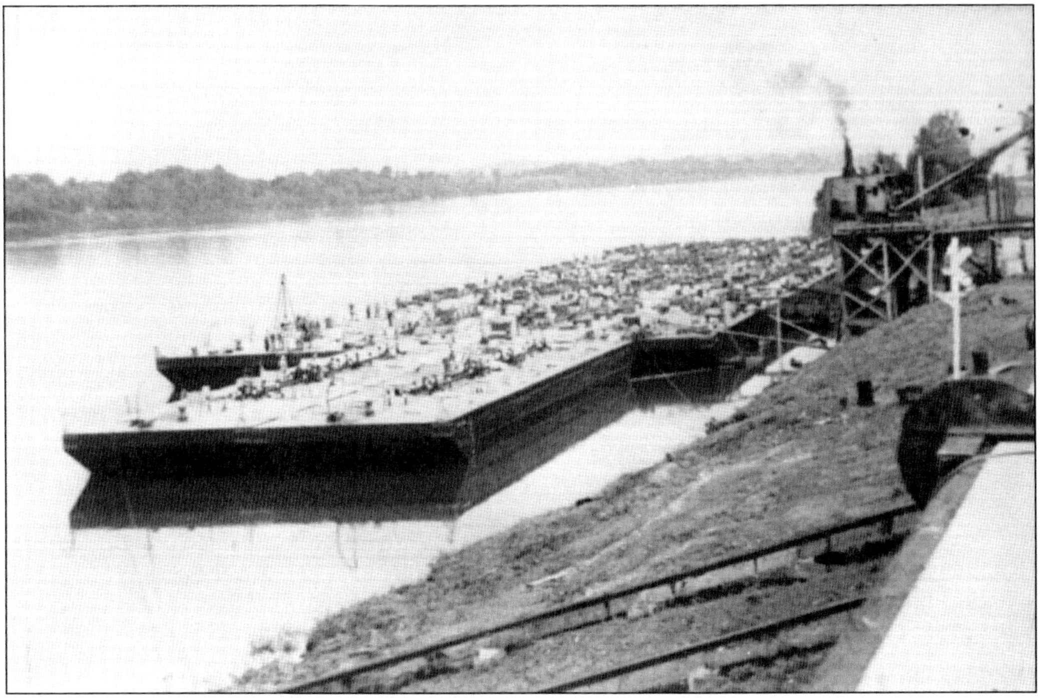

Pictured here around 1943 are large wooden oil barges that were built for the US Army. Note the workmen on the decks. Maxon Construction Company employed a number of men to build these barges; much of the work was done by hand. The seams were all caulked with a ropelike material treated with pitch and then pounded in between the seams with wooden mallets. The noise was terrific and with a large number at work could be heard quite a distance into town when other noisemaking works were shut down. (Courtesy of Tell City Historical Society.)

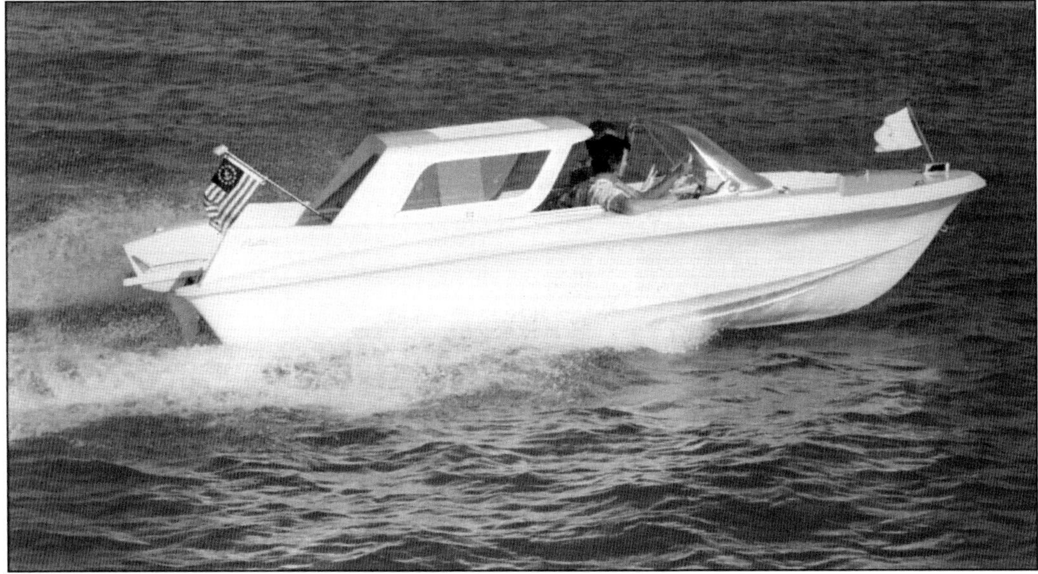

Cutter Boats, Inc., was located on State Road 66 on the north end of town, where Parker Hannifin (Commercial Filters) now operates. The company came to Tell City in 1958 and manufactured fiberglass boats.

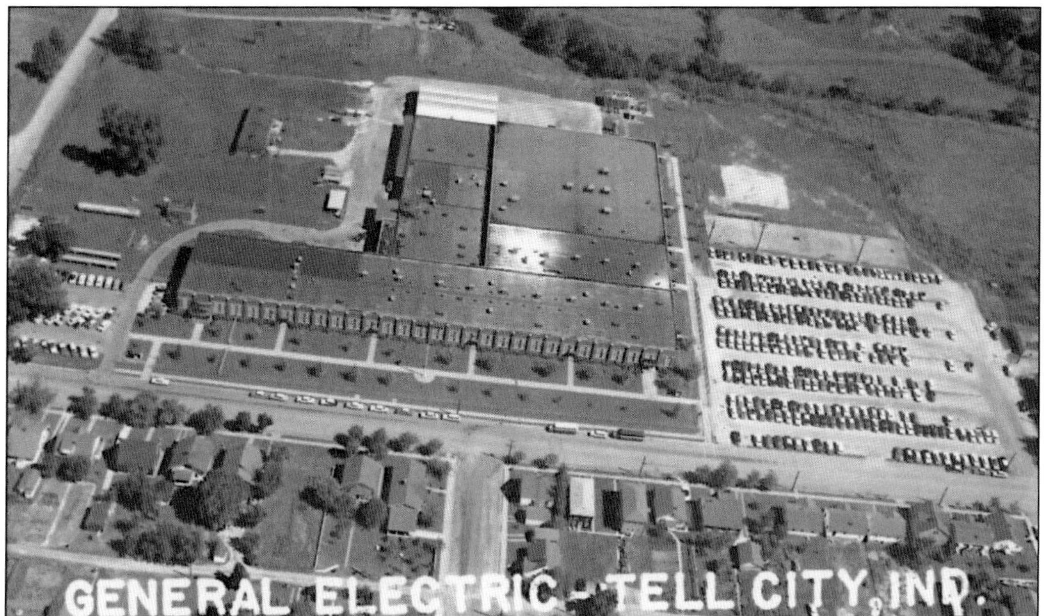

In March 1951, General Electric (GE) was producing tubes in Tell City. The plant began as a Ken-Rad facility, with production commencing on January 24, 1944. GE bought the tube-making division of Ken-Rad in 1945. In 1955, future president Ronald Reagan, as program director for the General Electric Theater television show, visited the plant and spent a busy day touring the city. Later, production was changed to small motors. The plant closed in November 2005.

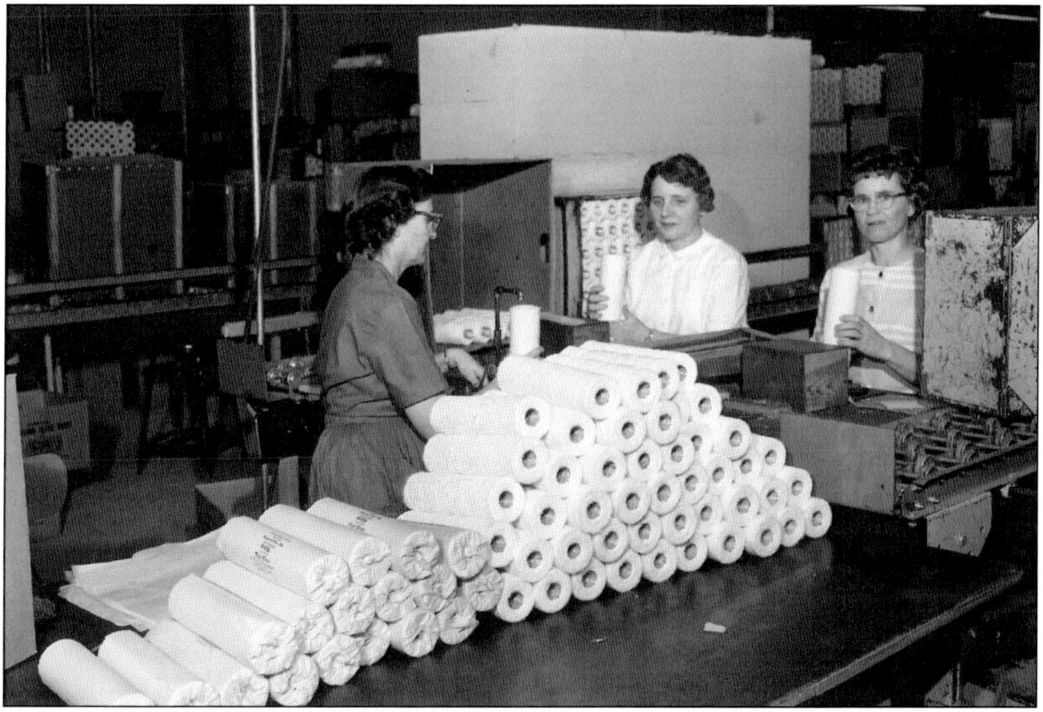

In 1963, Commercial Filters located in the former Cutter Boats building on State Road 66 on the north end of town. Today, this factory is part of the Parker Hannifin Corporation.

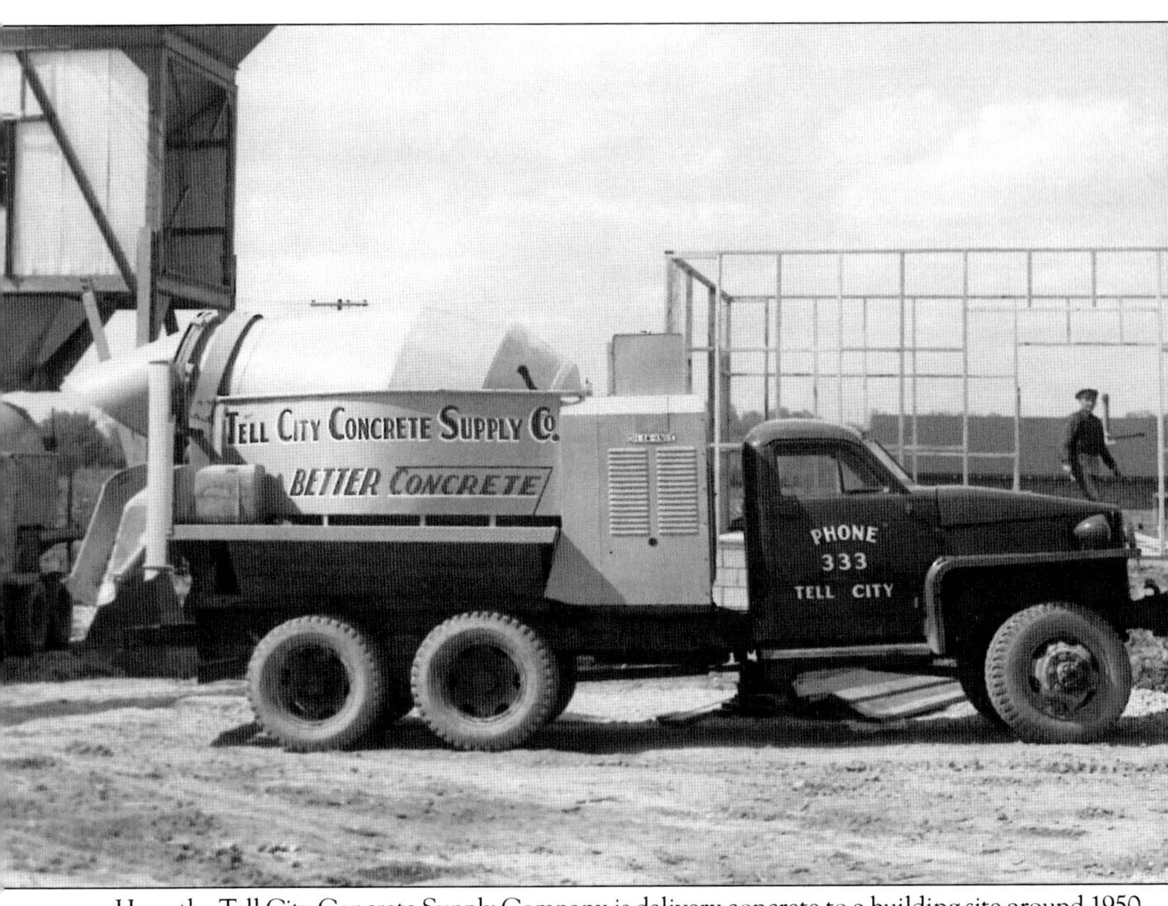

Here, the Tell City Concrete Supply Company is delivery concrete to a building site around 1950. The Tell City Concrete Supply Company is owned by the Mulzer family. (Courtesy of Tell City Historical Society.)

Four

DOWNTOWN

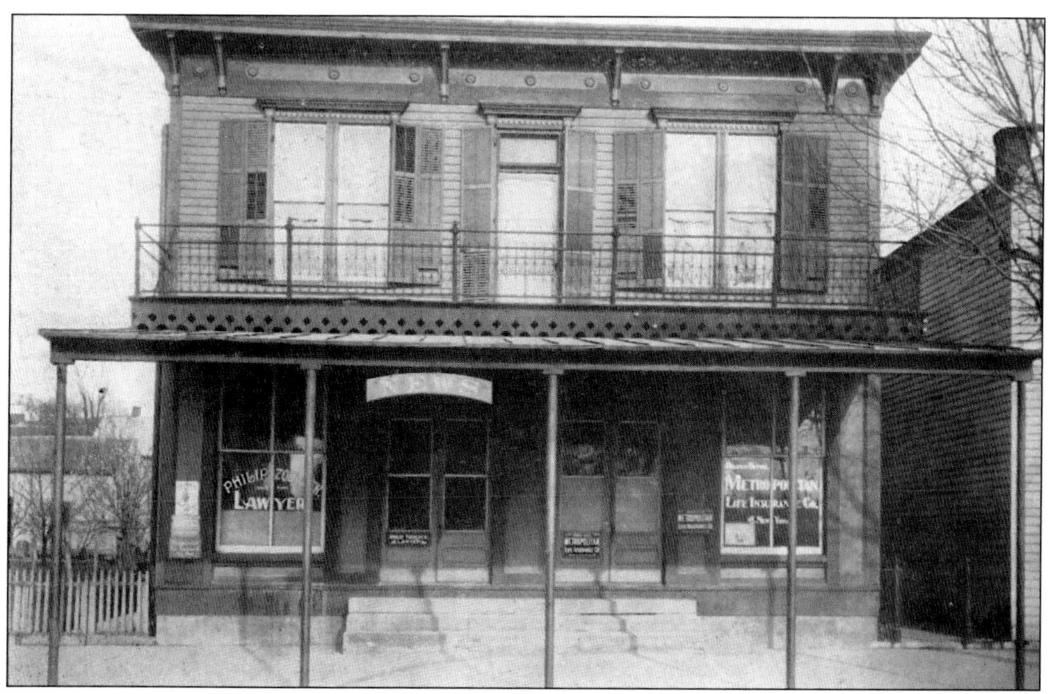

Pictured is the Tell City News Building, located in the 400 block of Main Street. The first floor was occupied by Metropolitan Life Insurance Company and Phillip Zoercher, attorney-at-law. The *Tell City News* was founded by Phillip Zoercher in 1891. In 1900, Louis Zoercher purchased the *Tell City News* from his brother and took over as editor of the paper.

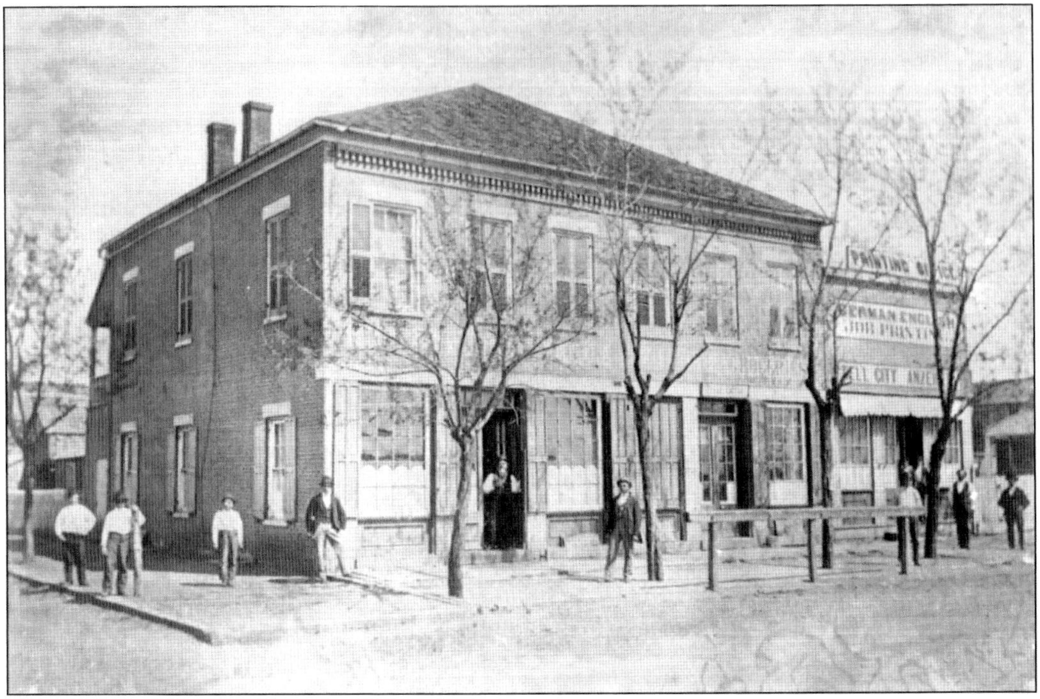

The Tell City Anzeiger Newspaper Building was constructed in 1866. In 1888, George Bott acquired half interest and moved into this building. There was a saloon operated by Adam Gruntz and a German grocery on the right side of the building. In 1891, the Botts started an English-language newspaper, the *Tell City Journal*, which continued until 1923. (Courtesy of Tell City Historical Society.)

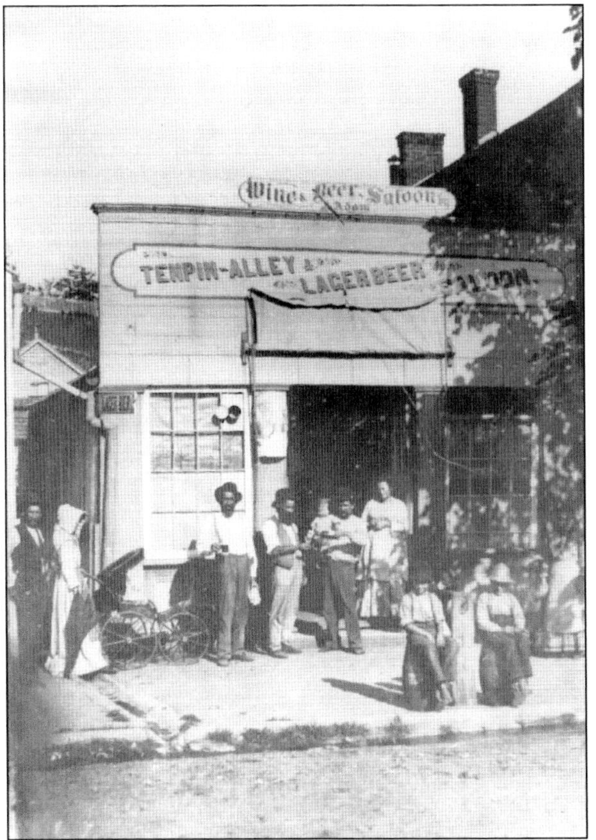

The Adam Saloon was located in the 500 block of Main Street. Pictured around 1890 are, from left to right, three unidentified; Magnus Kriesle (heavy beard), founder of Kriesle Manufacturing; Joseph Adam Sr. holding a baby; a Mrs. Adam (in the doorway); and three unidentified. (Courtesy of Tell City Historical Society.)

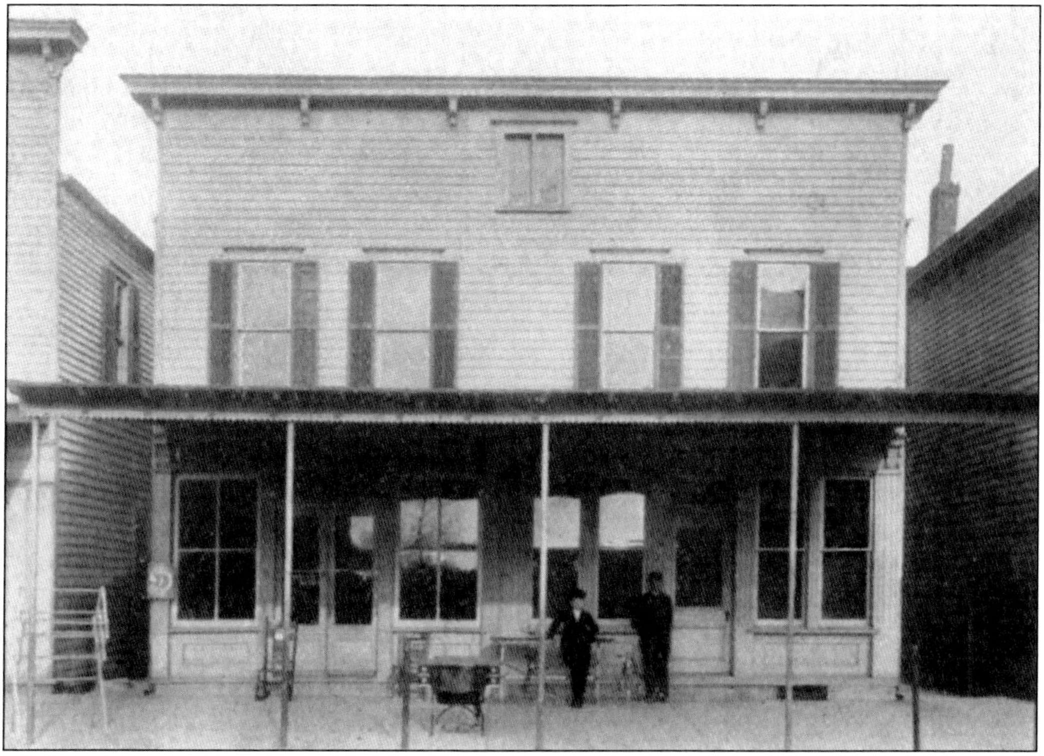

J.H. Schergens founded Schergens' Furniture Store in 1858. In 1893, his son Charles took over the business and erected this building in the 500 block of Main Street. Besides selling furniture, the firm was also an undertaking business. This structure was torn down to make way for the new Home Mutual Insurance building.

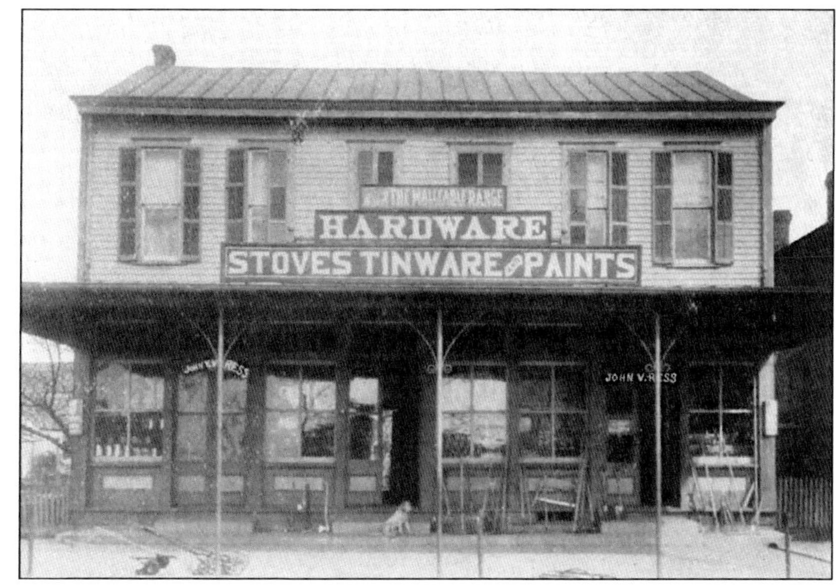

John V. Ress opened this business in 1878. Ress learned his skills with tinwork in Cincinnati. Besides tinware, he also sold a full line of hardware items.

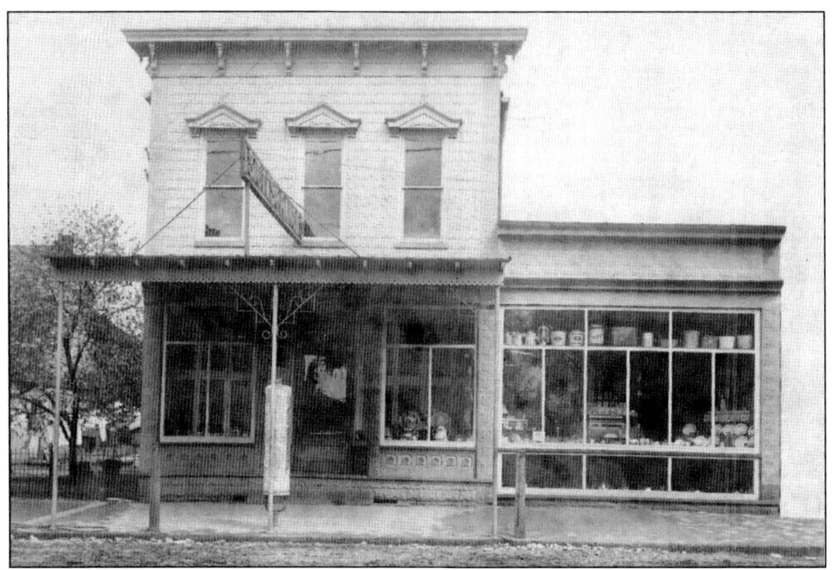

The Frank J. Ress Store was one of the early merchandising places in Tell City. This building once housed Gamble's Store as well.

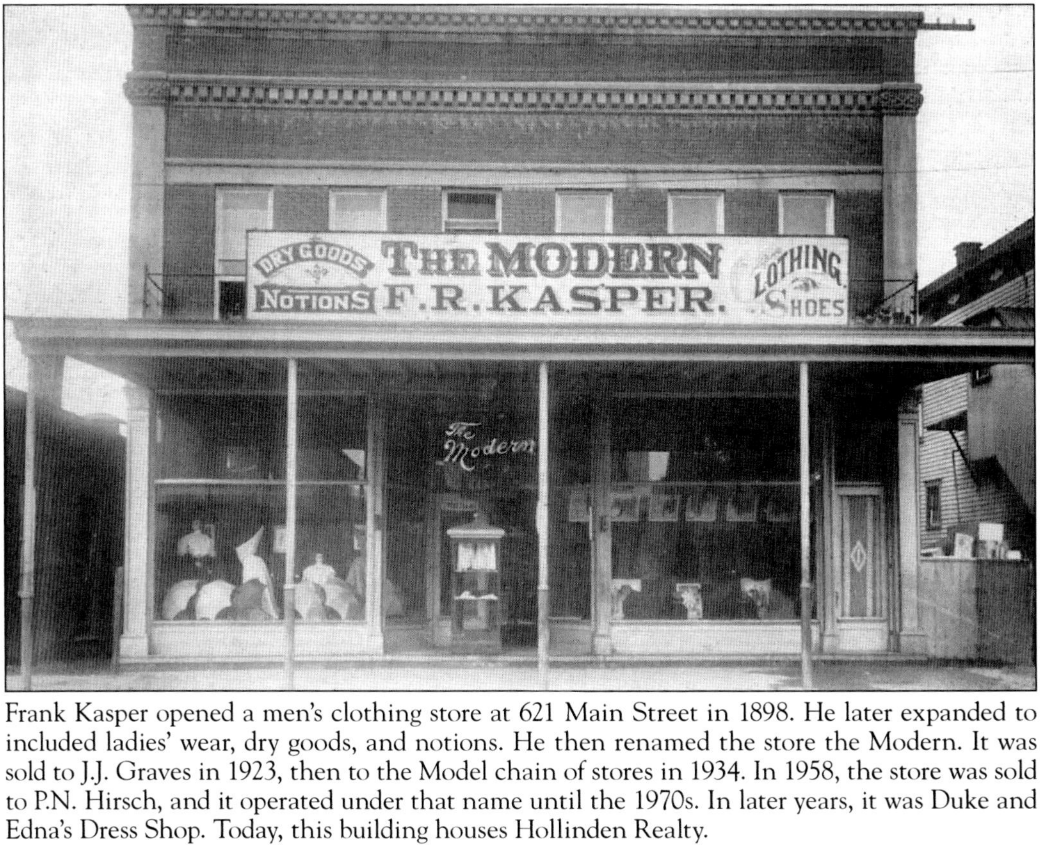

Frank Kasper opened a men's clothing store at 621 Main Street in 1898. He later expanded to included ladies' wear, dry goods, and notions. He then renamed the store the Modern. It was sold to J.J. Graves in 1923, then to the Model chain of stores in 1934. In 1958, the store was sold to P.N. Hirsch, and it operated under that name until the 1970s. In later years, it was Duke and Edna's Dress Shop. Today, this building houses Hollinden Realty.

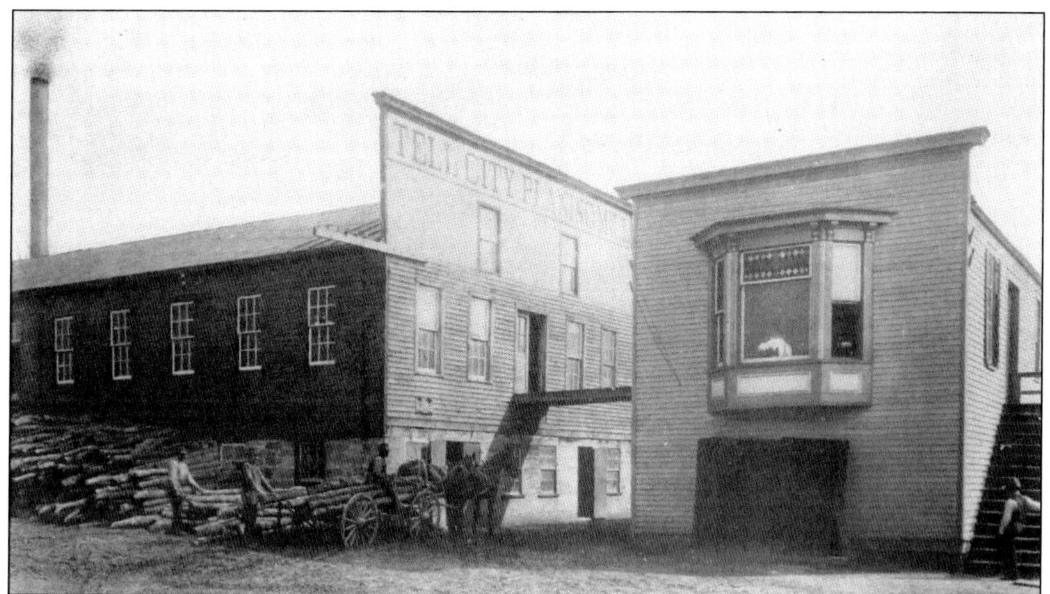

The Tell City Planing Mill, also known as Kreisle Manufacturing Company, was one of the oldest businesses in Tell City. It was founded in 1865 and occupied a wood-frame building, which was originally constructed as a brewery in the 1860s—but that business failed. A plank road once passed between the two buildings.

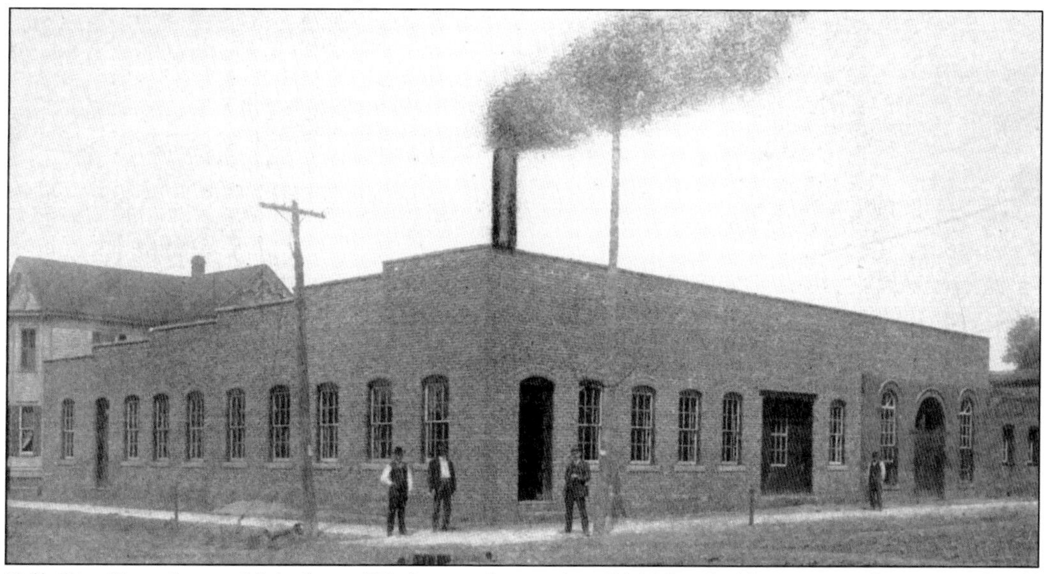

Tell City Foundry and Machine Works was located at 706 Humboldt Street. The original Tell City Foundry and Machine Works was owned by Wiedmer and Oboussier and opened around 1880. It was one of Tell City's earliest industries and was located in a frame structure that burned down. The new Tell City Foundry and Machine Works building was constructed in 1908 by its new owners—A.P. Fenn, Adolph Zuelly, R.P. Carr, Henry Boehman, and Guy LaRue. They only ran it until 1911 or 1912; they attempted to manufacture a grease pump, which was unsuccessful and depleted their resources. Note the steam engine visible in the front of the business. The home visible behind the building was razed. The Tell City Pour Haus, an eatery and live music venue, and the Tell City Brewery now occupy this structure.

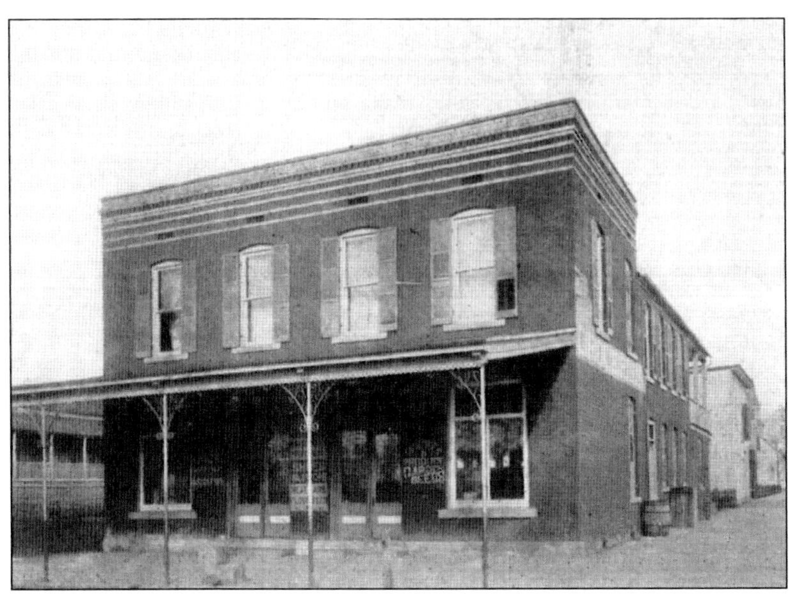

Henry Basedow, a Prussian immigrant, started a grocery store at the corner of Ninth and Mozart Streets. Today, it is an apartment building and, for the most part, still looks the same. This image was taken around 1908.

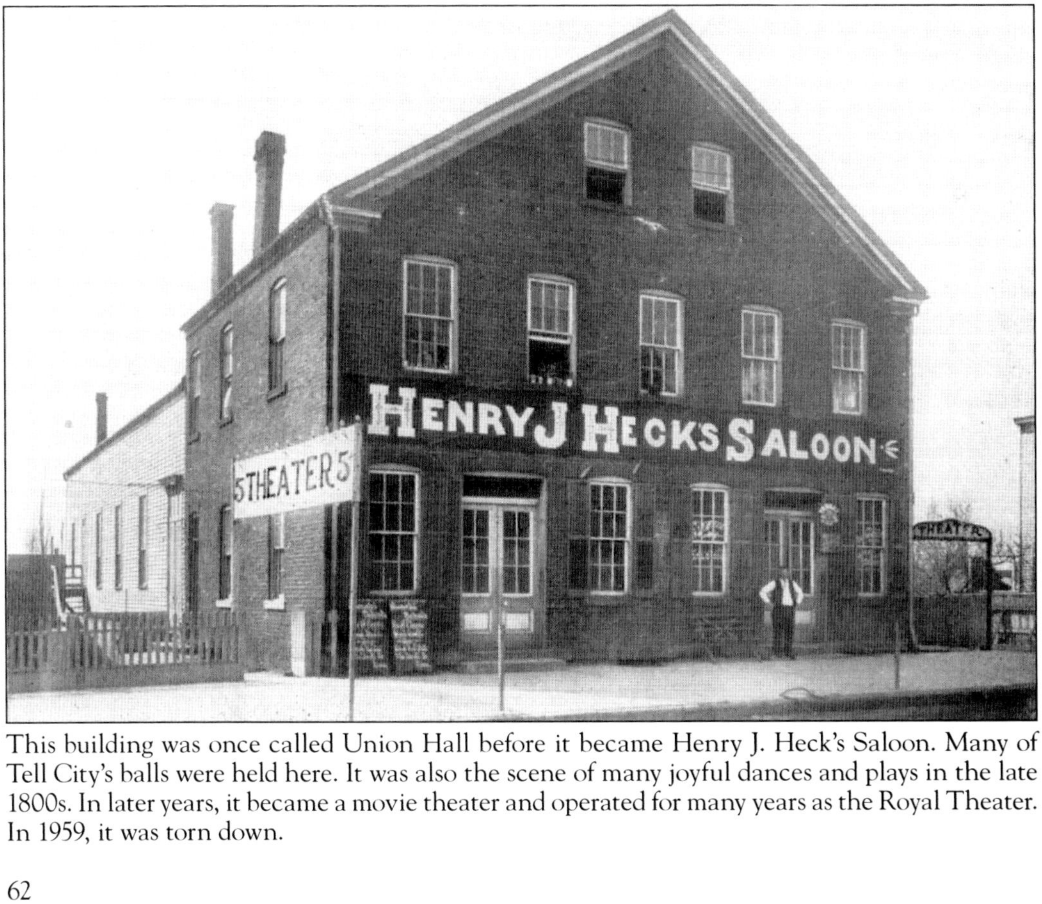

This building was once called Union Hall before it became Henry J. Heck's Saloon. Many of Tell City's balls were held here. It was also the scene of many joyful dances and plays in the late 1800s. In later years, it became a movie theater and operated for many years as the Royal Theater. In 1959, it was torn down.

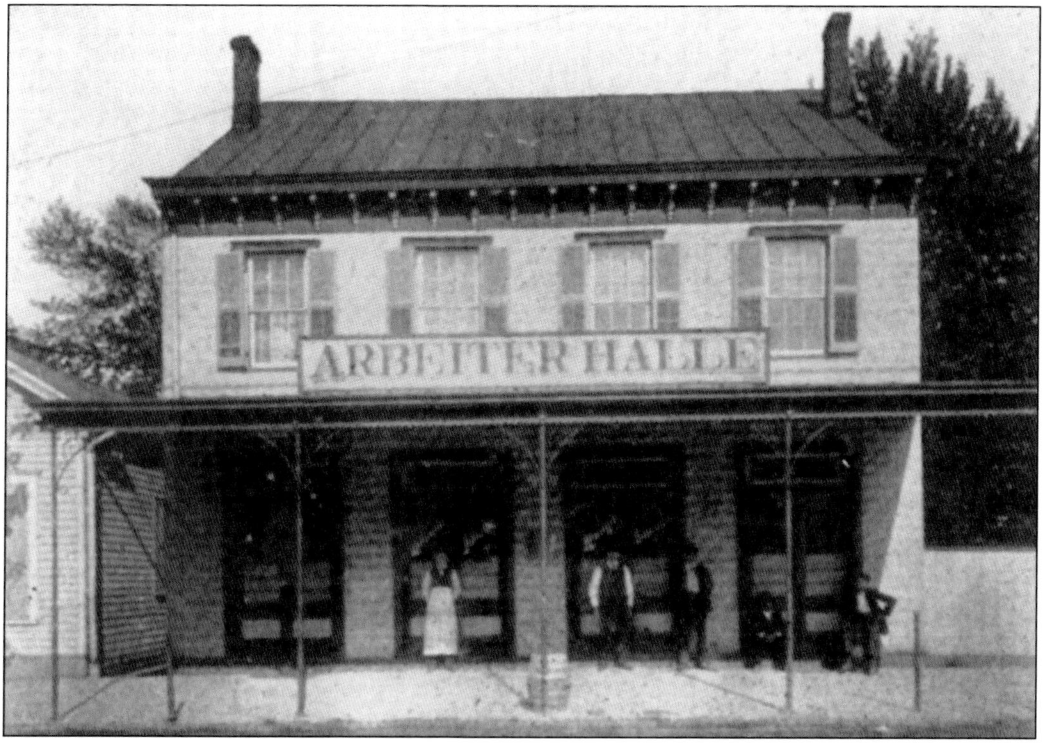

Originally called Arbeiter Halle (Worker's Hall), Einsiedler's Saloon was built in 1872 and served a free lunch with the beer. It was wired for electricity in 1899 by owner Reim Einsiedler. A competing bar owner, Dick Windphfennig, would come each morning and slap a dime on the bar for a shot of whiskey. Each evening, Einsiedler would take that same dime down the street to purchase a shot of whiskey from Windphfennig. This same dime exchanged hands in this manner for many years. In 1953, Vernon Braun purchased Einsiedler's Saloon. Today, it is known as Braunie's Bar. The original covered sidewalk still exists.

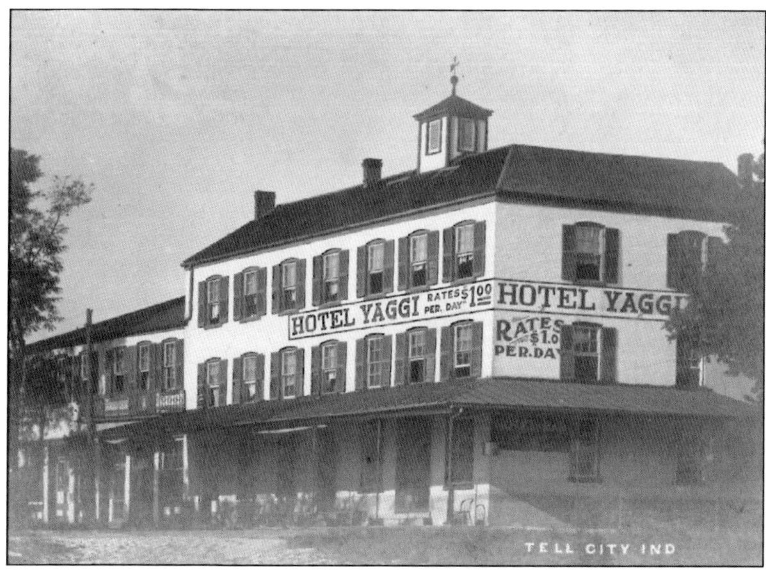

In 1858, Fredrick Steiner built the Steiner House Hotel at Seventh and Blum Streets. In 1876, Anton Moraweck purchased the hotel from Steiner and renamed it the Hotel Moraweck. It was then sold to Edward Yaggi, who changed the name to Hotel Yaggi. After that, it was the Kellems Hotel. In 1919, the structure was demolished. (Courtesy of Tell City Historical Society.)

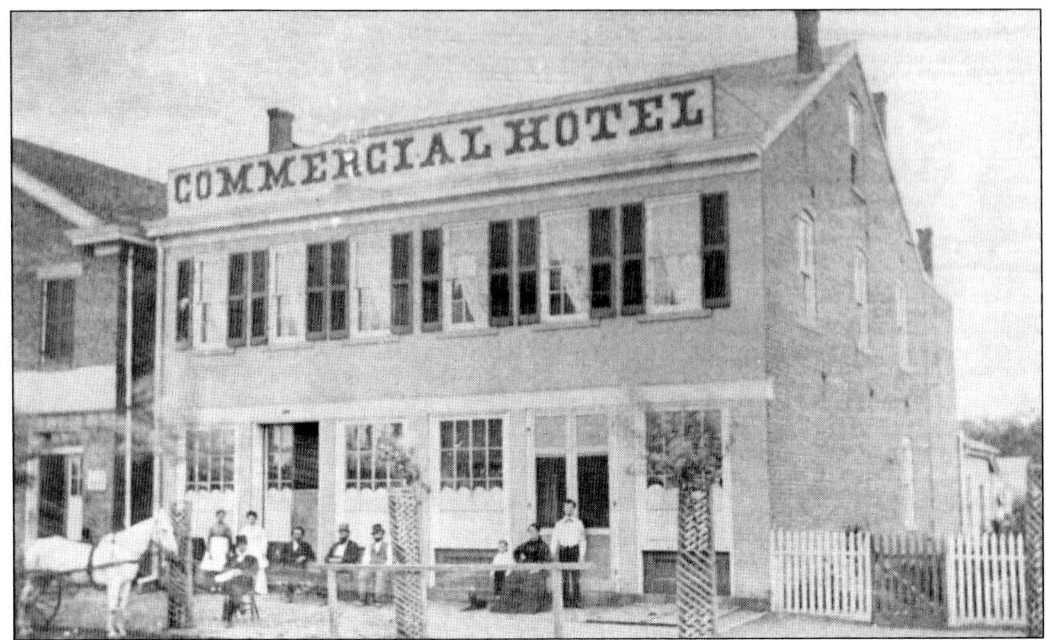

The Commercial Hotel was located in the 200 block of Main Street. It was originally only two stories; a third story was added in the early 1900s. The Masonic Lodge met on the third floor until its building was completed. In later years, the hotel was combined with the structure shown at left (Washington House) to form one building known as the William Tell Hotel. (Courtesy of Tell City Historical Society.)

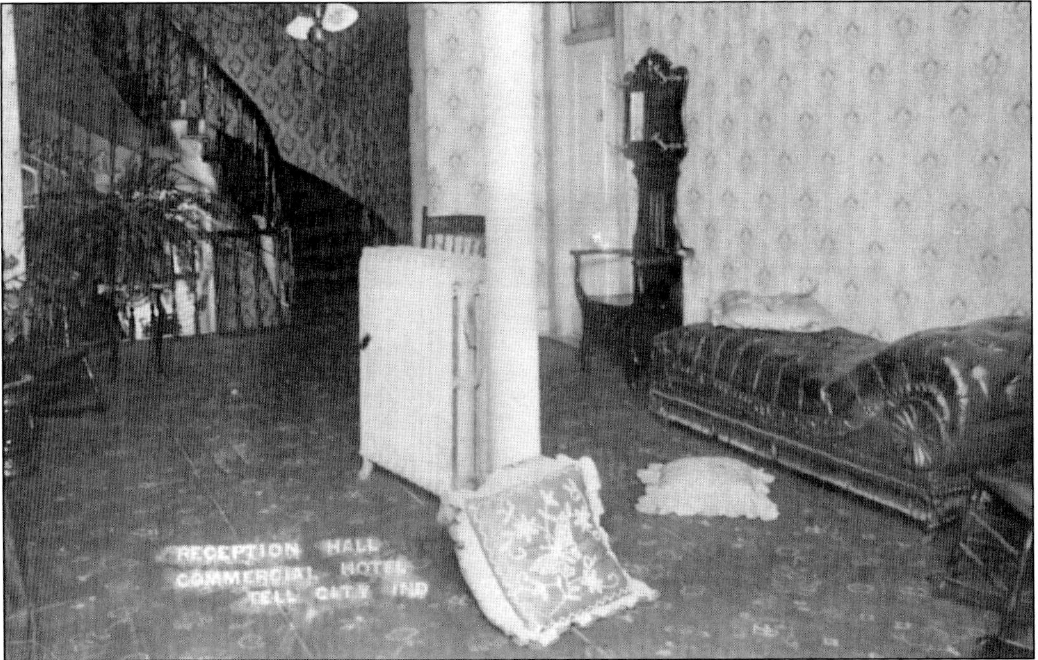

The Commercial Hotel's Reception Hall is pictured around 1910. This photograph was taken on the second floor of the hotel. The building had a beautiful spiral staircase, which remained until the hotel was demolished in 2009. (Courtesy of Tell City Historical Society.)

Washington House, a hotel, was located on the corner of Washington and Main Streets. It was built around 1875, and the proprietor was Henry Plumeyer. The hotel went through multiple additions, with the largest being the construction of a third story. This happened when it was combined with the Commercial Hotel (at right) in 1920 to form the William Tell Hotel. In 2009, a collapse occurred that caused the William Tell Hotel to be demolished.

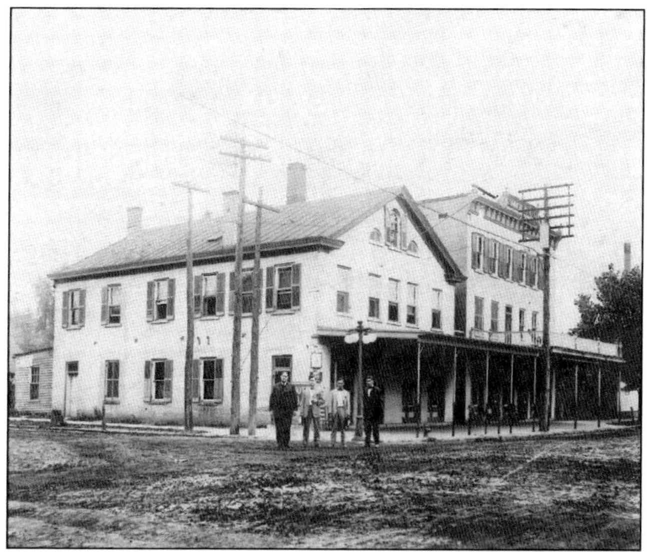

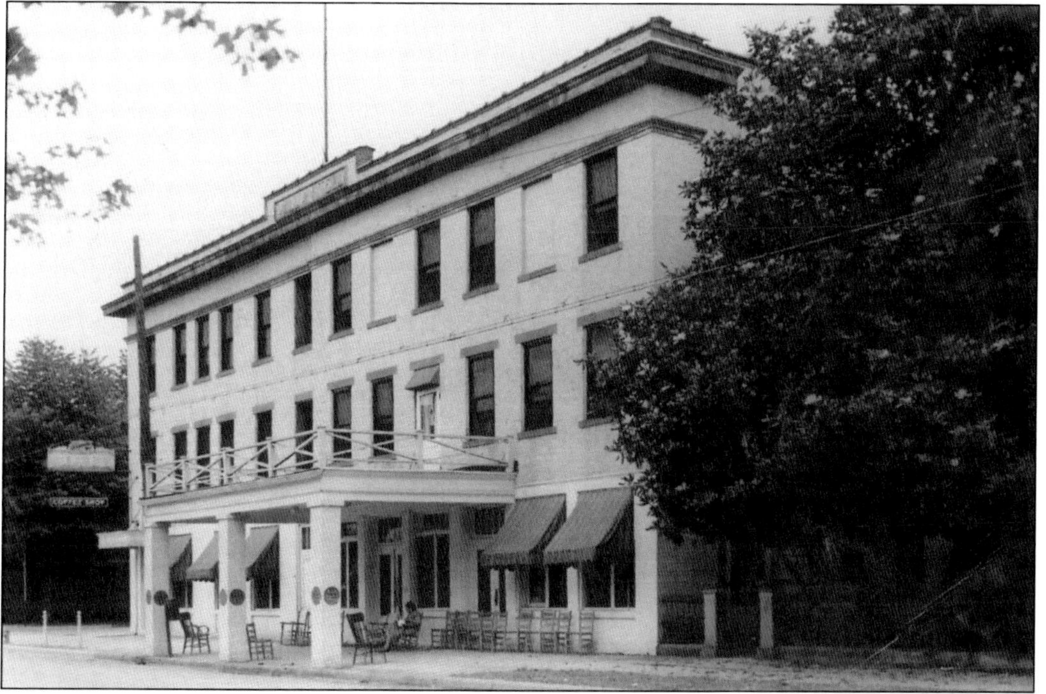

The William Tell Hotel was originally two separate hotels. In the 1920s, the Commercial Hotel and Washington House were combined into one. This project was undertaken by a group of citizens who formed a company in order to do this. They saw a need for a modern establishment, and it brought many customers into town. Ronald Reagan had accommodations here when he visited Tell City in 1955. The hotel had a very noteworthy restaurant located in the corner of the building on the first floor. The hotel closed in the 1970s. After its closure, the top floors remained empty but the bottom floor housed several different types of businesses, such as the License branch, Tell City Video, Cole Insurance, Travel Connections, and many others. In 2009, the building partially collapsed along Washington Street. Sometime after that, the entire structure was demolished.

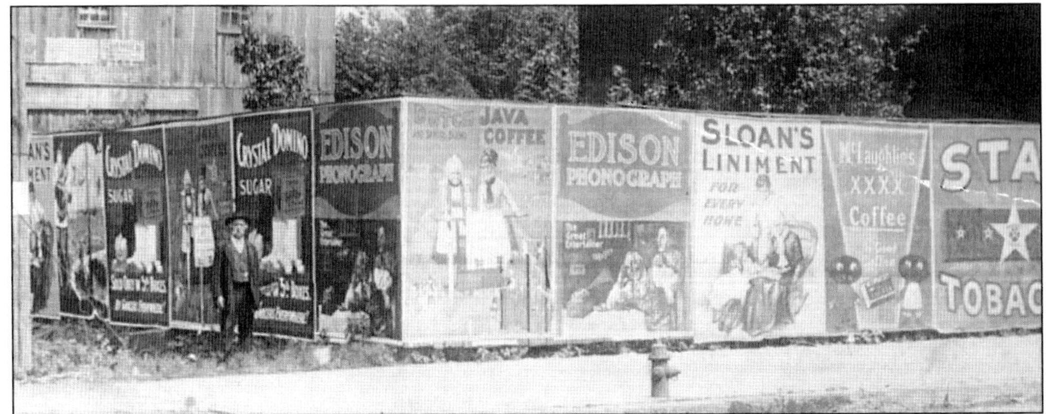

These signboards were near the southeast corner of Main and Pestalozzi Streets. The billboard franchise in Tell City at that time was owned by G.S. Dusch & Son. Dusch was a local pharmacist and owned a pharmacy just across the street. The building seen in the right background was the Obrecht Brothers Manufacturing Company's hubs storage facility. Both buildings, as well as the signboards, are no longer there as today there is a service station at this location. (Courtesy of Tell City Historical Society.)

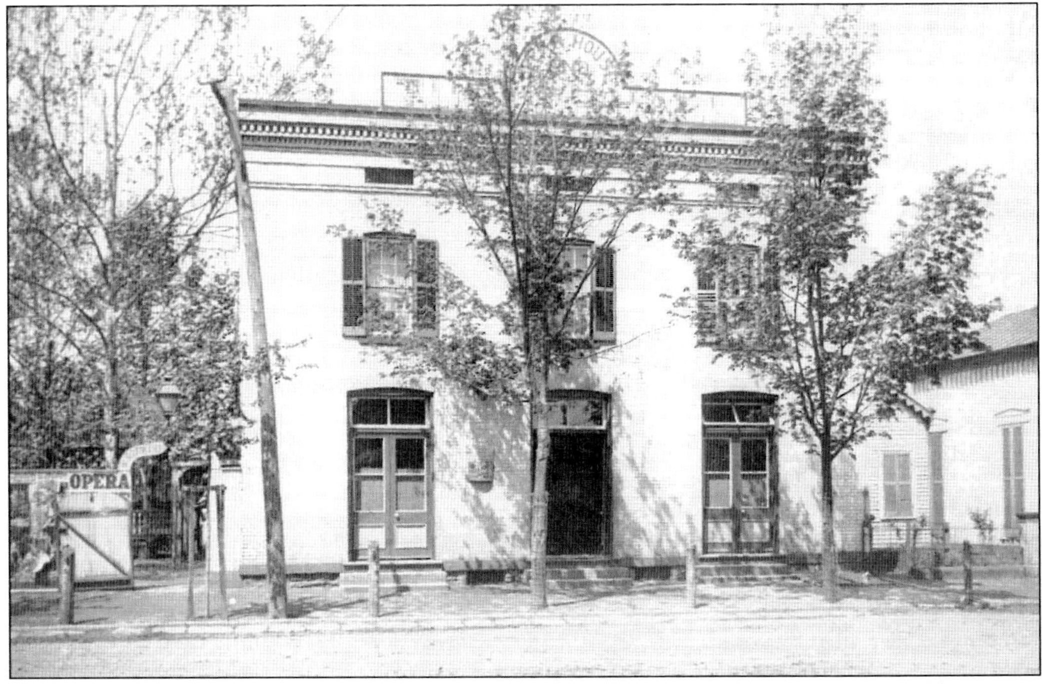

Known as Turner Hall, Hofmann's Garden, or the Tell City Opera House, this building once housed the Turner Society, which was an athletic and social club. In 1870, Wendell Hofmann bought the building and operated a saloon and beer garden, skating rink, and a playhouse. In the late 1800s, the building was remodeled—and the roofline was changed—and it became the Tell City Opera House. It was the location for shows by traveling groups of players, as well as home talent groups. In the 1900s, it was converted to a moving picture theater and later used as a showroom for automobiles by the Werner Motor Company, which at one time was the oldest Ford dealership in Indiana. It has been said that Gene Autry and his horse Champion performed here. (Courtesy of Tell City Historical Society.)

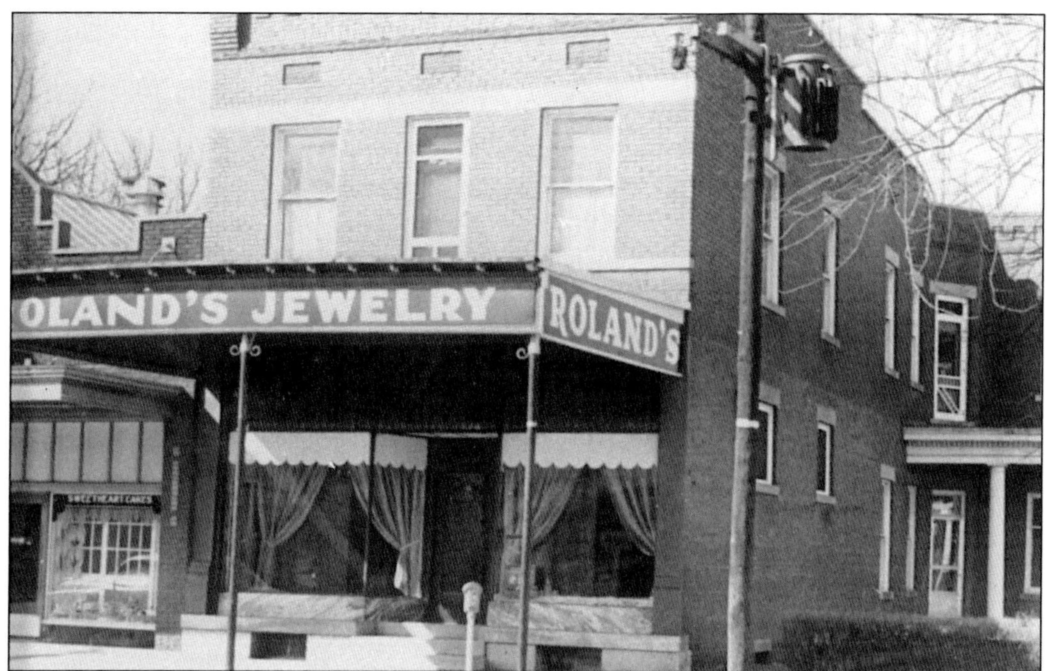

In 1884, Fred G. Heinzle purchased the Huber Jewelry Store. The Heinzles' stock included a wide assortment of watches, clocks, jewelry, and silverware. In 1908, the old building was razed and replaced by this two-story redbrick structure. In 1956, Kenneth Roland Sr. purchased the jewelry store, moved his grandfathers' jewelry store from Cannelton to this location, and renamed it Roland's Jewelry. Later, it was moved to another location. The building at left was Van's Bakery. The front of this building still looks the same today. After the bakery closed in the 1960s, Dorothy Kessner opened her carpet business at this location. (Courtesy of Tell City Historical Society.)

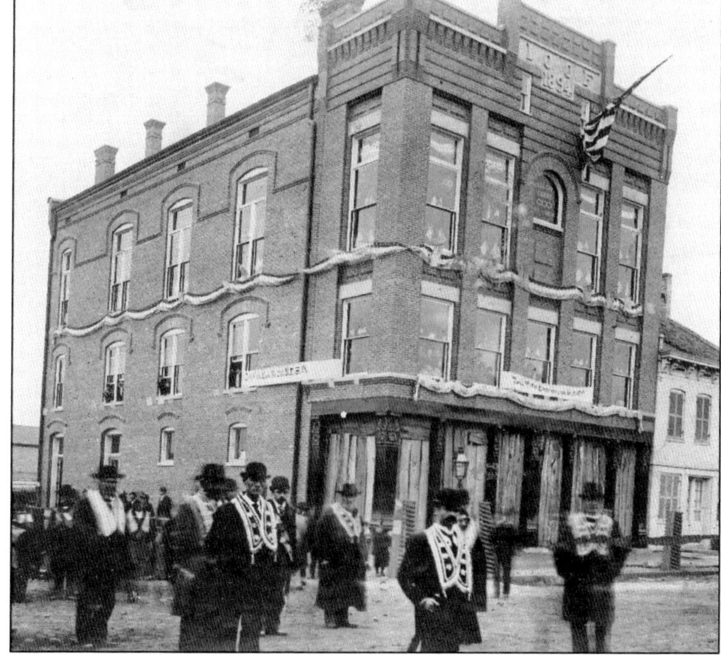

The dedication of the Odd Fellows Lodge at Main and Mozart Streets took place on Thanksgiving Day, November 29, 1894. A grand ball took place that night with music by the Star Band. This building housed Cassidy and Vitoe, later Jim & Jim's Menswear, on the first floor, apartments on the second floor, and the Odd Fellows Lodge on the third floor. The last occupant of the building was Capers restaurant. The building burned down on October 13, 2013. (Courtesy of Tell City Historical Society.)

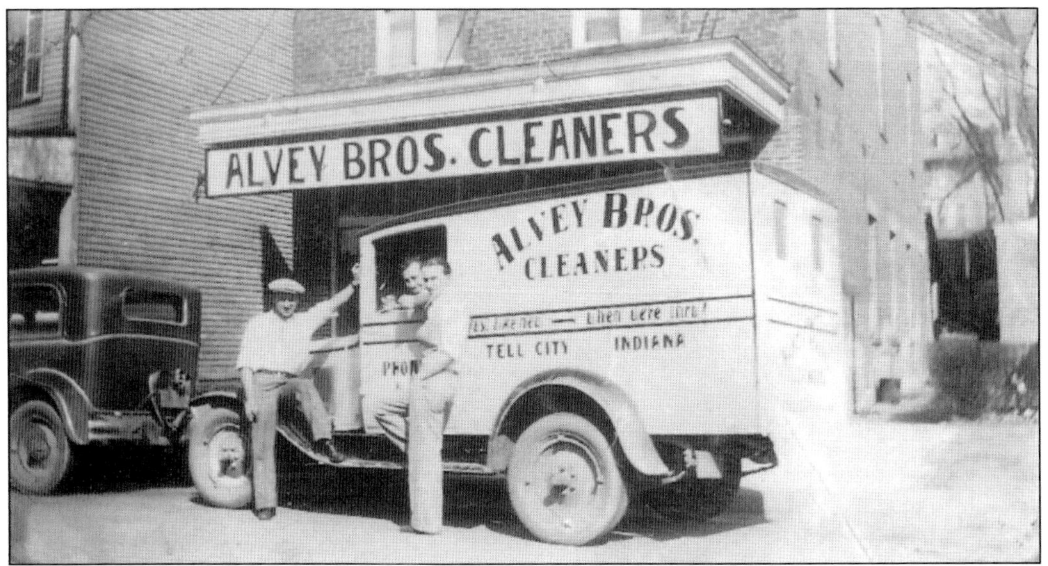

Alveys Cleaners, located at 606 Main Street, opened for business in 1927. It is still in operation today. Pictured are, from left to right, Jade Alvey, unidentified driver, and Harry Alvey. (Courtesy of Tell City Historical Society.)

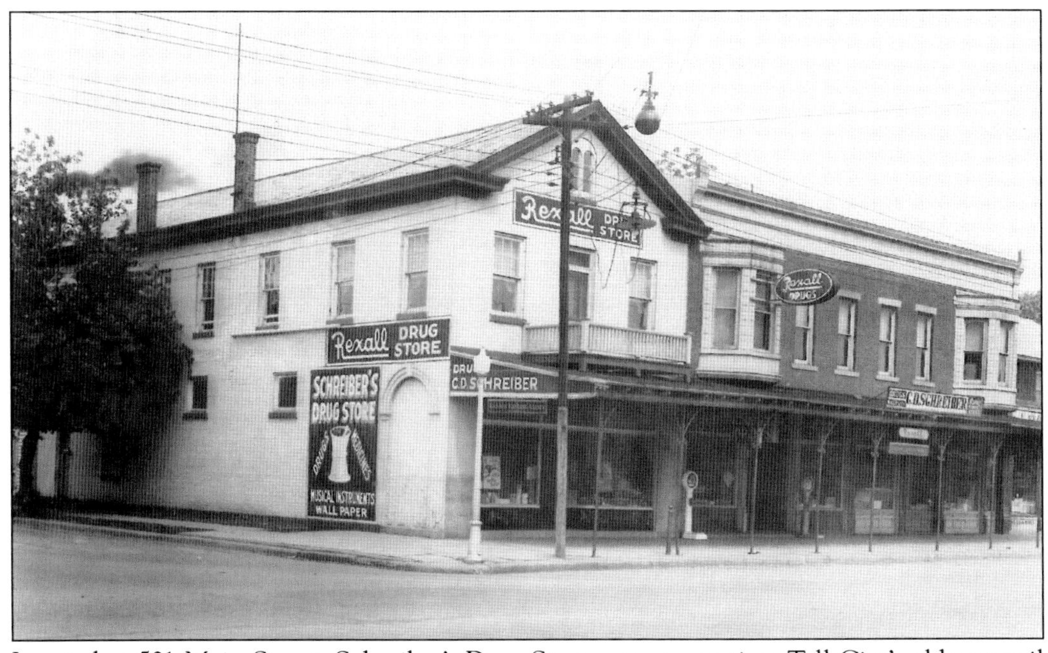

Located at 501 Main Street, Schreiber's Drug Store was at one time Tell City's oldest retail establishment. It was originally located in the market square in 1861, and was operated continuously by the Schreiber family beginning in 1866. The drugstore also sold musical instruments and wallpaper. The building had a fire in 1989 and was razed to make room for a Citizens National Bank drive-through. Note the fire ball, an early signaling device, hanging in the middle of the street. (Courtesy of Tell City Historical Society.)

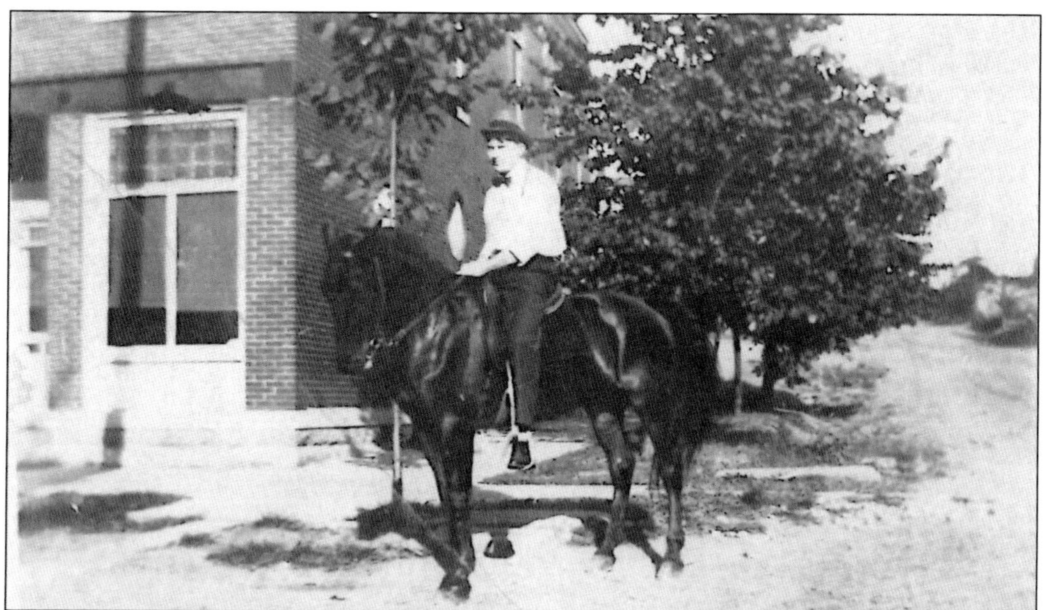

Basedow Bottling Works, located at 302 Ninth Street, was built in 1895 by Oscar Basedow (pictured) for his soda water business. Part of the building was said to be the one of the first commercial ice-cream plants in Tell City. In the 1950s, it became Wheelers Grocery and Meats, which remained in business until the 1990s. Most noteworthy is the Coca-Cola mural painted along the Washington Street side of the building. In 2004, the building was purchased by the author, who restored the structure. Today, it is an antique store.

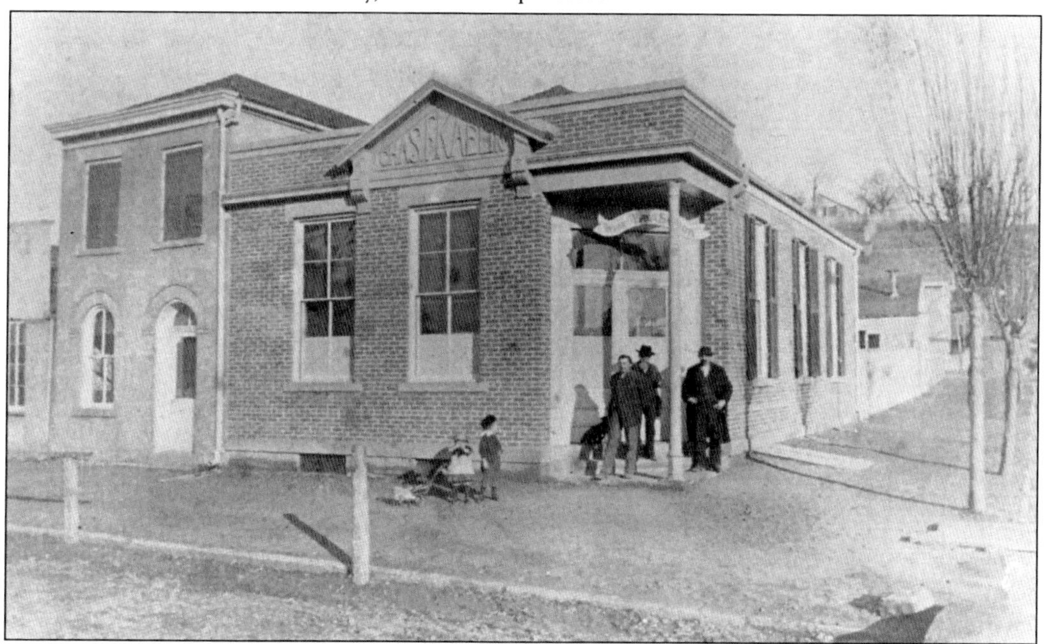

The Charles F. Kaelin Building was constructed around the 1880s. The Heubi family later owned a tavern there called the White Swan Saloon. After White Swan Saloon closed, the structure housed several different businesses, most recently a financial lending company. The building at left was constructed in the 1870s and was a residence for the Heubi family.

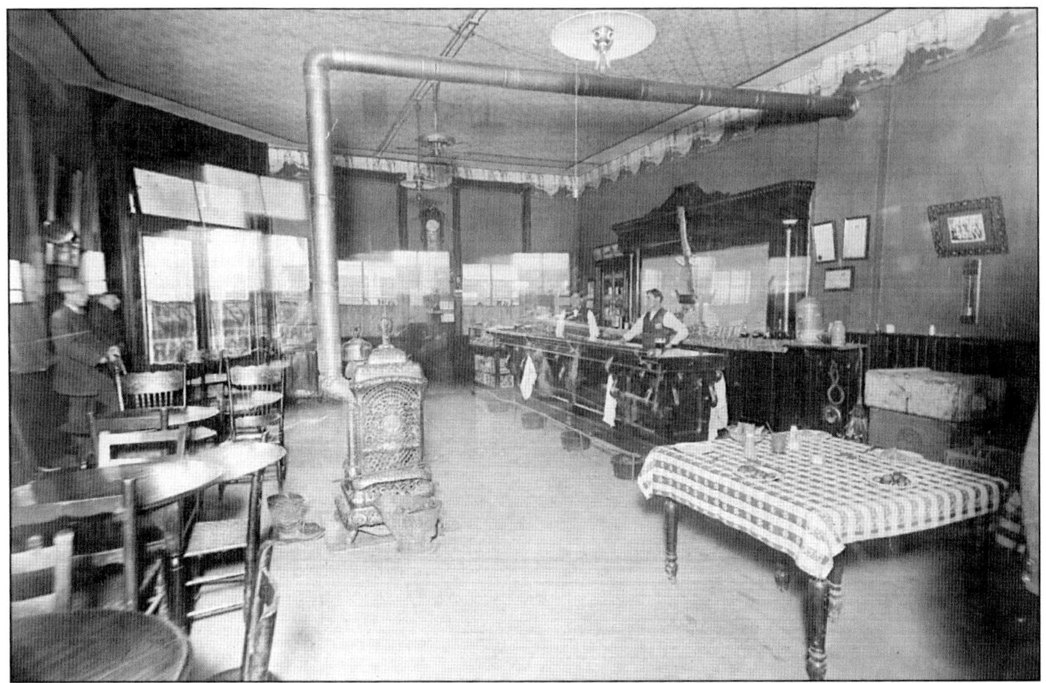

The White Swan Saloon was located at 502 Main Street. Before it was the White Swan Saloon, it was the Charles F. Kaelin Saloon. It later housed a men's clothing store and a financial loan office. This building still stands today.

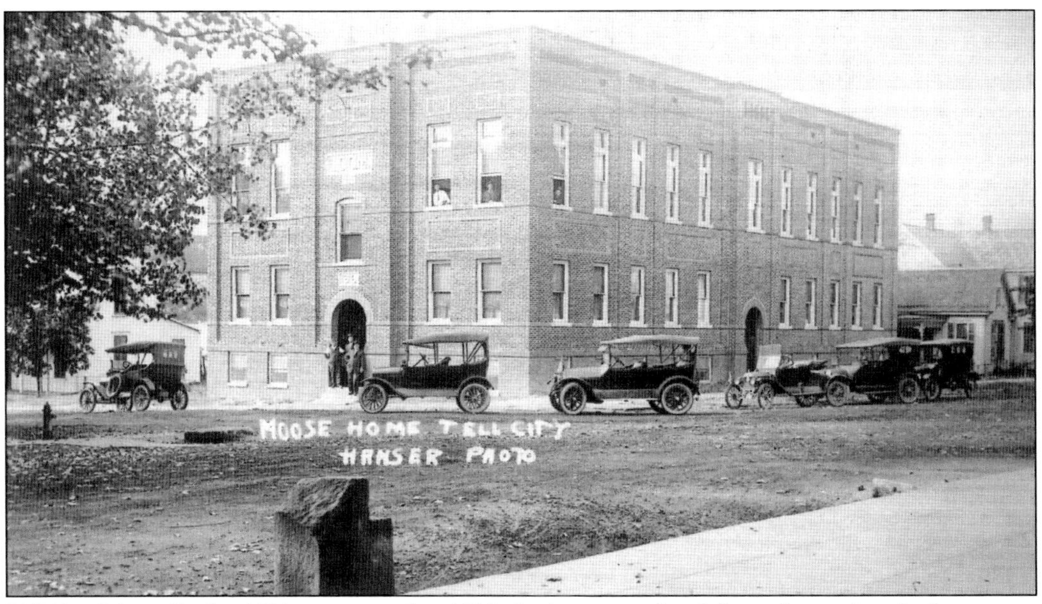

Tell City Moose Lodge 1424 was erected in 1916. At that time, the club was located in the basement, and on the second floor was the lodge room. The first floor had a large dining hall. The building was remodeled, and the club was moved to the first floor. After the Moose constructed their new building on Dauby Lane in 2004, this structure was razed to make room for St. Paul Catholic Church's new parish hall. (Courtesy of Tell City Historical Society.)

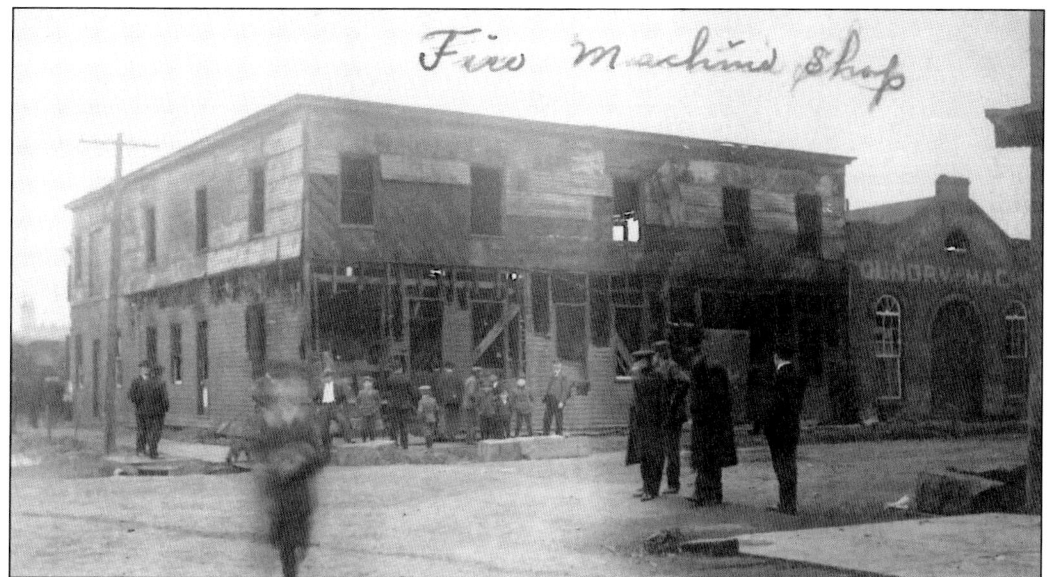

The Tell City Foundry and Machine Works was located at 706 Humboldt Street. Originally, it was a two-story wooden structure; however, after a fire, as seen here, it was replaced with a one-story brick building. Today, the building houses the Tell City Pour Haus and the Tell City Brewing Company. (Courtesy of Tell City Historical Society.)

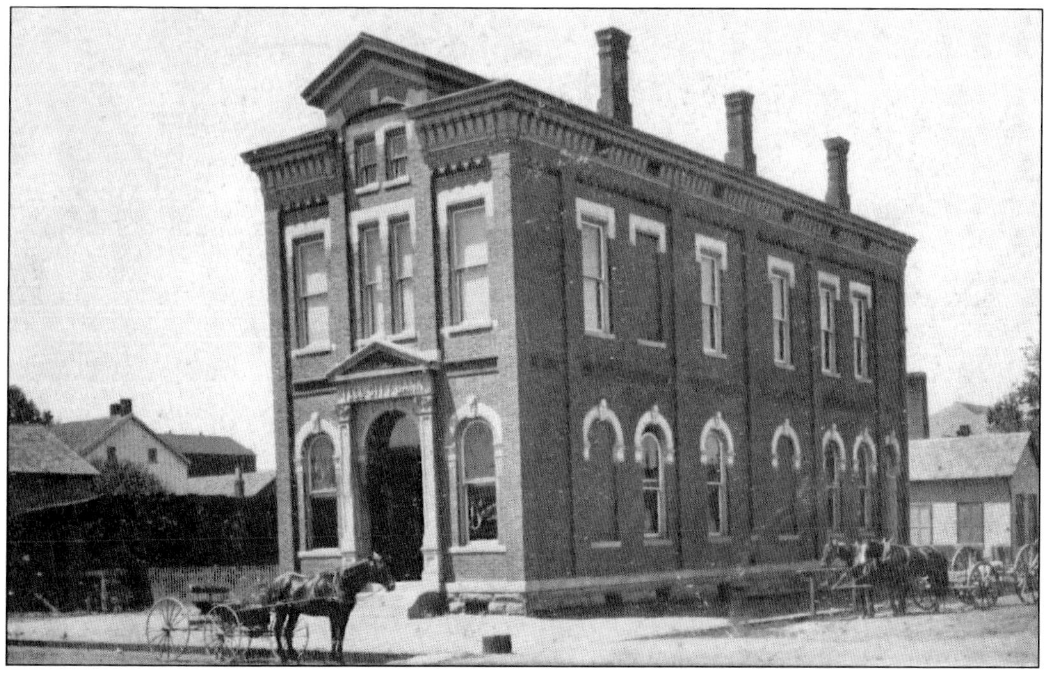

Tell City National Bank was established in 1894 and remained at this location until 1947, when the company built a new facility. During the 1937 flood, the bank was underwater. When the floodwaters finally subsided, the employees washed the money in a washing machine and ironed it dry. After the bank moved, the structure became the Glow Room Tavern. The building was painted a bright green/teal color. It glowed! The building was later bought by the Casebolt family and restored. (Courtesy of Tell City Historical Society.)

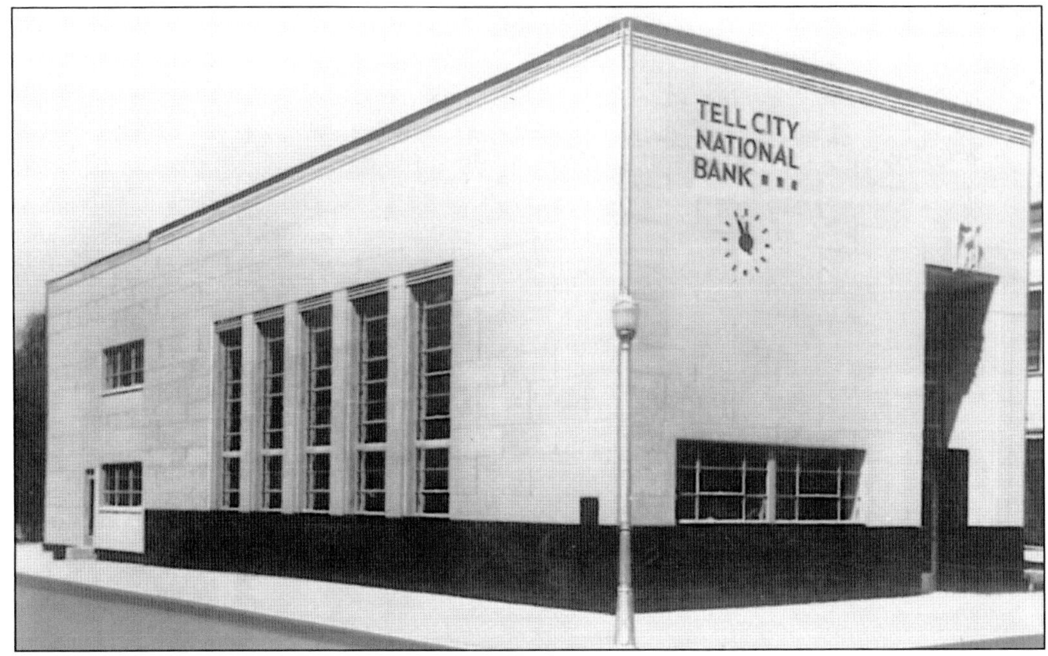

Tell City National Bank constructed this building in 1947. There were two major renovations undertaken to this building. A three-story addition was constructed on the back of the building. Later, an overall update and addition were made. After the bank was purchased by Fifth Third Bank and moved to its new location, the Tell City Electric Department located here. Note the eagle above the door. This was removed and now resides at the Tell City Historical Society.

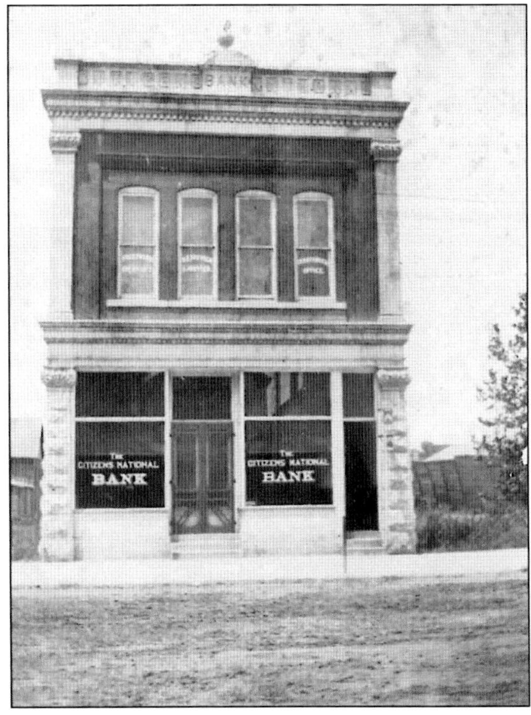

Citizens National Bank was built in 1904. In 1954, a new building was erected next to the original structure, and in 1975, another addition was made. Over the years, the interior was remodeled at various times to modernize the facilities. In 1998, Citizens National was purchased by Old National Bank. (Courtesy of Tell City Historical Society.)

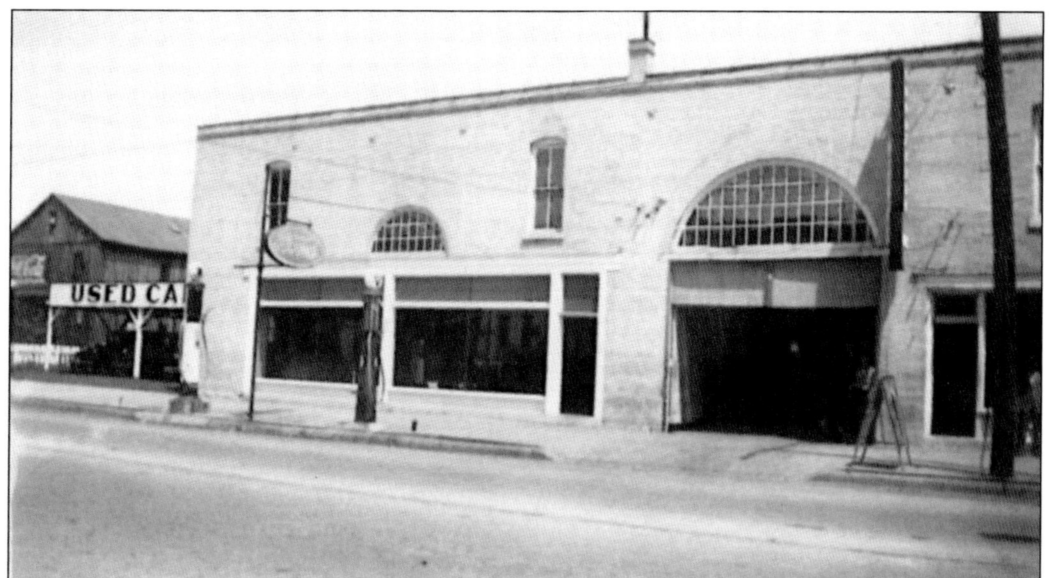

This barn first housed a stave-making factory in 1880. Flooding ruined this endeavor, and the property was sold and turned into a livery stable owned by Charles Werner and Alois Birchler. After a fire in 1908, the structure was rebuilt in brick. The livery was a booming business, housing as many as 40 horses and buggies for hire. Later, the Werner Motor Company, at one time the oldest Ford dealership in Indiana, was established here. After it was a Ford dealership, this structure became a Chevrolet dealership under Cambron Chevrolet. The Werner family still owns this building, which underwent a major renovation in recent years. (Courtesy of Tell City Historical Society.)

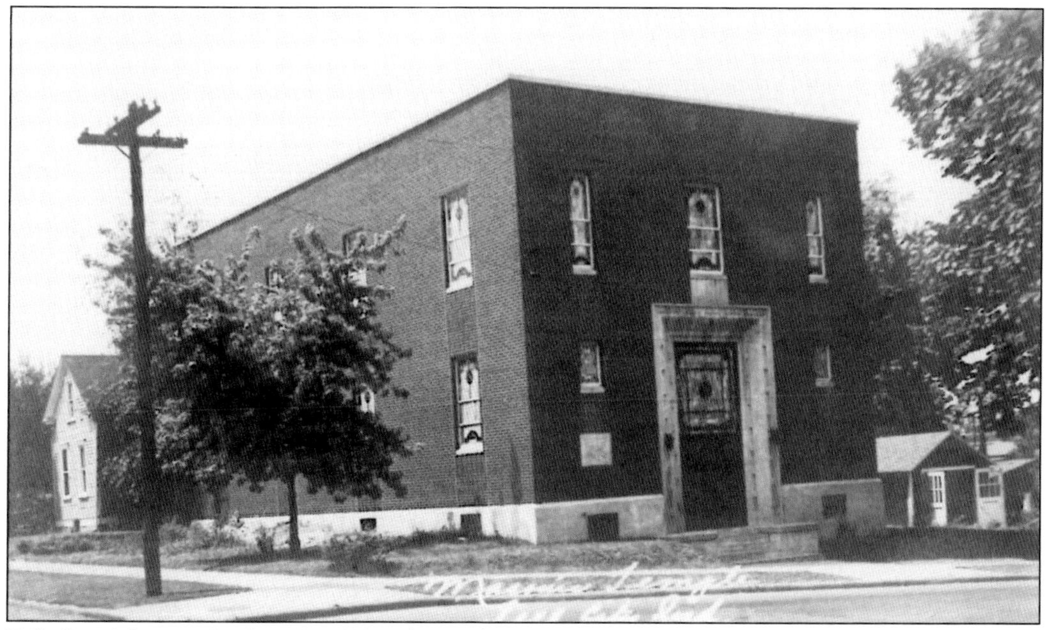

Tell City Masonic Lodge No. 623 is located at 827 Mozart Street. The lodge was built in 1937 and chartered in 1899. The Masonic Lodge is still very active in the community, hosting various events throughout the year. Today's building remains the same as it appears in this photograph.

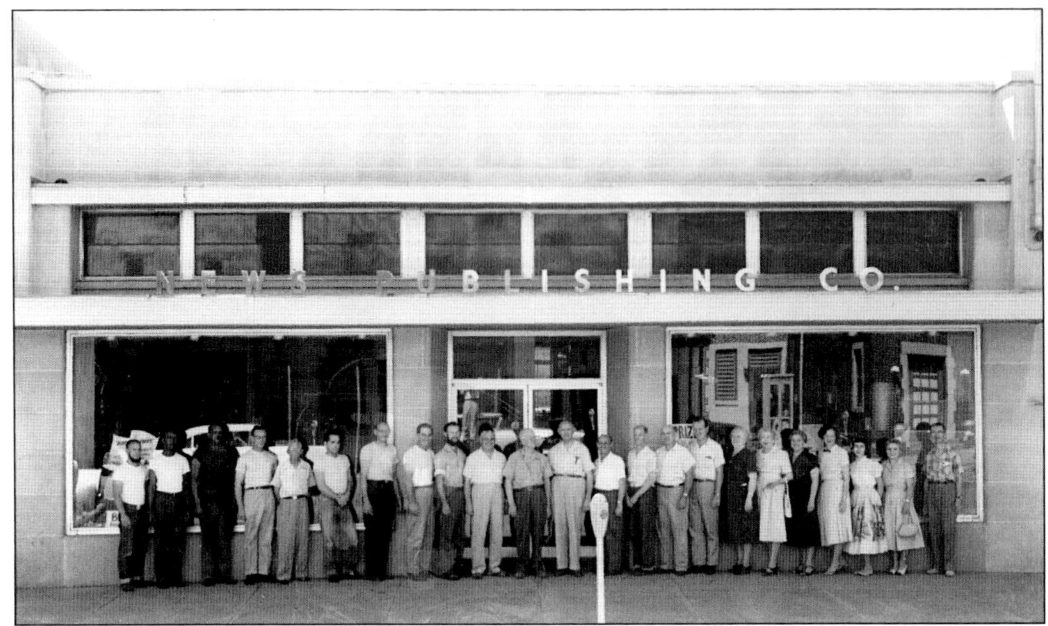

Employees of the News Publishing Company are pictured here around 1963. From left to right are Gene Scheible, Allen Owen, Jim Slaughter, John Scheidegger, Ed Buchser, Ernie Graybill, Hugo Reckulhoff, Norman Hudson, Marvin Longest, Bob Cummings, U.B. Cummings, Edgar Schergens, Jack Collins, Austin Hemphill, Charles U. Clark, Schles Scheidegger, Althea Rohn, Lucille Gerber, Mary M. Goffinet, Lucille Schergens, Ruth Ann Coyle, Lucille Steinsberger, and Clarence Schultz. (Courtesy of Tell City Historical Society.)

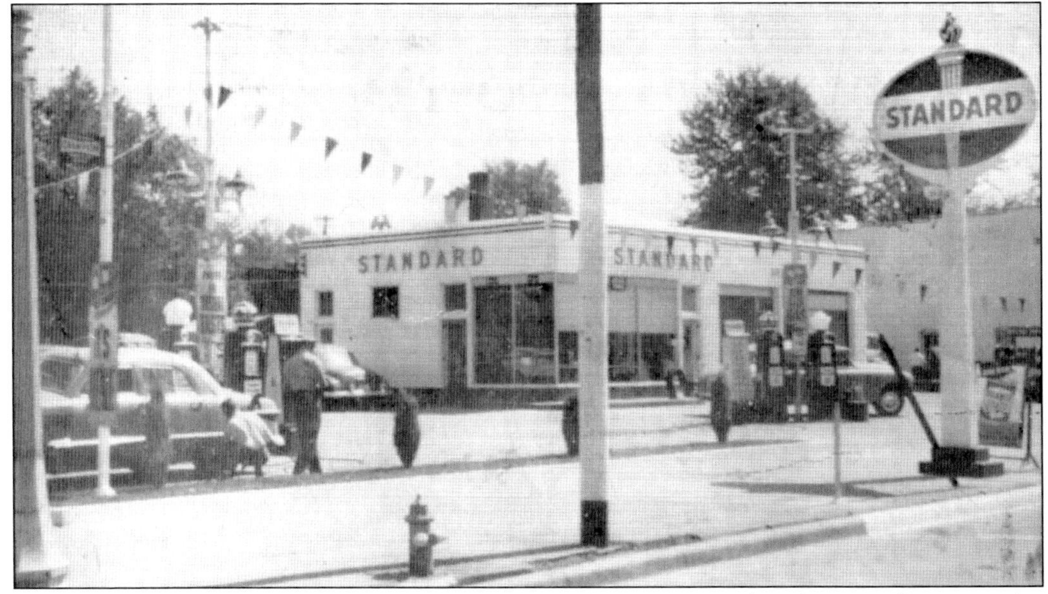

Young's Service Station was located at Main and Pestolozzi Streets. This place is still in use today as a senior center.

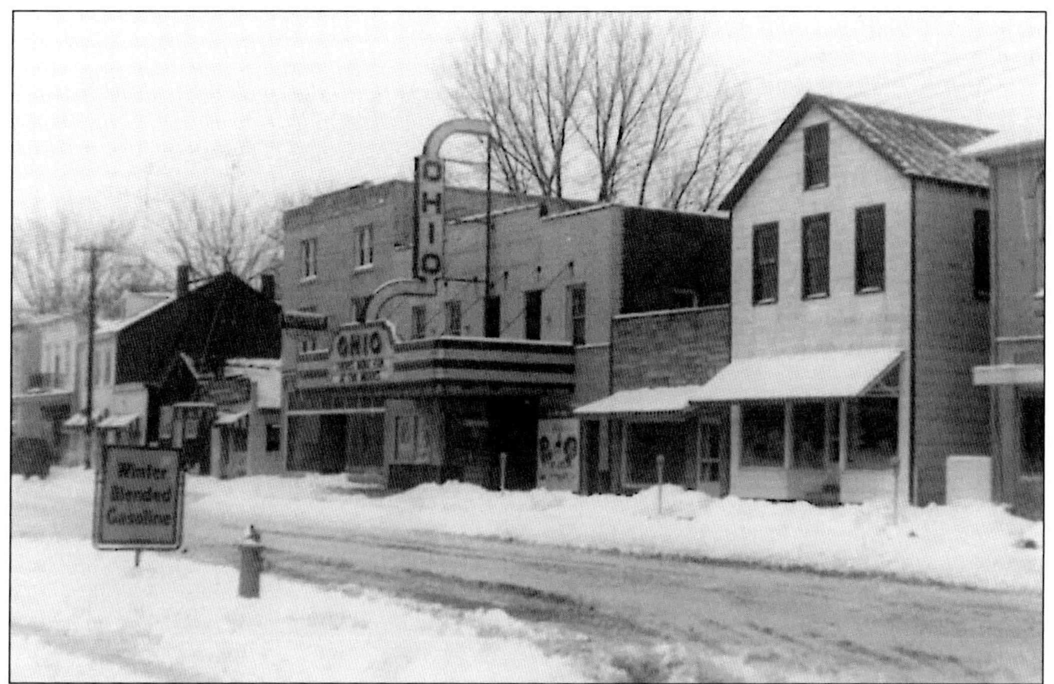

Located in the 400 block of Main Street was the Ohio Theater (at center). It later became Liberty Church. The structure subsequently burned and was torn down. Today, Edward Jones financial advisors has erected a new building on this site. (Courtesy of Tell City Historical Society.)

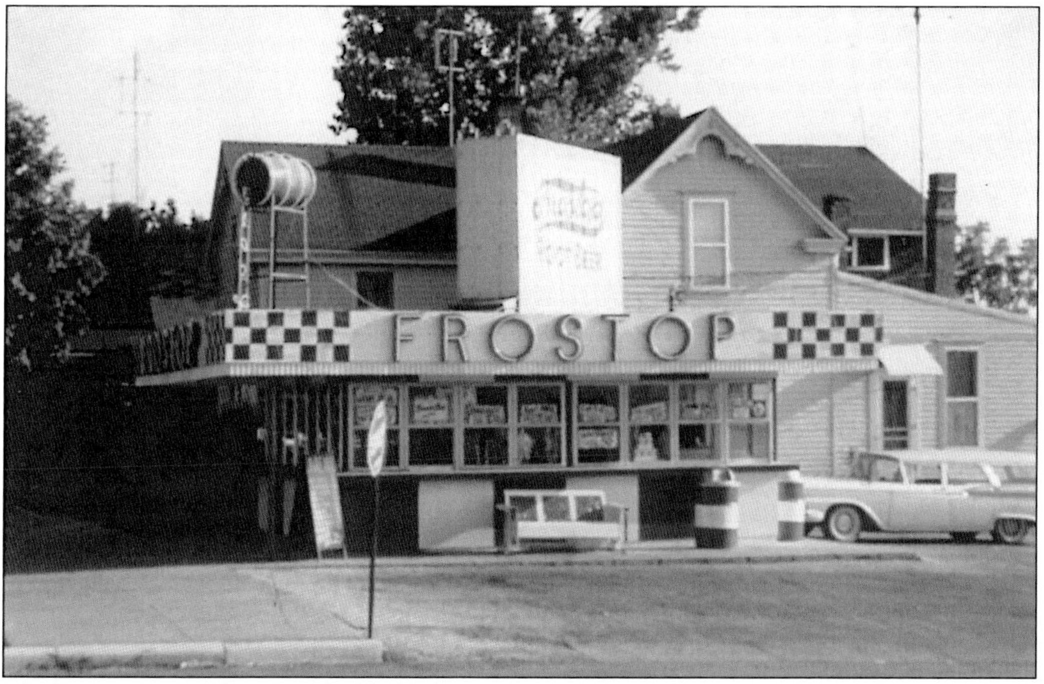

The Frostop, opened in 1955, holds fond memories of an era gone by. Most people remember its famous root beer and Pronto Pups. Today, the building has had some modifications—the iconic root beer on top has been removed. The restaurant operates seasonally.

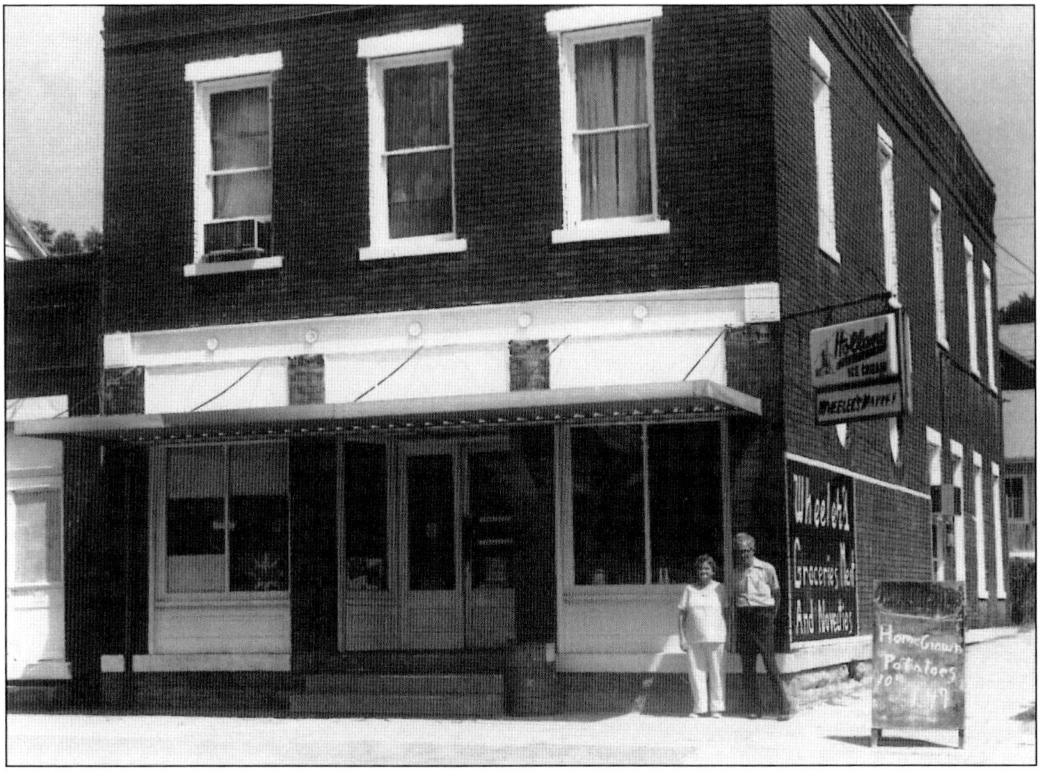

Constructed in 1895 by Oscar Basedow, this building was used as a bottling plant for his soda water. Later, it was the first commercial ice-cream plant in town. In the 1960s, it became Wheelers Grocery and Meats. Today, it houses William Tell Antiques. (Courtesy of Charles and Janet Wheeler.)

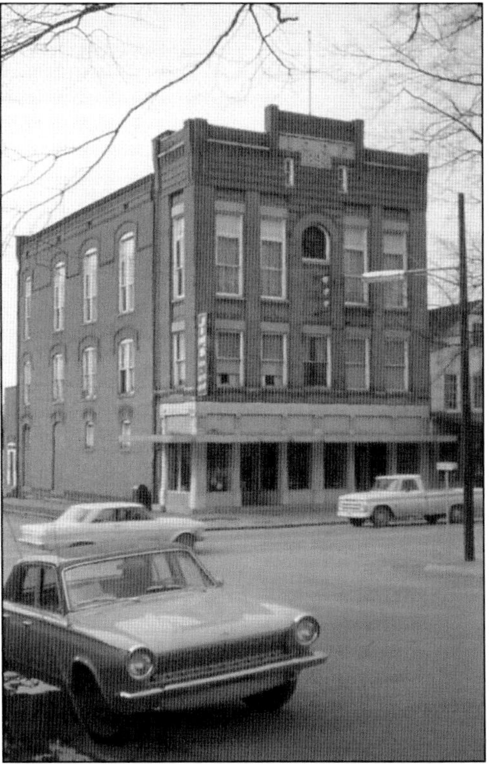

Jim & Jim's Menswear was located at 701 Main Street. Many remember going here to buy their first suit. The second floor of the building housed apartments, and the third floor was used as the Odd Fellows Lodge. In later years, the building was Capers restaurant. On October 13, 2013, the building burned and was demolished. (Courtesy of Tell City Historical Society.)

Franzman's Meat Market was located in the 400 block of Main Street, where Hagedorn Law Office now stands. This photograph was taken in 1979 as the old structure was being torn down. (Courtesy of Tell City Historical Society.)

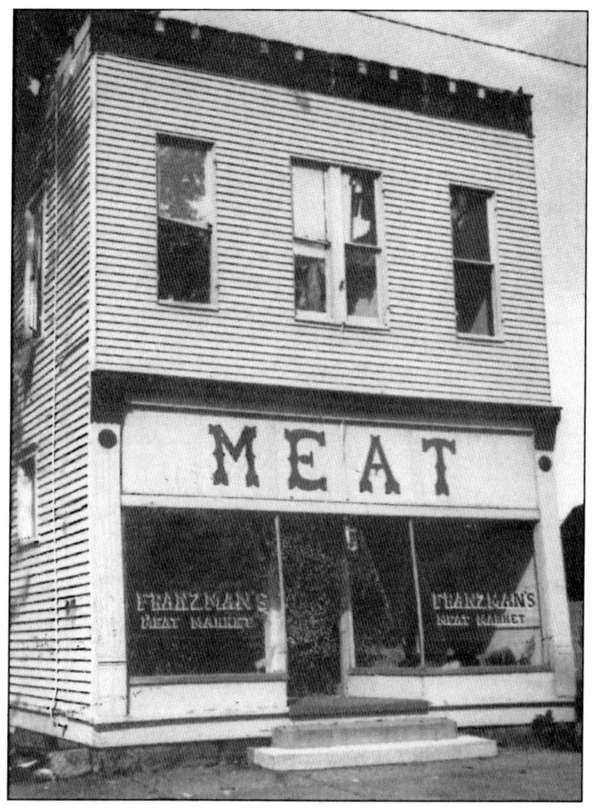

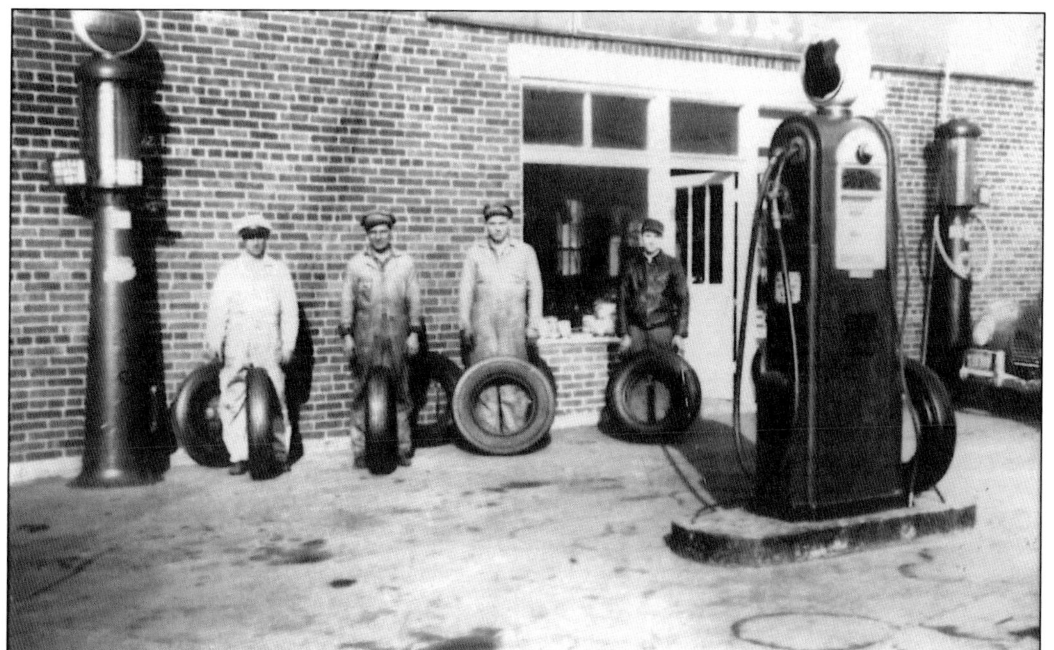

Blackie Tire & Battery was located at Mozart and Seventh Streets. Pictured, from left to right, are Blackie Paulin, Bob Haff, Arthur Tanner, and an unidentified man. (Courtesy of Tell City Historical Society.)

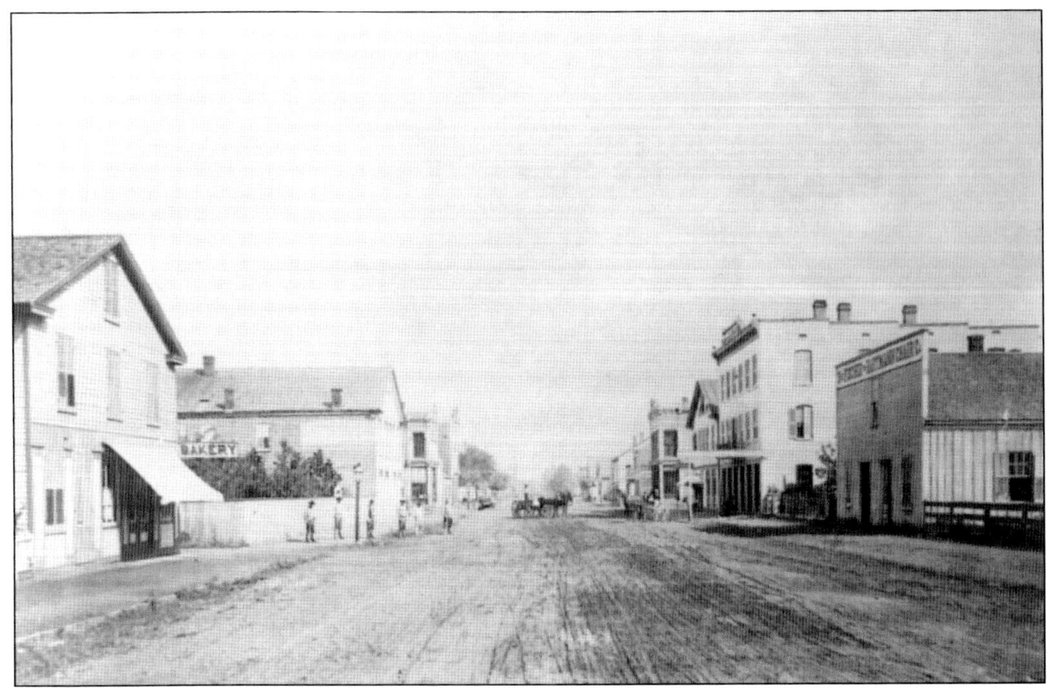

On the far left in this view looking north on Main Street from the corner of Blum and Main Streets is Gloors Bakery, owned by Casper Gloor. Down the street, the fence surrounding Nimsgern's garden can be seen, next to Windphfennig's Saloon. On the right is Fischer & Hartman Chair Company. This building was more of a warehouse for the factory. Farther down the block are the Commercial Hotel and Washington House. The Gloors were said to befriend many refugees, giving them sanctuary in their home. (Courtesy of Tell City Historical Society.)

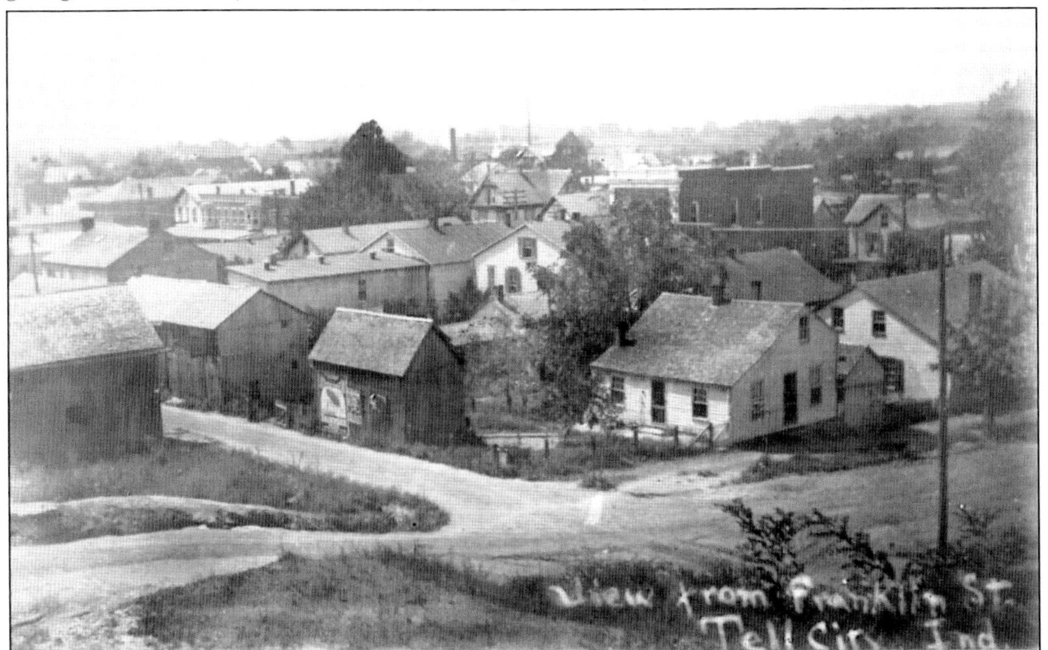

This aerial view is looking southwest from Franklin Street.

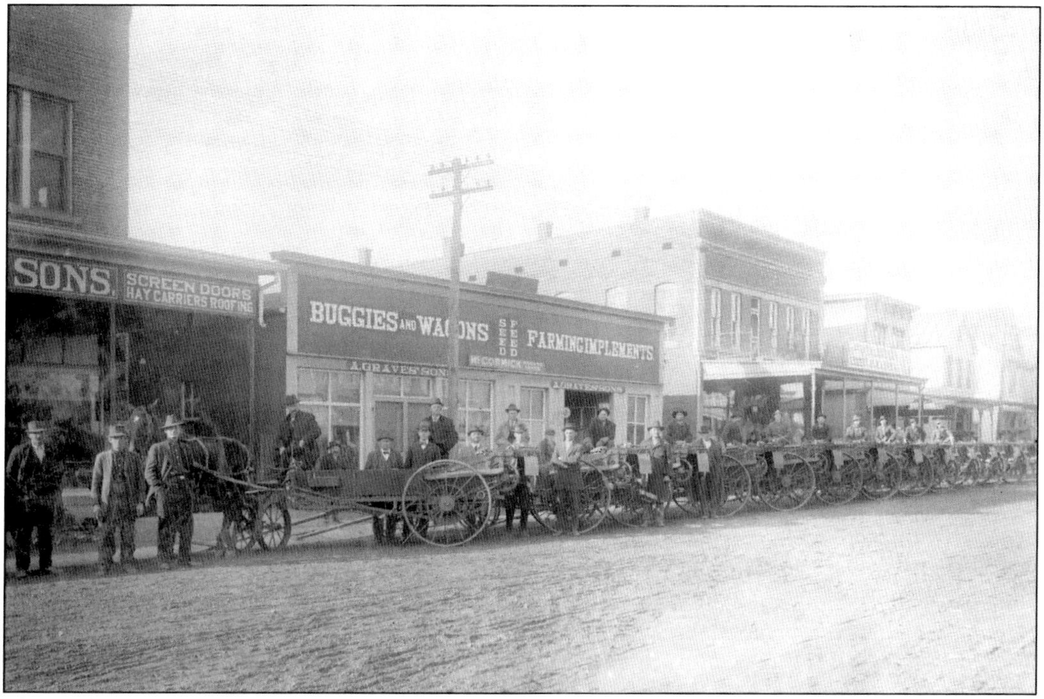

Shown here is the 600 block of Main Street around 1900. Among those pictured are Johnson Peckenpaugh (far left) and Claude Howell (11th from left). The rest are unidentified. (Courtesy of Tell City Historical Society.)

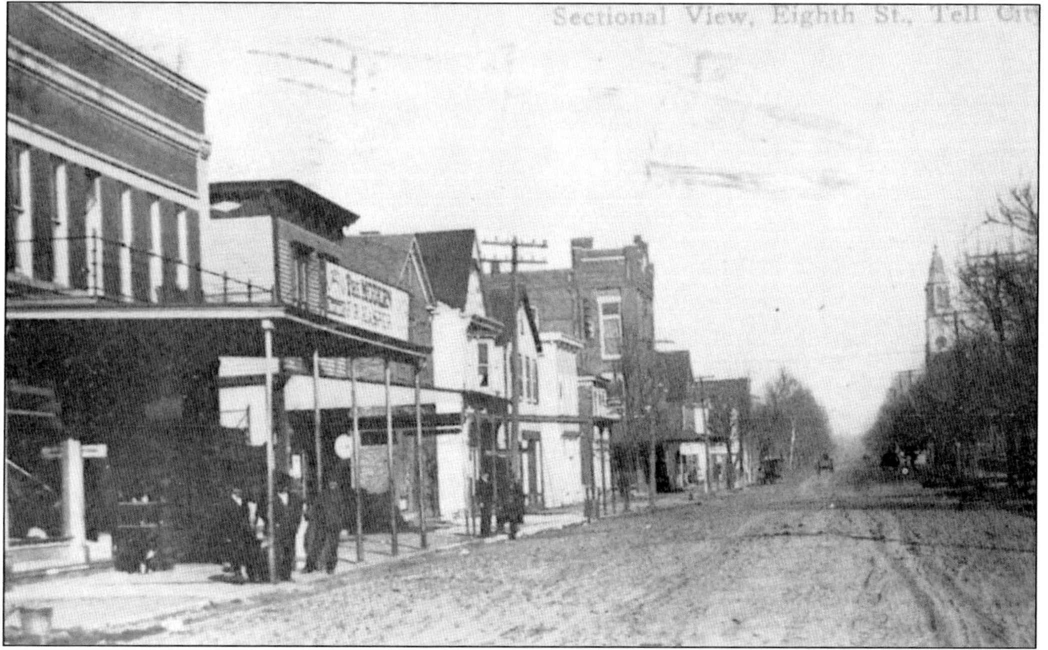

The Modern was owned by F.R. Kasper and located in the 600 block of Main Street. It is the only building in the photograph that is still standing today. (Courtesy of Tell City Historical Society.)

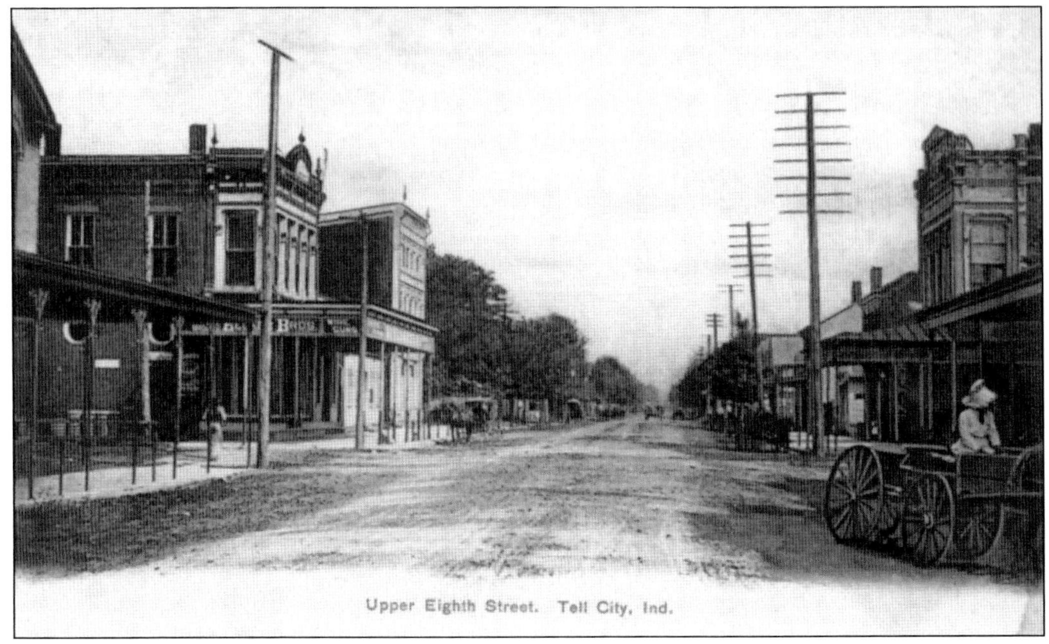

Depicted here is the 300 block on upper Main Street. The Becker Bros. store is on the left, and on the right is Stadlers Store.

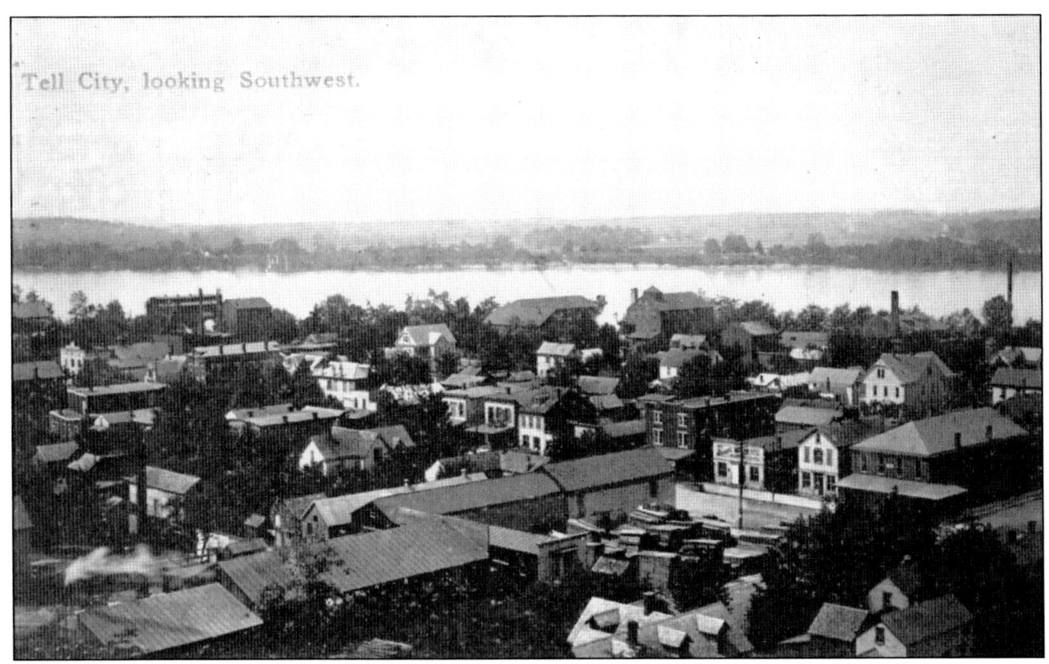

Shown is an aerial view of Tell City looking southwest toward the Ohio River.

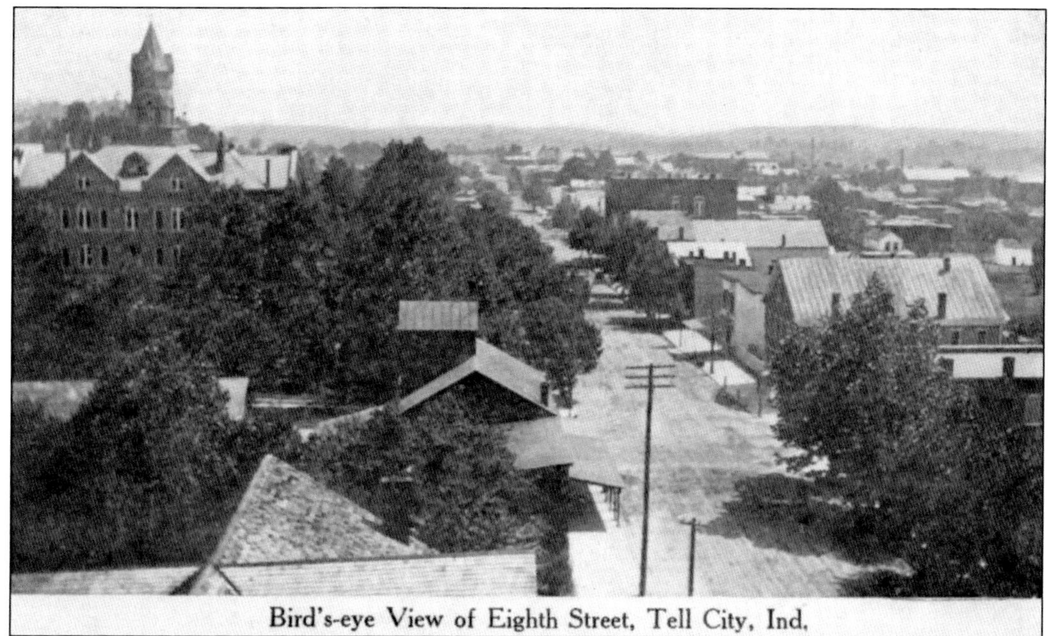

This bird's-eye view of Main Street shows the lovely wide streets.

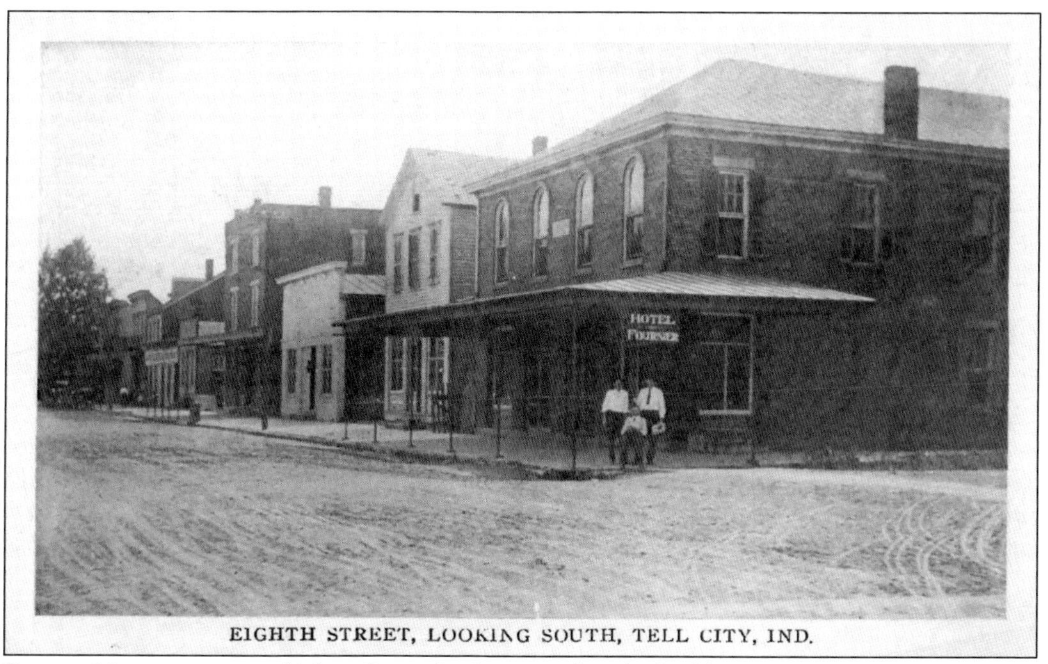

Depicted here is a view of Main Street looking south. The building at front right is the Hotel Fourner. The three-story building, fourth from right, was the Kampschaefer Meat Market.

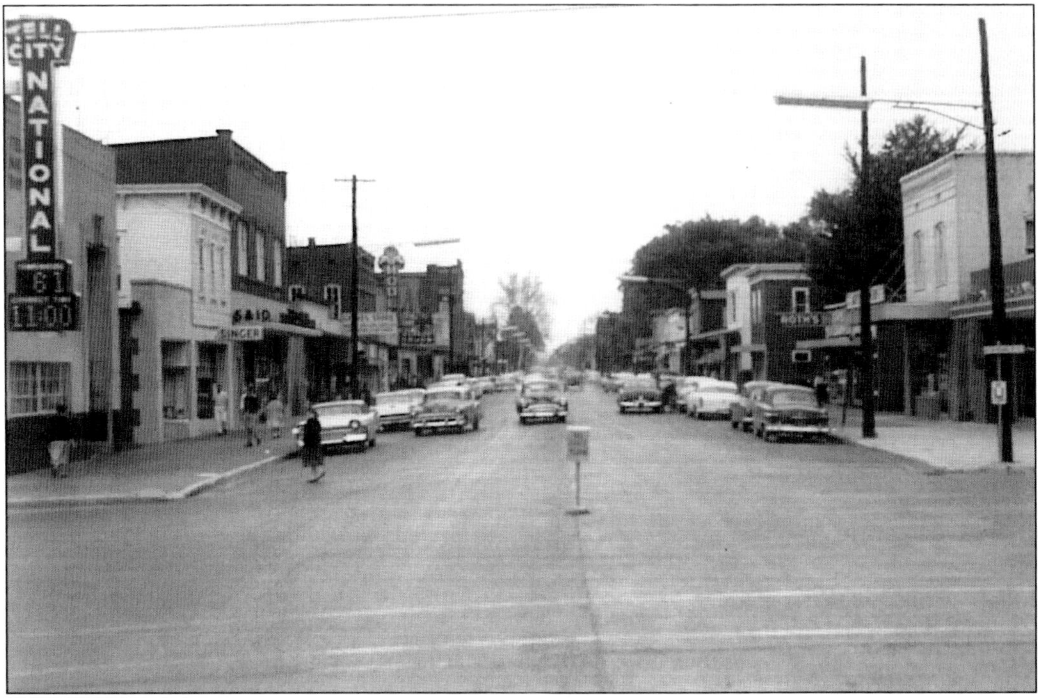

Shown is a typical Friday morning on Main Street. In the intersection is a No Left Turn sign, which was only used on Fridays and Saturdays. This view is looking north from the 500 block of Main Street, at the intersection of Franklin and Main Streets. (Courtesy of Tell City Historical Society.)

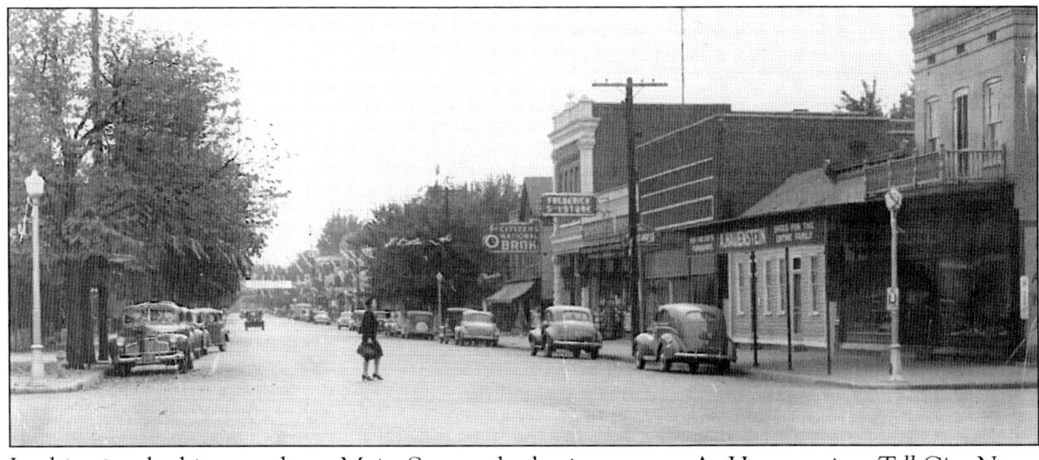

In this view looking south on Main Street, the businesses are A. Hauensteins, *Tell City News*, Frederick's 5 & 10 Store, and Citizens National Bank.

An aerial view of Tell City looking north shows the city's growth.

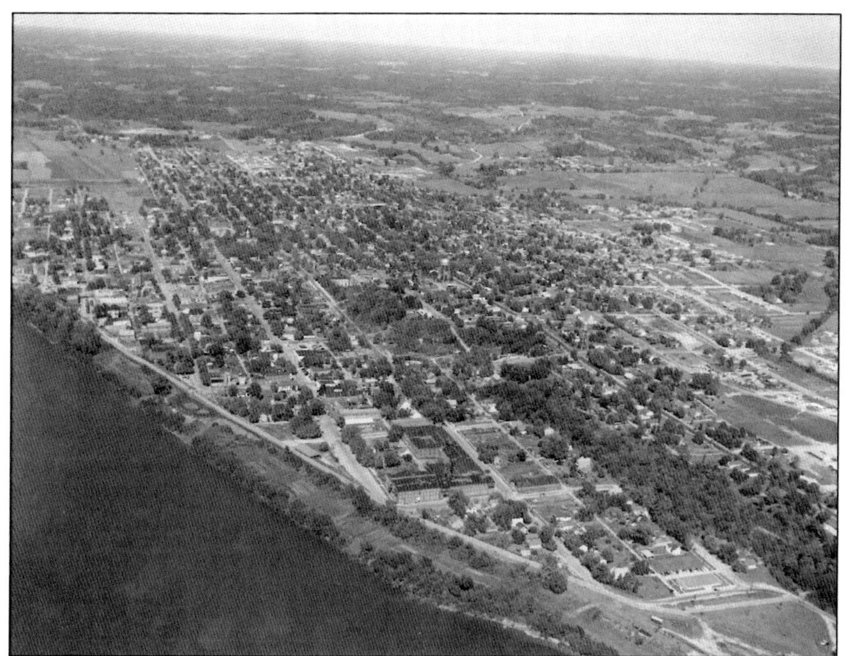

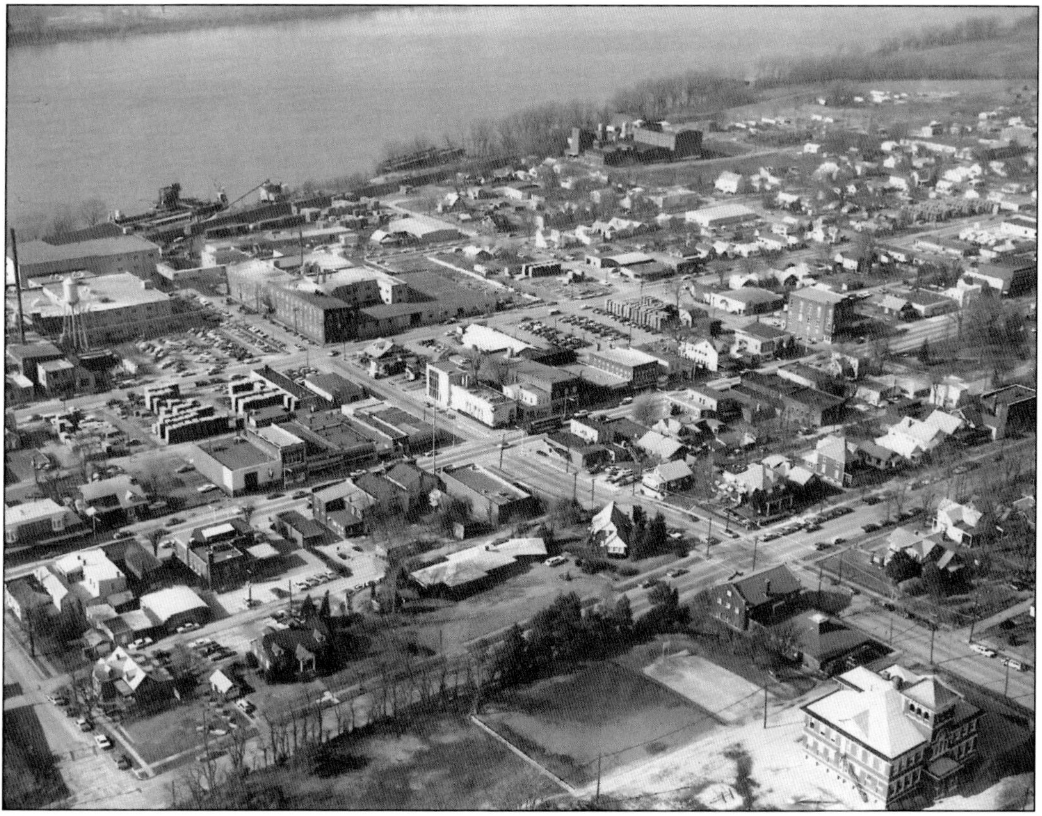

This aerial view of Tell City looks northwest in the modern era.

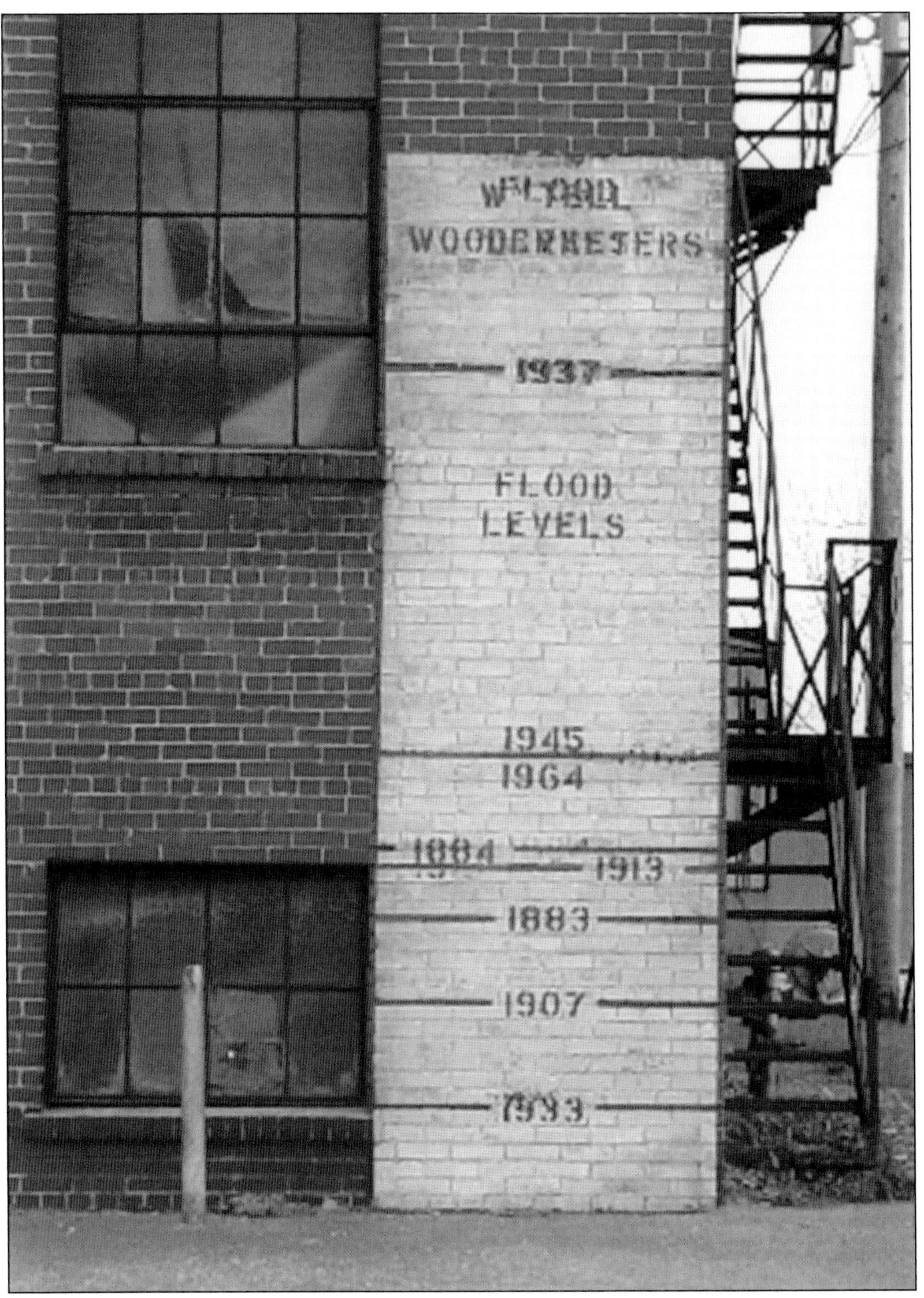

Pictured are Ohio River flood level markings on the William Tell Woodcrafters building, located in the 300 block of Seventh Street. The marks show flood levels from multiple years. In 2010, the building and markings were torn down after a fire during demolition.

Five

Churches, Schools, and Sports

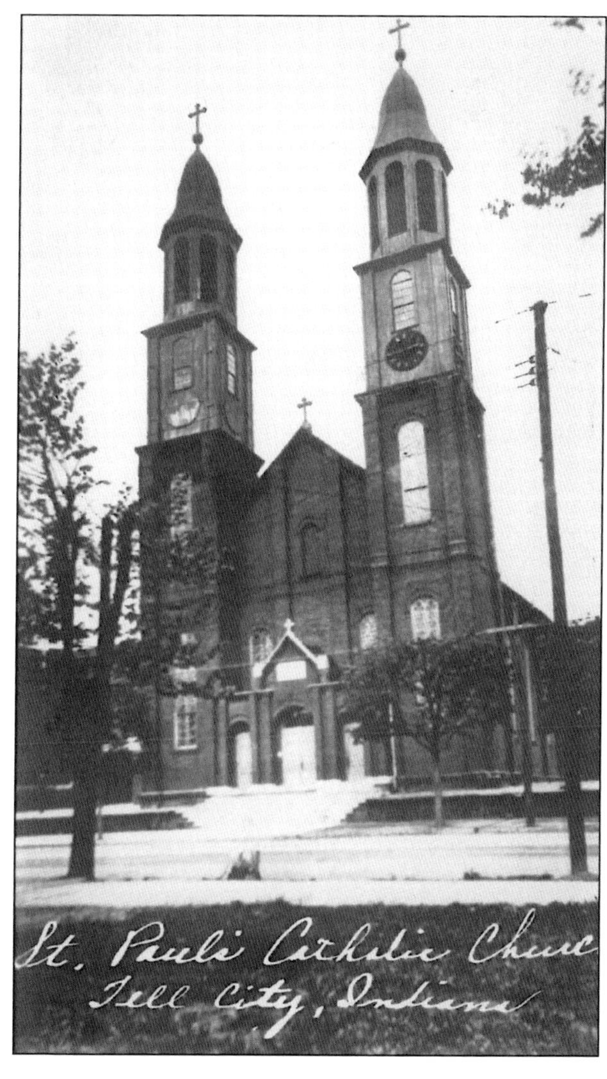

The original St. Paul Catholic Church was built in 1878. It was razed in 1954.

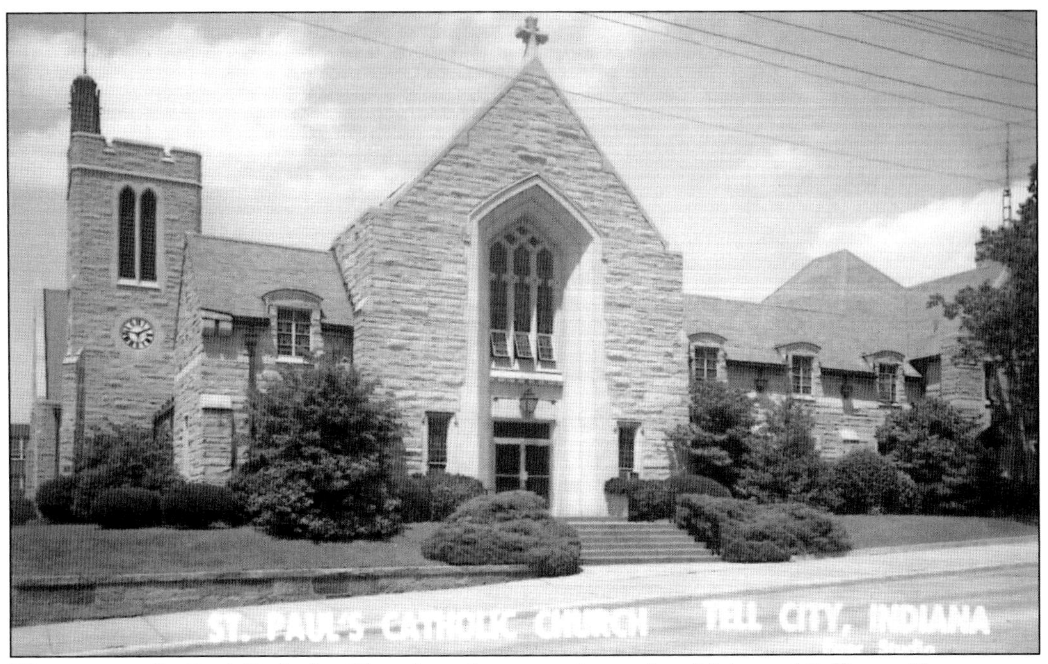

The current St. Paul Catholic Church and rectory, located at Main and Jefferson Streets, was built in 1954.

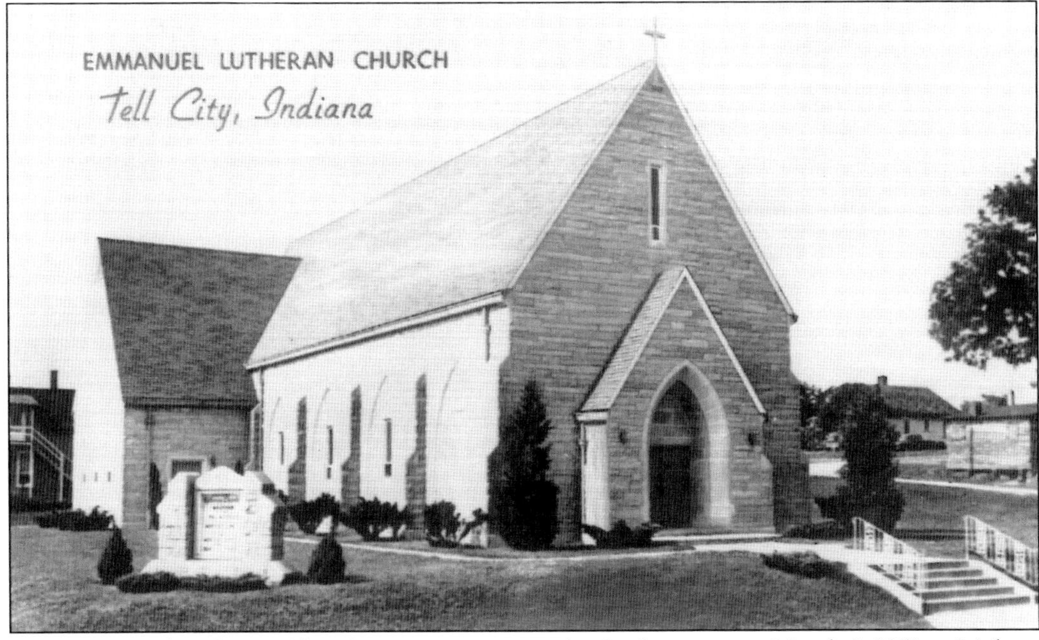

The Emmanuel Lutheran Church congregation met for the first time on March 4, 1951, at Mulzers Camp. The cornerstone was laid for the church in April 1952 at the corner lot on Pestalozzi and Twelfth Streets.

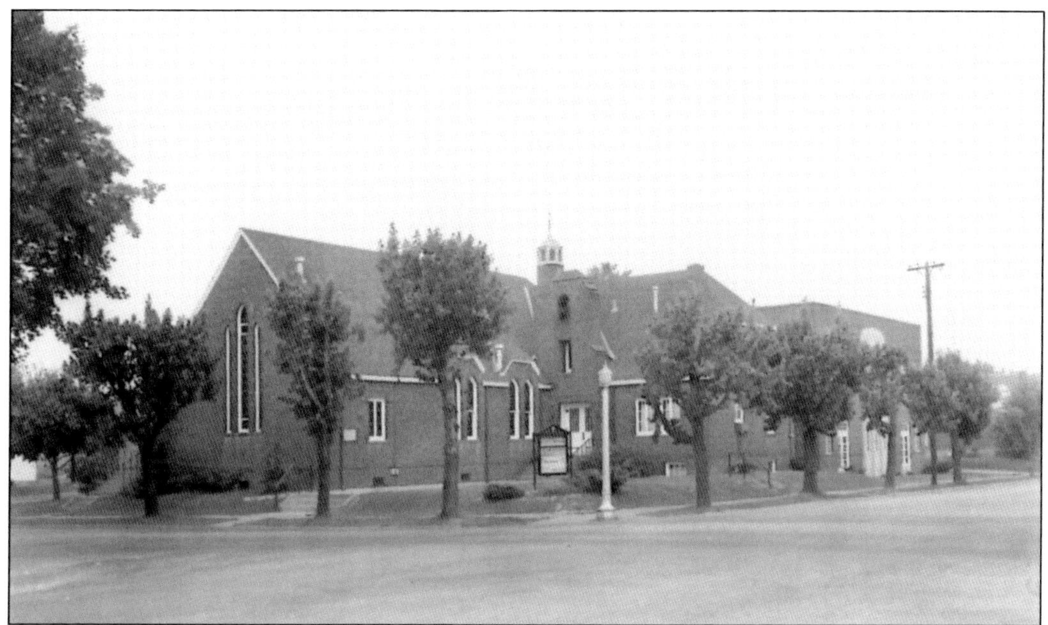

The congregation of First Baptist Church, located at 802 Thirteenth Street, originally met at city hall for 18 years. This church was built in 1939.

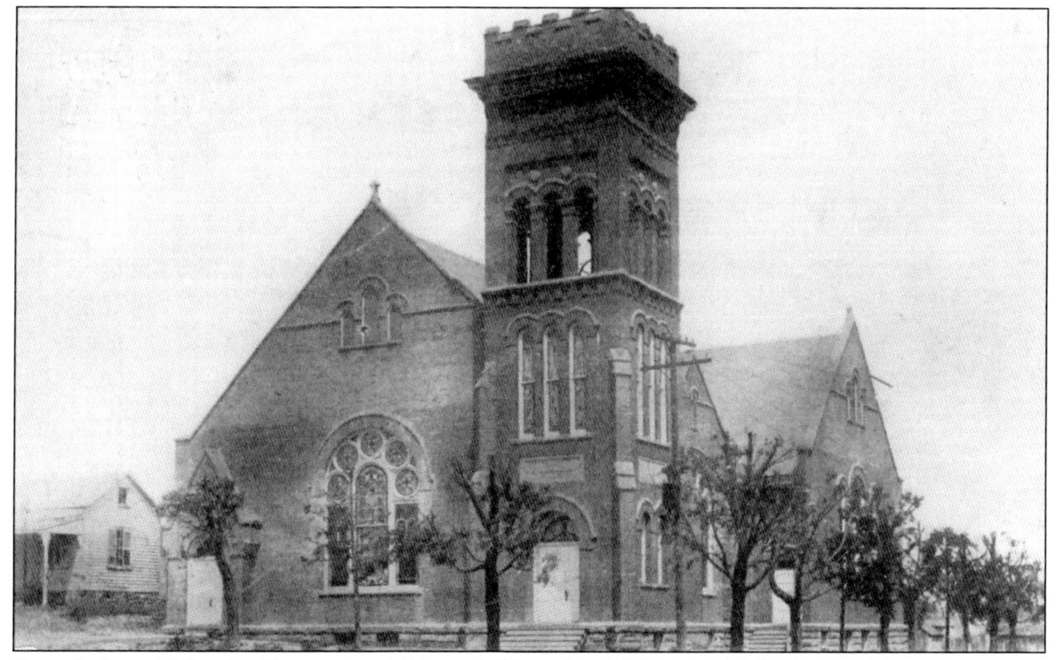

Founded in 1861, the Evangelical United Church of Christ is Tell City's oldest Protestant congregation. In 1907, this building was constructed to replace the original redbrick church. During the 1937 flood, the church provided beds and daily meals to flood victims.

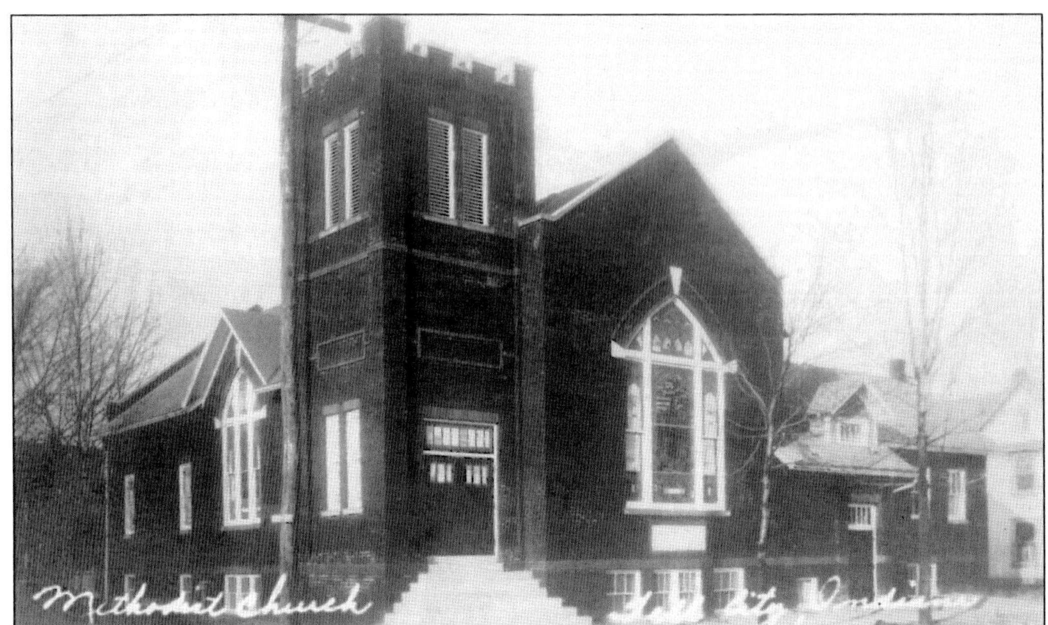

The Methodist Church began in Tell City in 1892 with the erection of a white church building. It was known as the "Little White Church" and was located on the corner of Tenth and Mozart Streets. By 1923, the congregation has outgrown this structure, and the current building was erected. A fundraiser was held with a goal of $16,000. Not only did church members give, but people from the community donated as well. The goal was met within four days' time.

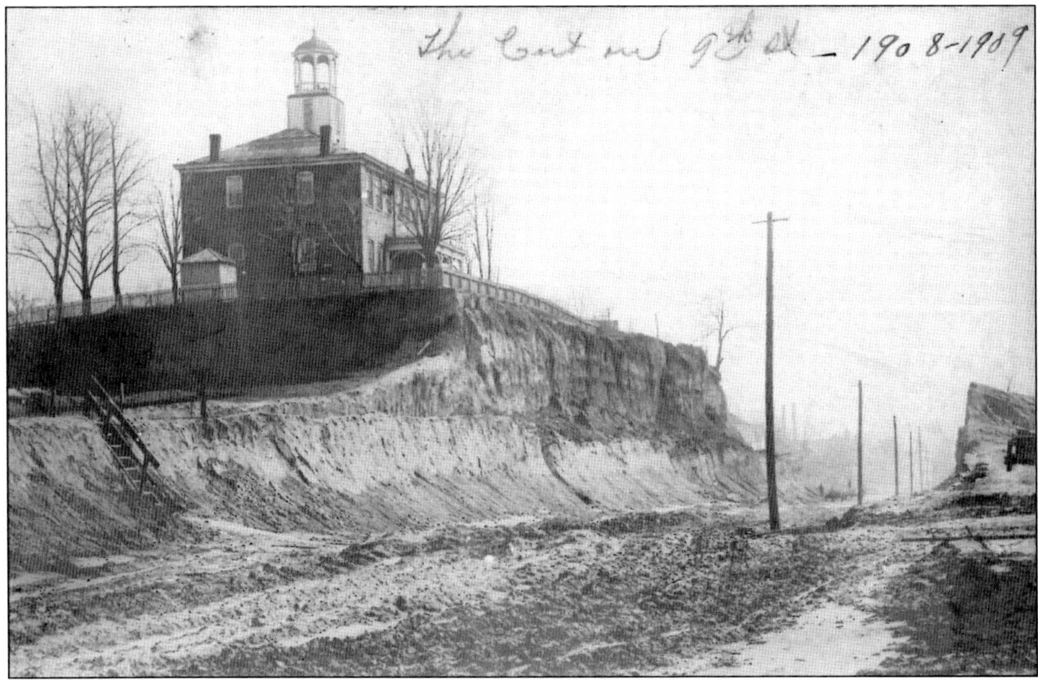

The South School was built in 1863. It was torn down in 1910 and replaced by the present Franklin School, which was built in 1909. The steep hill is from where Ninth Street was cut through. (Courtesy of Tell City Historical Society.)

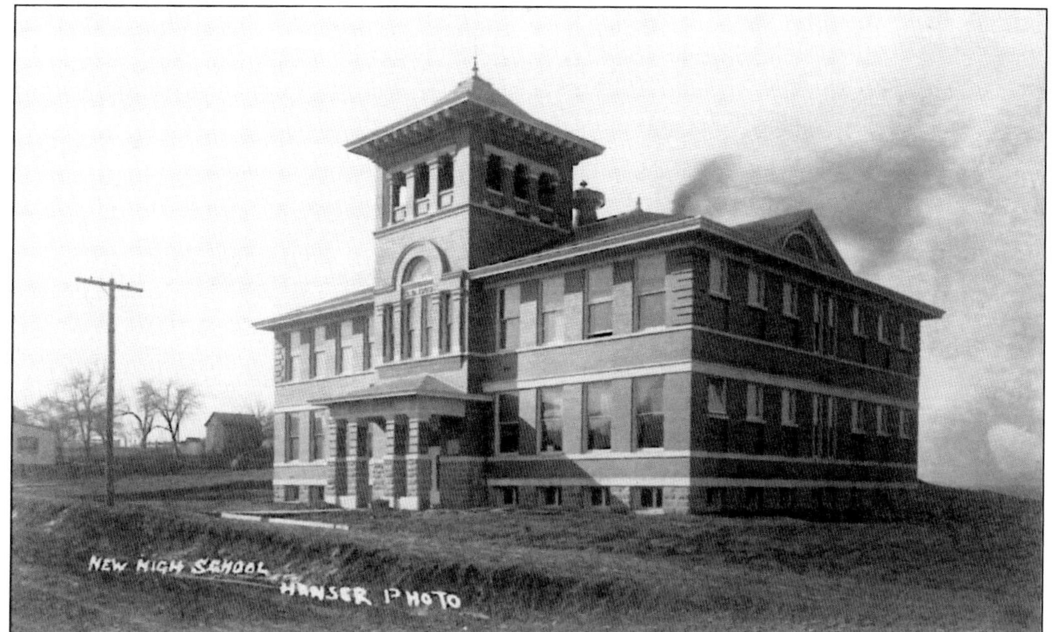

Franklin School was built in 1909 to replace the South School, located just to the west. It was the first school to have indoor plumbing. The elementary grades were on the first floor, and the high school occupied the second floor. After the new high school was built in 1928, Franklin School remained a grade school until 1980. (Courtesy of Tell City Historical Society.)

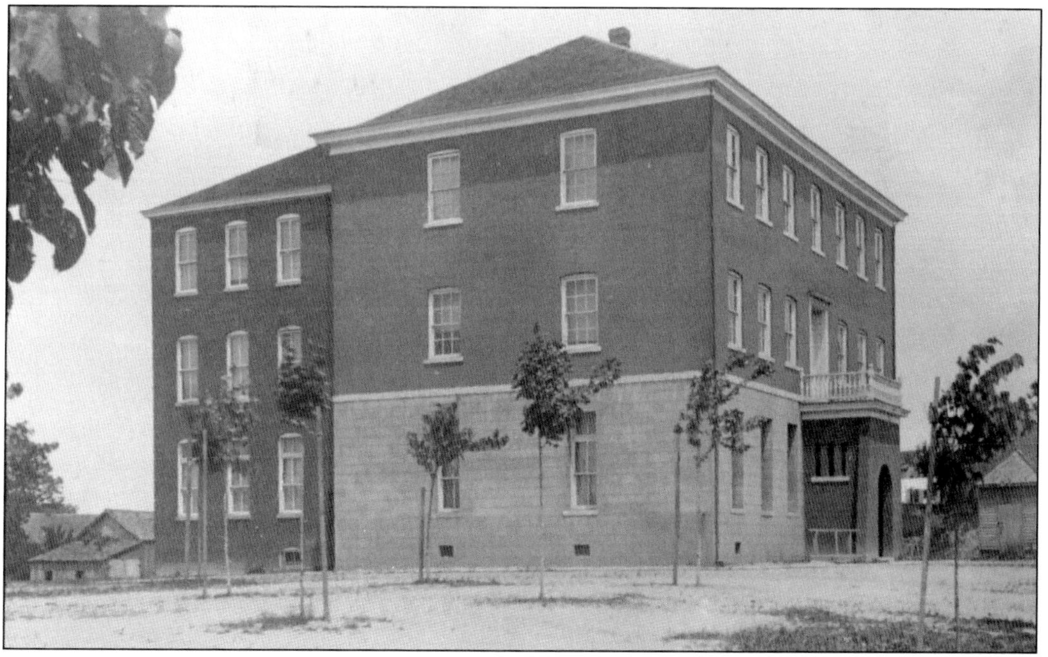

The old North School for many years housed most elementary grades. Originally, the second floor was the first floor. When the city cut the grading on Tenth Street, it made the basement area the first floor. Old North School was replaced by Newman School in 1920. (Courtesy of Tell City Historical Society.)

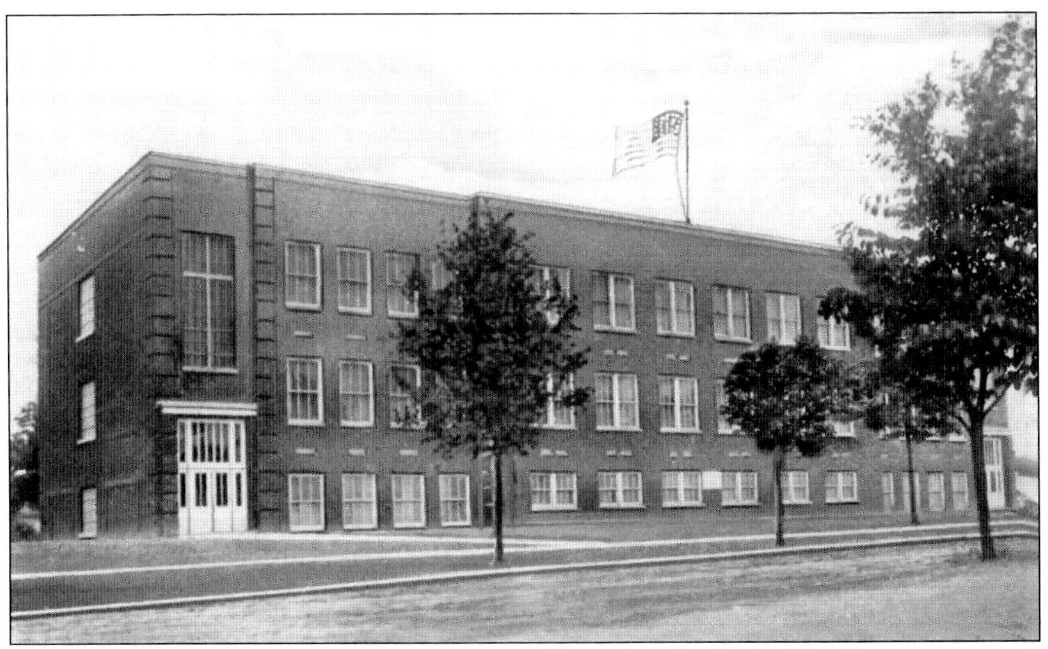

Newman School was built in 1920 to replace the old North School, which had been constructed at the same location in 1867. The school was named for Christian Newman, who was school superintendent from 1889 until his death in 1923. It is believed that he died as a result of pneumonia he developed at the ground-breaking ceremony for the new school. Before completion of Tell City High School in 1928, graduation ceremonies were held here. The building continued to be used as a school until 1999.

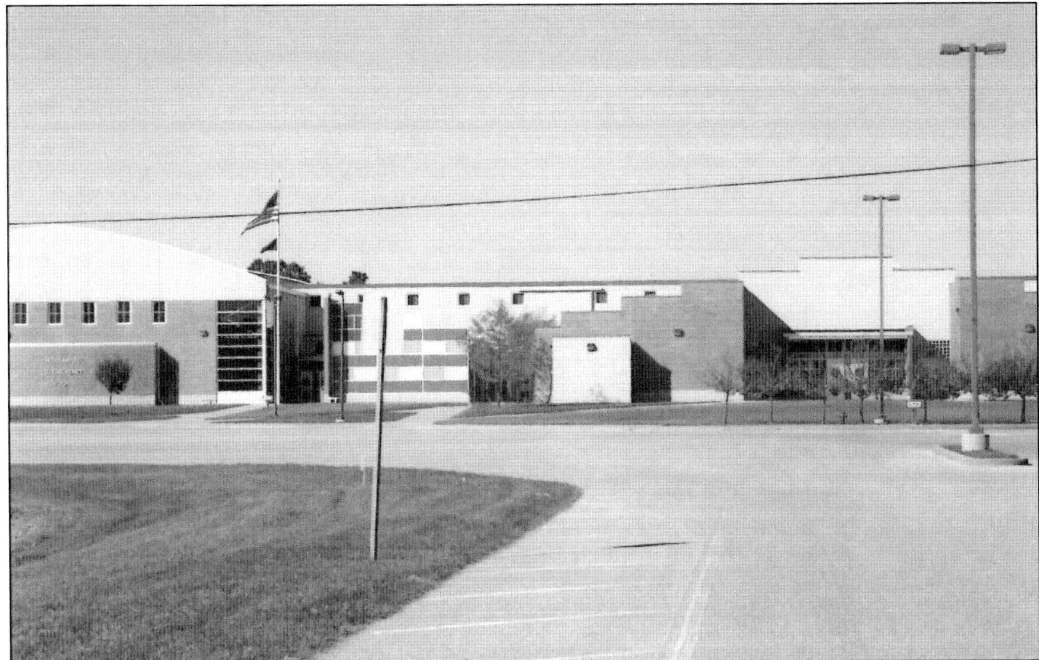

William Tell Elementary School is located at 1235 Thirty-First Street. Today, this school has grades K–6. (Courtesy of Tell City Historical Society.)

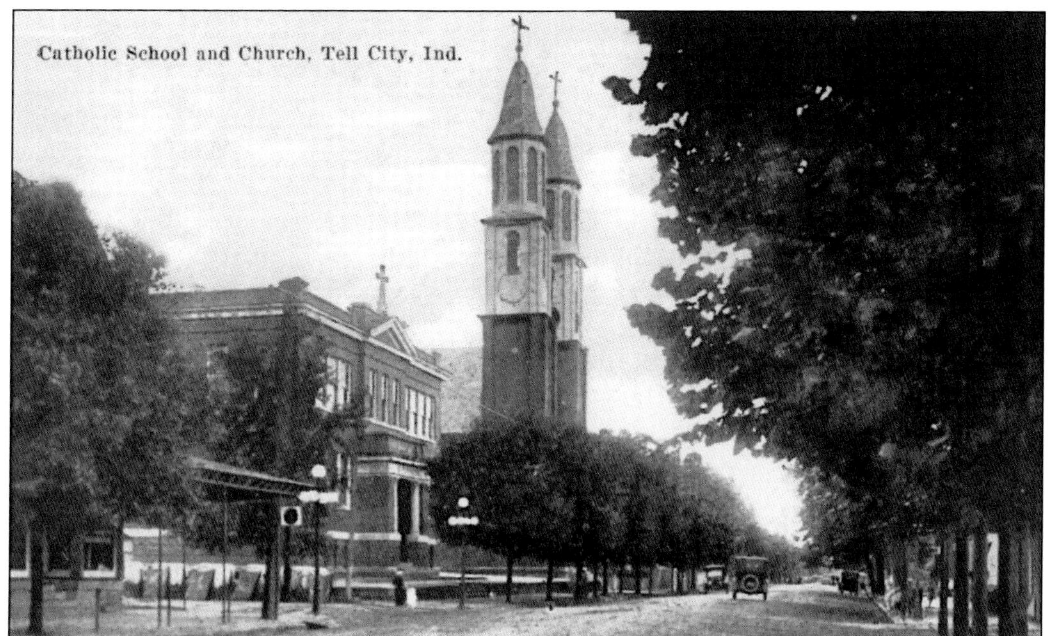

St. Paul School was established in 1859, and a five-room brick school building and the church were completed in 1877. A new school was built in 1914, with additions added in later years. The school continued until 1999. The school buildings were razed in 2006.

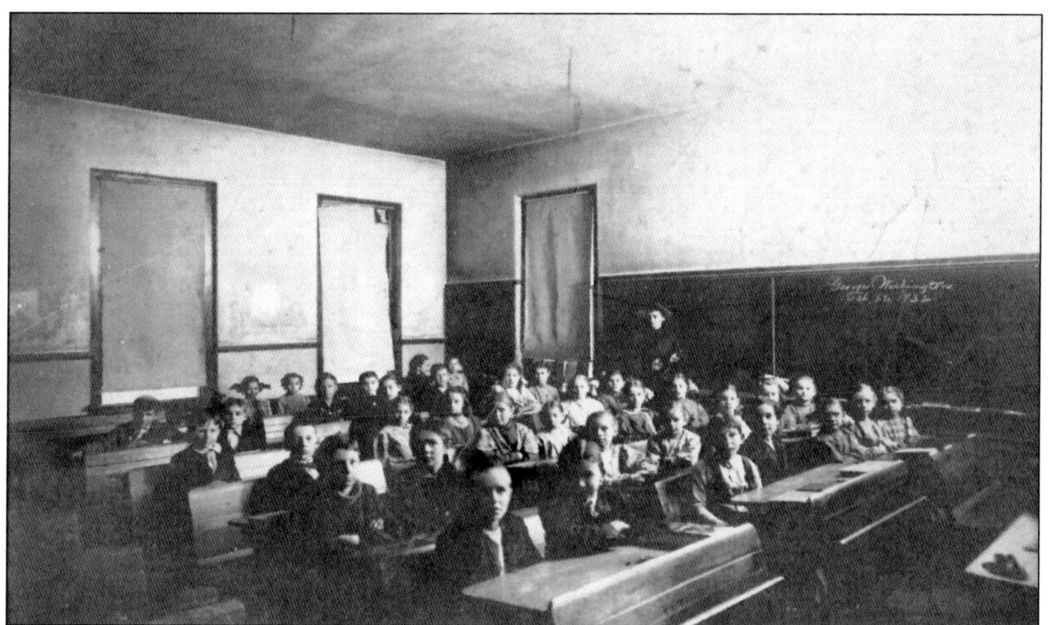

Pictured is a group of fourth and fifth graders at North School around 1911. The teacher was Edith Stewart. Included in the image are John "Hans" Begert, Henry Laflin, Luella Lehman, Estelle Kuster, Estelle Cassidey Paulin, Mary Prueher, Curtis Ress, Blanche Taylor, and Frieda Wagner.

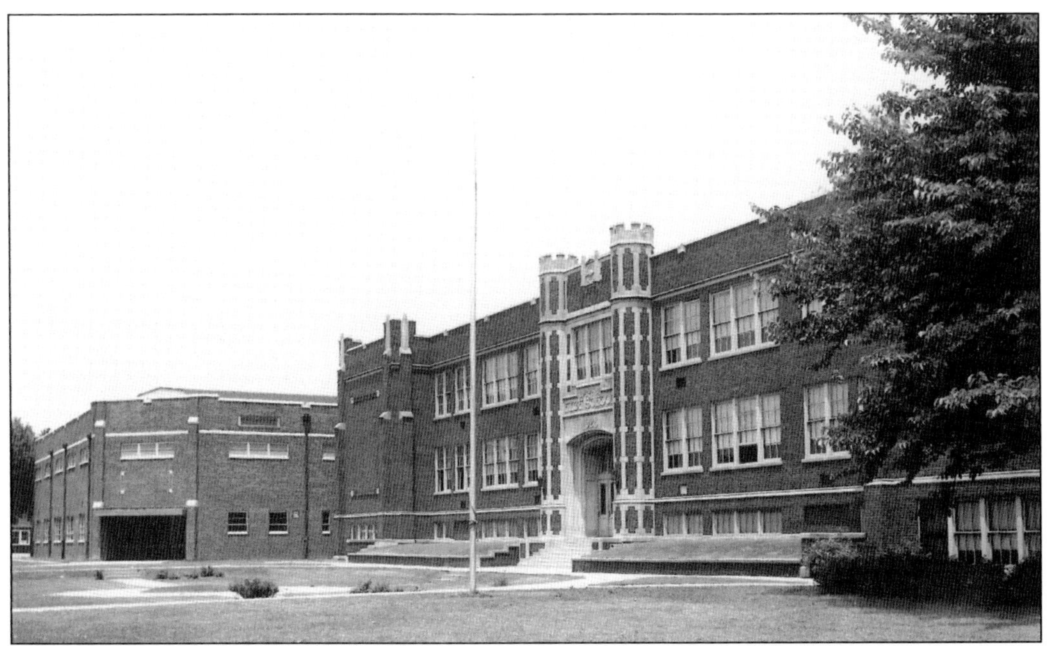

Tell City High School was built in 1928. Two of the major additions to the school were the gym in 1955 and the library in the summer of 1964. Several more additions occurred throughout the years, including an indoor swimming pool. Today, this is the Tell City Jr.-Sr. High School.

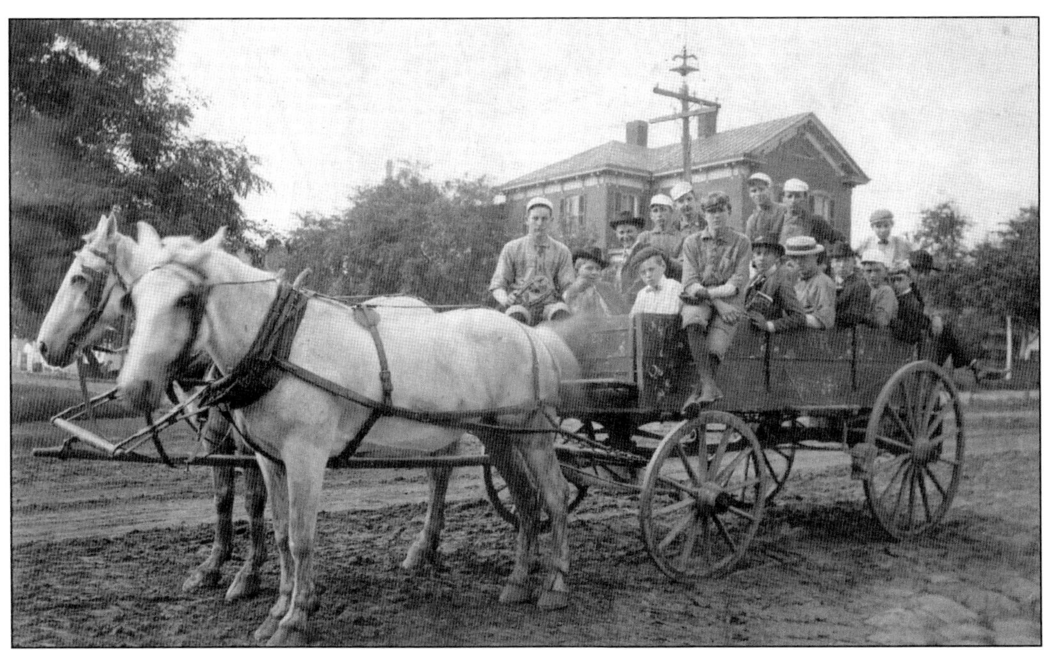

Baseball team members and fans piled into Albert Fenn's wagon for this picture, taken around 1907 near the intersection of Seventh and Humboldt Streets. Sitting at far left is Edwin Arndt, followed by, from left to right, Oscar Basedow, Roy Fenn (in white shirt), and Walter Hartman. Behind Fenn is Harry Greiner, and behind Greiner is Herb Patrick. Others included are, from left to right, Alphonse Kaelin, Bert Fenn, Frank Becker, Chris Fenn, David Bielefld, and Harry Krecker.

The Tell City Athletic Club is posing on the steps of city hall in 1906. Pictured are, from left to right, (first row) Charles Jehle, unidentified, Fred Greiner, and John F. Ress; (second row) John Haerle, Franke Jehle, Joe Adams, Louis Schroeder, and John A. "Hans" Muelchi; (third row) Harry Kaercher, George Kreisle, Edwin Grimmeisen, Harry Schergens, Frank Ball, and George Lehman; (fourth row) Hugo Bott, Krank Casper, Fred C. Ress, and Jack Kiefer.

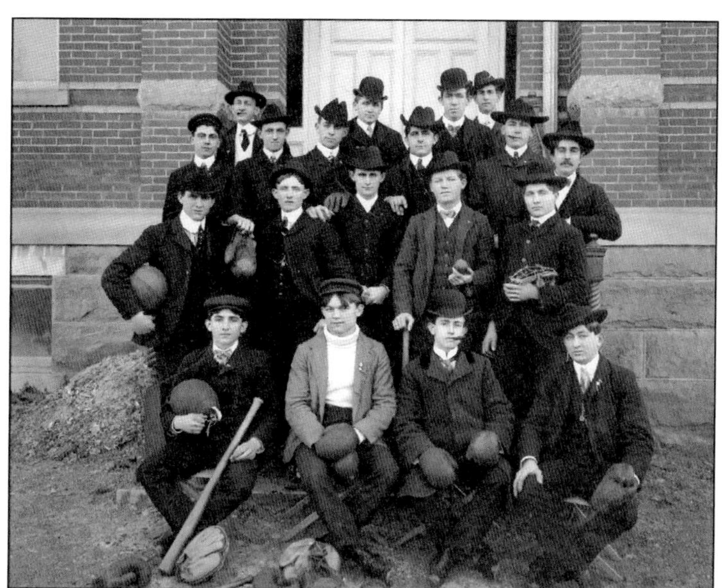

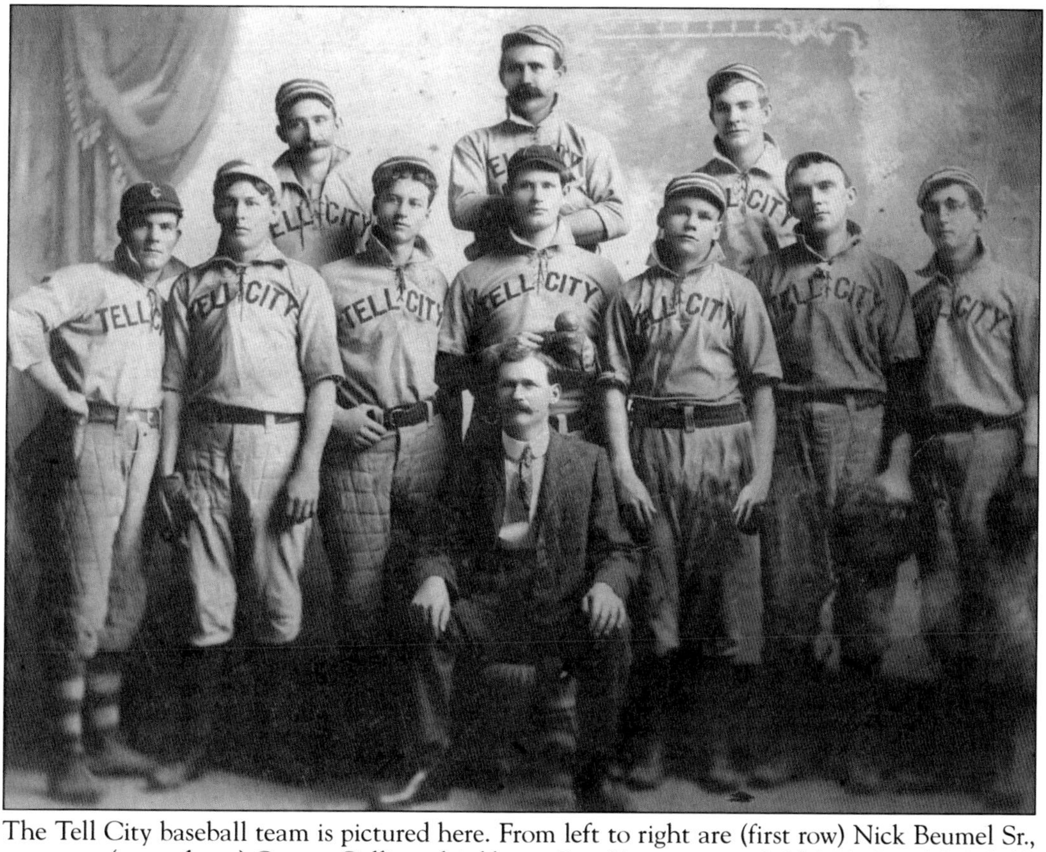

The Tell City baseball team is pictured here. From left to right are (first row) Nick Beumel Sr., manager; (second row) George Collins, third base; Curt Yaggi, center field; Milo Land, left field; Fred "Bud" Eggers, pitcher; Jack Murphy, shortstop; Jake Kelly, catcher; and Albert "Jack" Kiefer, utility; (third row) Albert "Bunch" Futterer, first base; Joe Schuh, second base; and Ed Goffinet, right field. (Courtesy of Tell City Historical Society.)

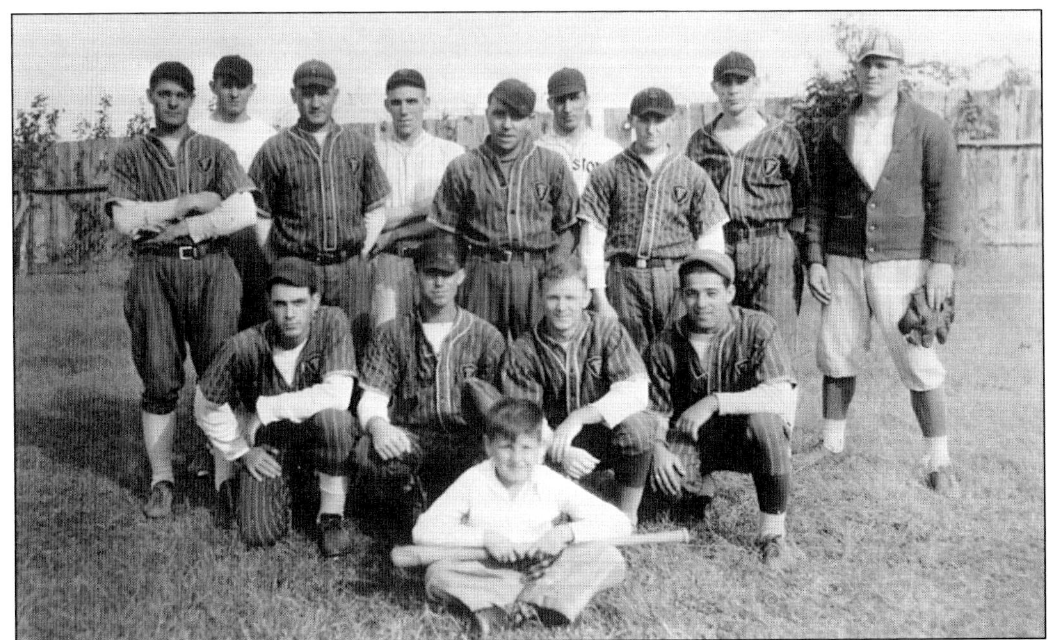

The Firestones baseball team was sponsored by Dick Winchell and Blackie Paulin. Those pictured include batboy Walter Lindauer, Everett Sanders, Curly Gilliland, Swat Anderson, George Kays, Johnny Northernor, Eddie Lindauer, Don Stiles, Bill Naegle, Lathrop "Hops" Reid, Charlie Braun Jr., Frank Gaynor, Alvin Ruxer, and one unidentified. (Courtesy of Tell City Historical Society.)

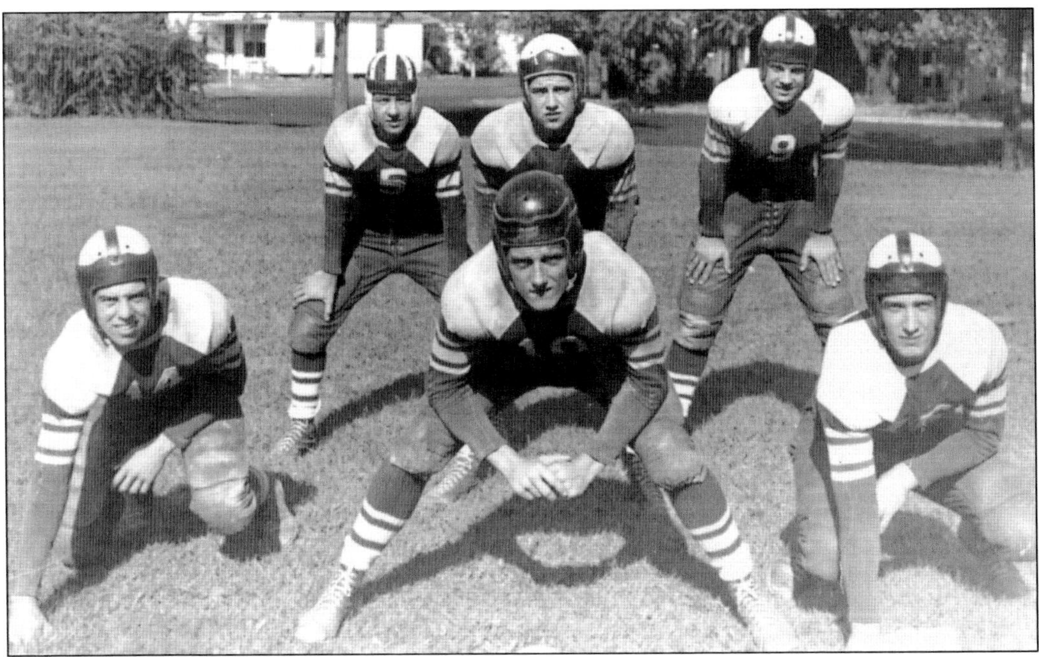

The 1939–1940 Tell City High School six-man football team includes, from left to right, (first row) Junior Dickman, Eddie Stevens, and Bob Morris; (second row) Jim Hartz, Tom Byrd, and Bill Kreisle. (Courtesy of Tell City Historical Society.)

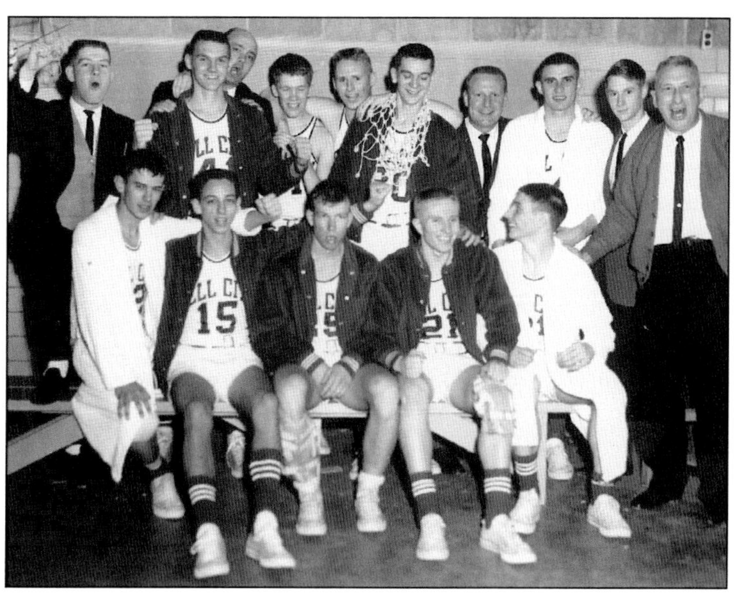

The Tell City High School basketball team was the sectional champion in 1963. Pictured are, from left to right, (first row) Larry Reynolds, Ronnie Arnold, Kermit Quick, Jim Meek, and Gary Hubert; (second row) Alan Kessler, Jerry Brunner, assistant coach Jim Stubblefield, Dave Clark, John Arnold, Gary Kleaving, head coach Jerry Gray, Jerry Kuntz, Gene Bender, and Grady Swadley. (Courtesy of Tell City Historical Society.)

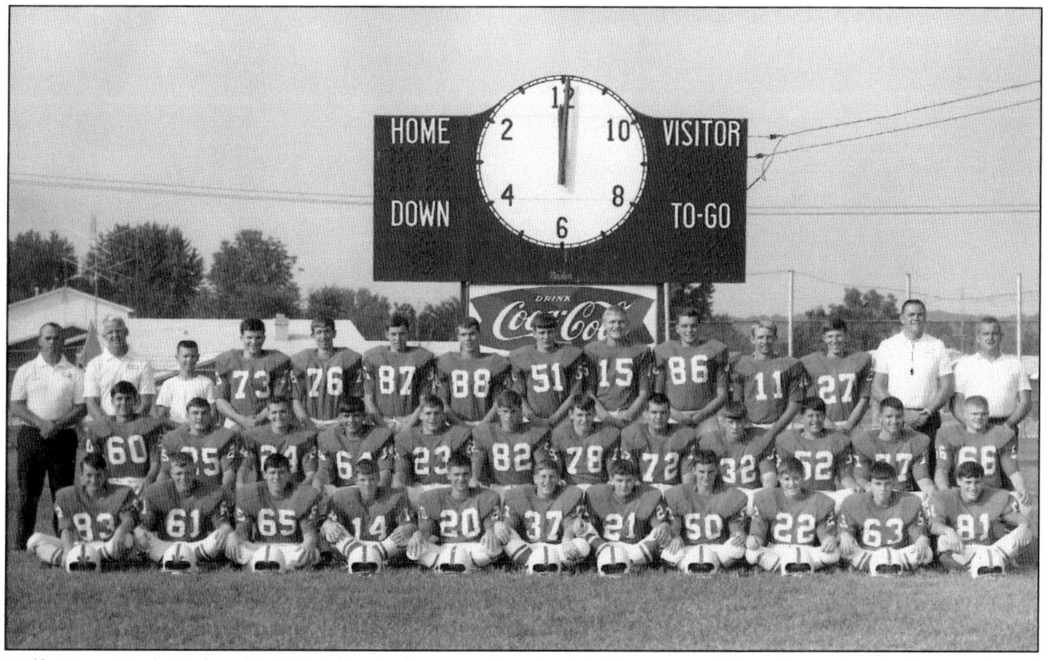

Tell City High School's 1966 football team finished 7-2, a record for the school. Pictured are, from left to right, (first row) Dennis Humston, Roger Kieser, Dave Mahoney, Paul Saalman, Dave Pyle, Mike Malone, Steve Richardt, Gary Lohoff, Danny Tapley, Gary Burden, and John Lauer; (second row) Boise Macon, Harold Goffinet, Ronnie LaGrange, Paul Biever, Dave LeClere, Richard Buckmaster, Kenny Schwartz, Lee Gengelbach, Jack Little, Tom Wint, Sam Oberhausen, and Joe Richard; (third row) Coach Jewell, Coach Busse, Steve Dauby, Steve Houghland, Don Foerster, Stanley Austin, Norvin Esarey, Ronnie Hauser, Craig Blackford, John Austin, Steve Peckinpaugh, Rodney Jordon, Coach Curry, and Coach Talley. (Courtesy of Tell City Historical Society.)

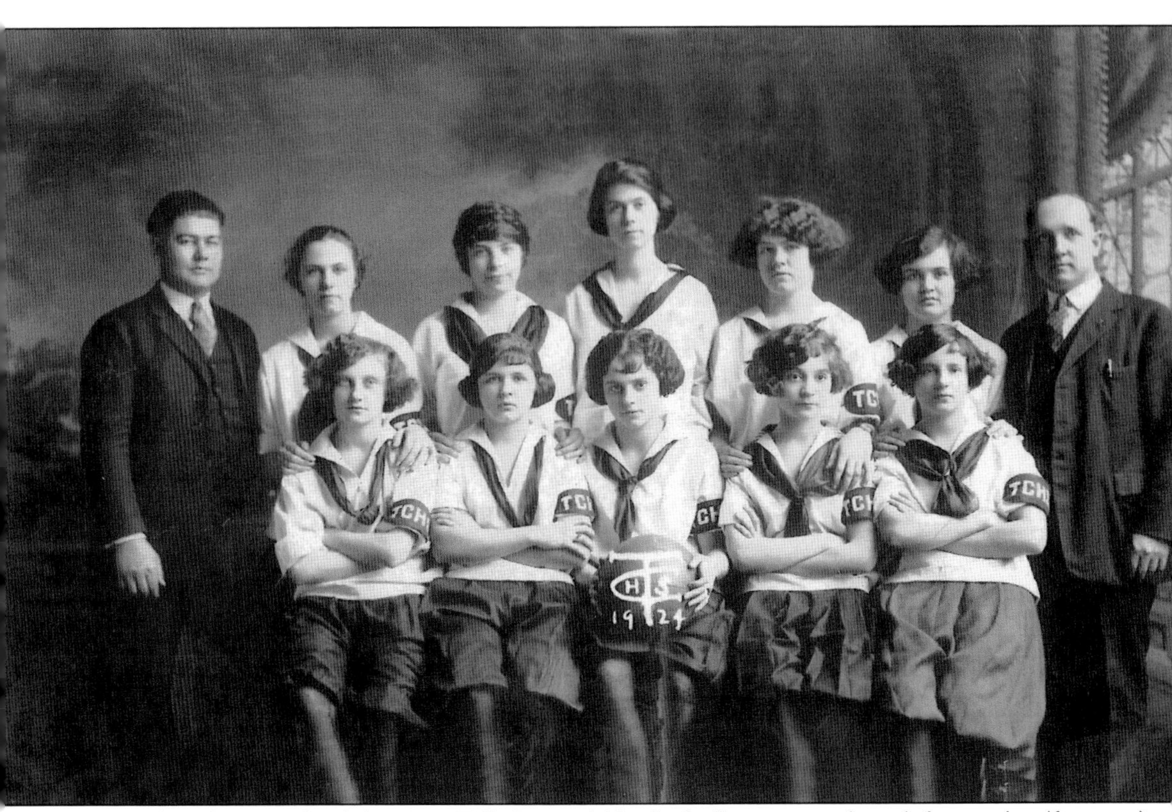

In this photograph of the 1924 Tell City girls' basketball team are, from left to right, (first row) Catharine Brenner, Marie Hugger, Helen Scheible, Cathryn Zoercher, and Olga Scheible; (second row) coach Clyde Walters, Helen Bader, Winifred Herrmann, a Miss Thrasher (chaperone), Leona Moutschka, Othello Ress, and business manager Eugene O'Bryan. (Courtesy of Tell City Historical Society.)

Six

Fun and Celebration

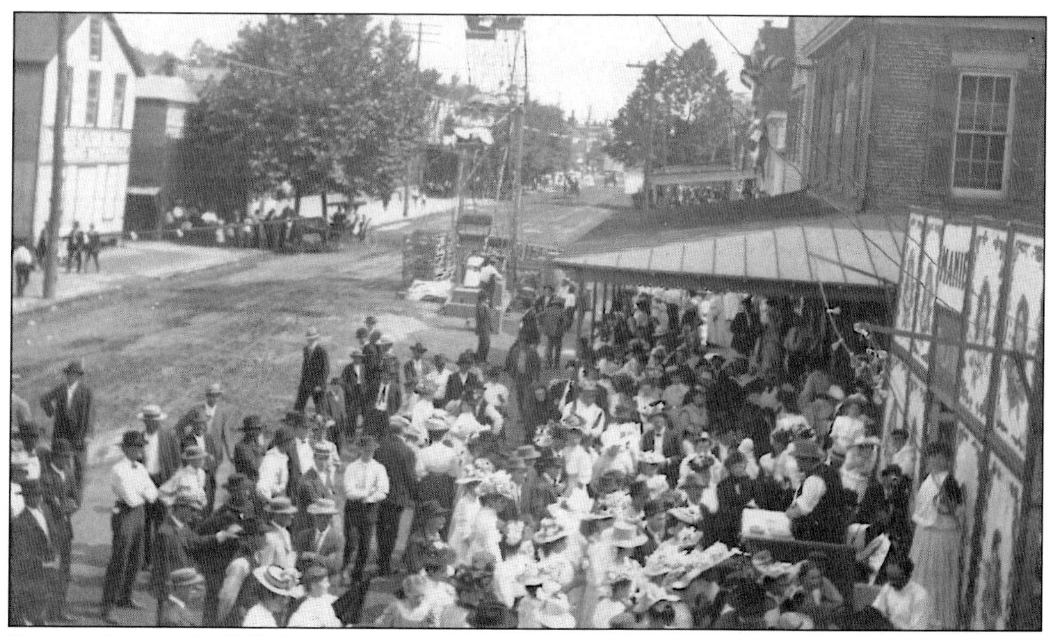

Pictured here is the Tell City Homecoming in 1916. This photograph was taken at the corner of Main and Humboldt Streets. (Courtesy of Tell City Historical Society.)

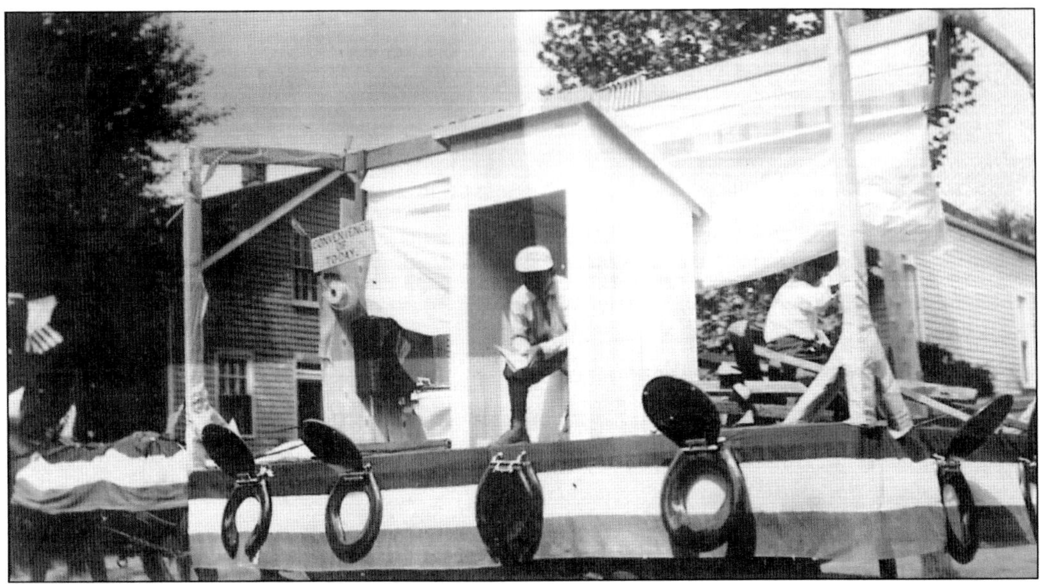

The Knott Manufacturing built a parade float for the Tell City Homecoming in 1916. The company made wooden toilet seats. Its factory was located at Sixth and Tell Streets.

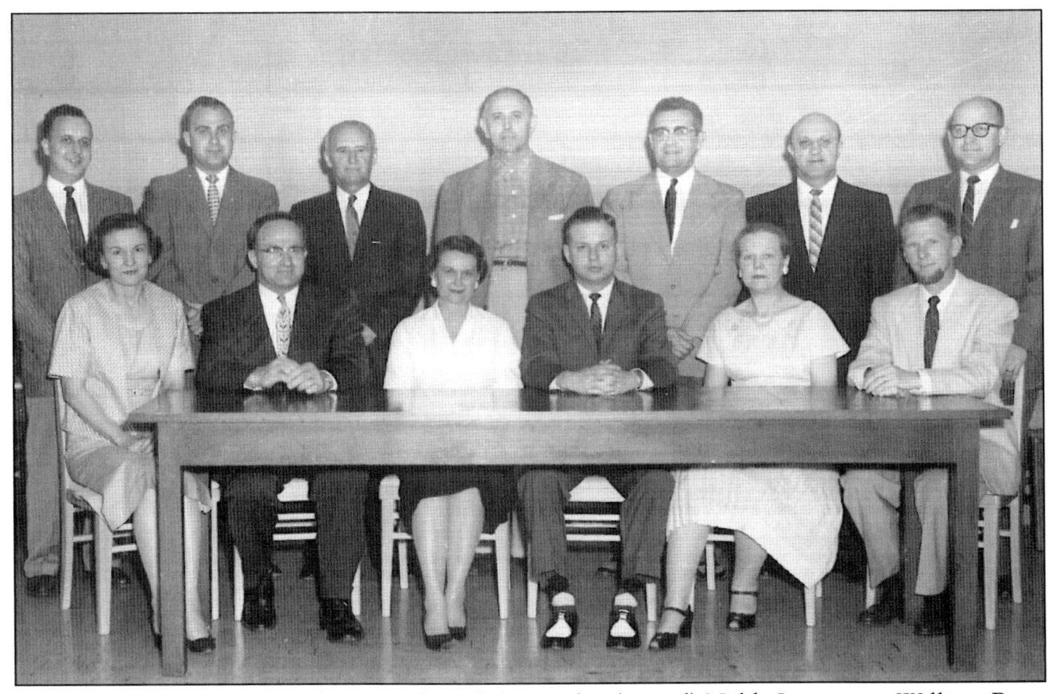

Centennial committee members are, from left to right, (seated) Nelda Lawrence, William Ress, Ruth Ann Kennedy Werner, Jim Wittmer, Verna Graves Johnson Hill, and Walter Graves; (standing) Frank Simpson, Ralph Reed, Harold Kennedy, E.W. Schergens, Anthony Oberhausen, Frank Clemens, and Dr. Bernard Bosler. This photograph was taken in 1958.

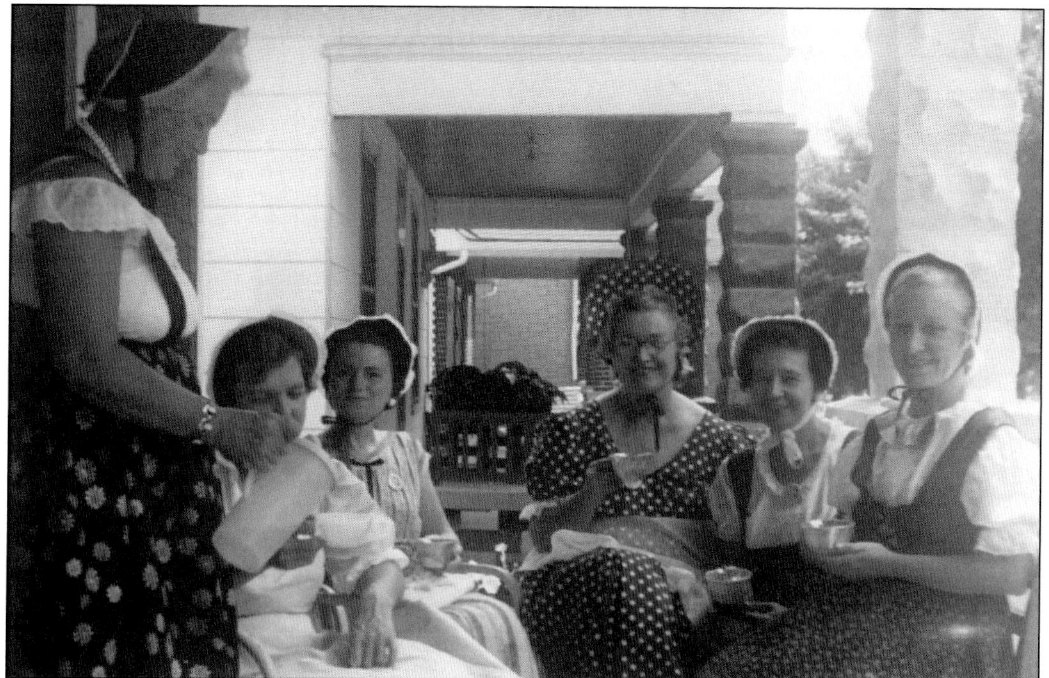

During the Tell City Centennial in 1958, residents were encouraged to dress up in period clothing. These ladies had afternoon tea wearing their outfits. From left to right are two unidentified, Louis Esarey, Opal Snyder, Mae Sandage, and Zelda Cail.

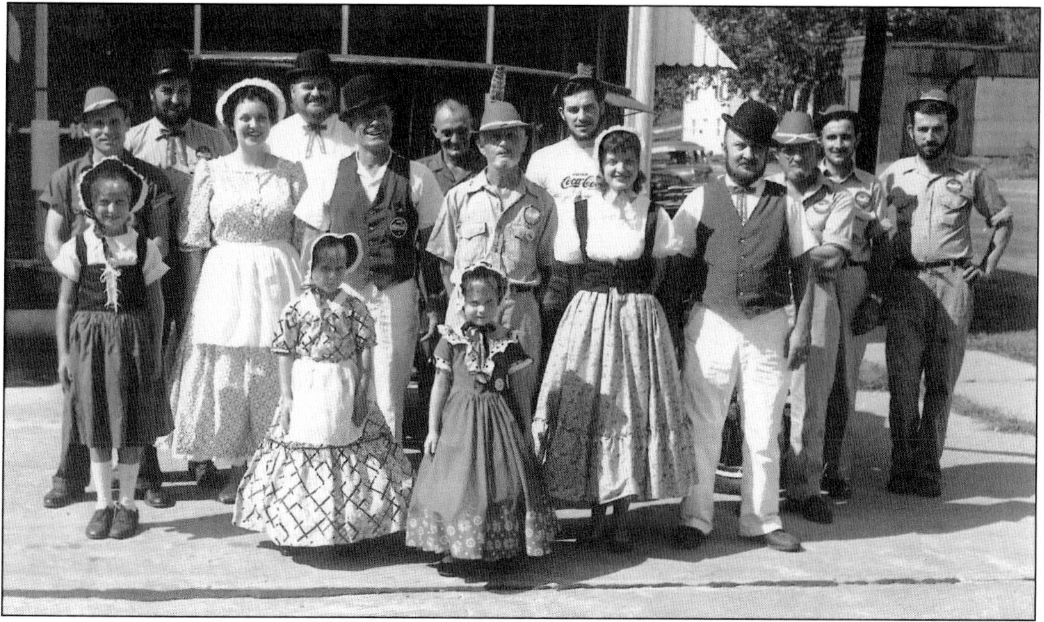

Coca-Cola employees and a few of their children are dressed up for the Tell City centennial in 1958. From left to right are (first row) Mary Jane Miller Heeke, Cathy Miller Frizzell, and Mary Jane Owen; (second row) unidentified, Sharon Feix, Urey Chambers, Walter Tableman, unidentified, and Gabe Miller; (third row) Burnell Richter, Hughes Owen, Leo James, Delmar Alvey, Gilbet Huebschman, Bob Ransom, and Earl Alvey. (Courtesy of Mary Emma Owen.)

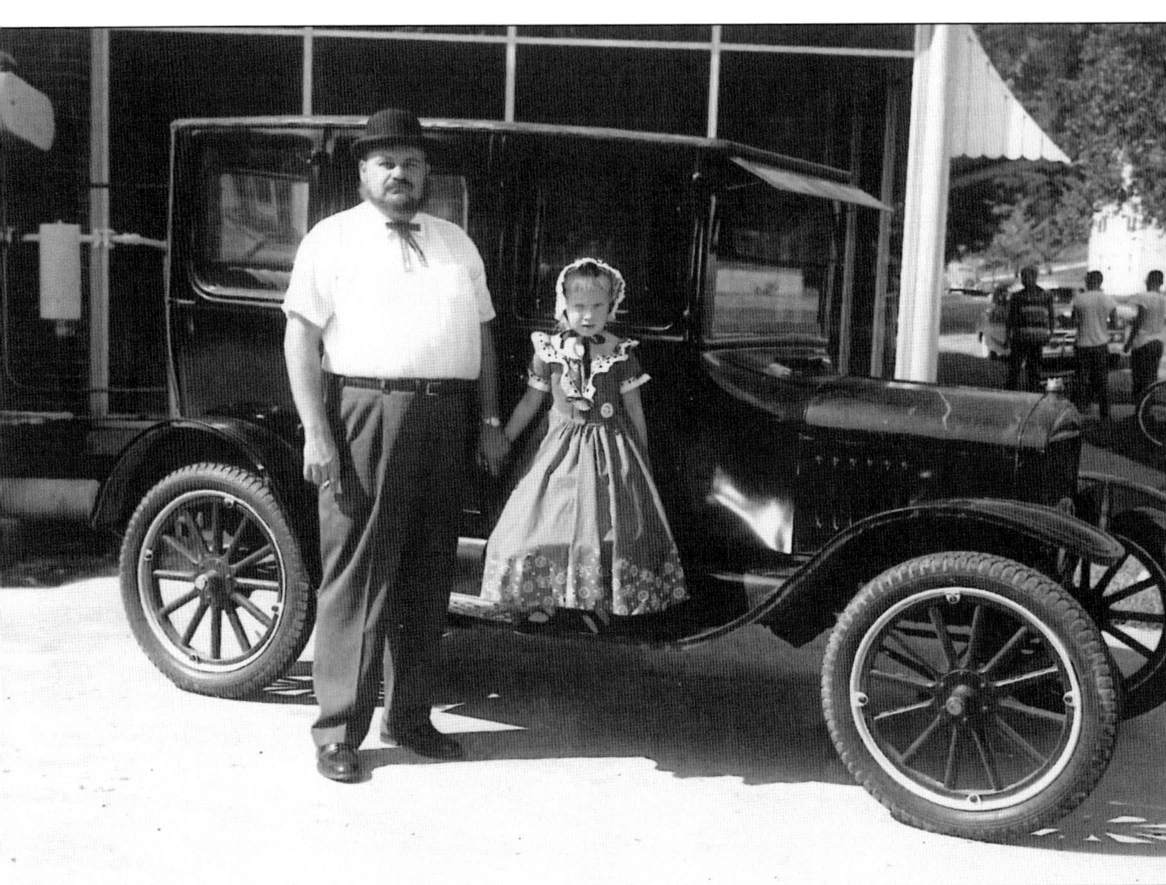

Hughes Owen and his daughter Mary Jane Owen pose with "Old Tom" during the 1958 centennial. "Old Tom" was Hughes's 1925 Ford Model T; he drove this car in nearly every parade. The car still resides in Tell City today and is owned by the author. (Courtesy of Mary Emma Owen.)

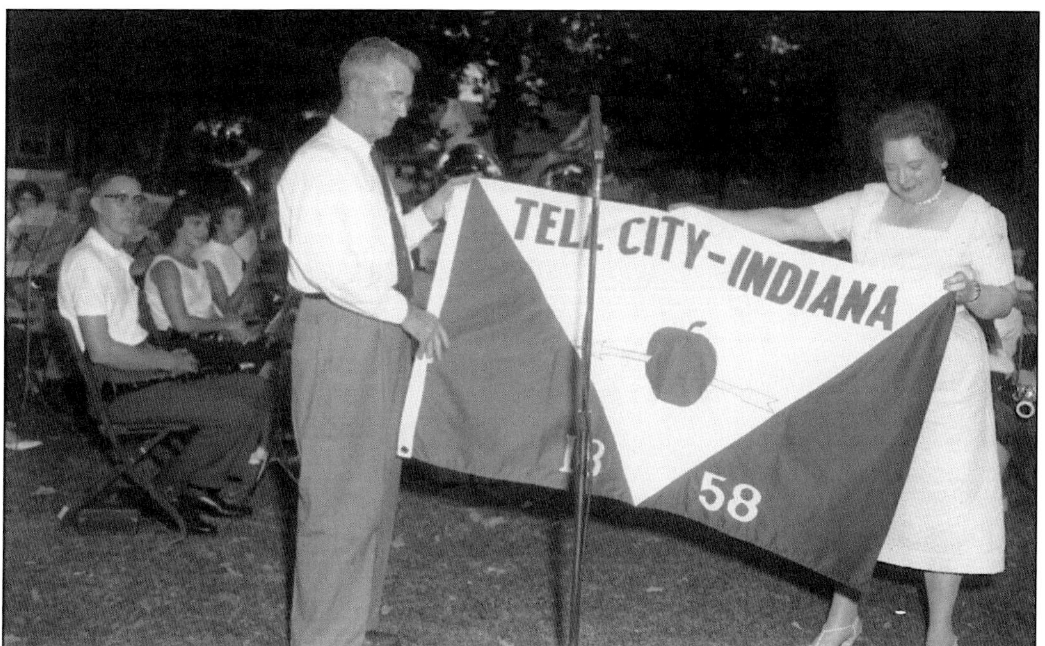

The Tell City Historical Society sponsored a contest for a flag design for Tell City. Marie Clemens submitted this winning entry. Here, Louise A. Becker presents the official flag to Mayor William Howe. Becker and Dr. James Current were cochairs of this project. (Courtesy of Tell City Historical Society.)

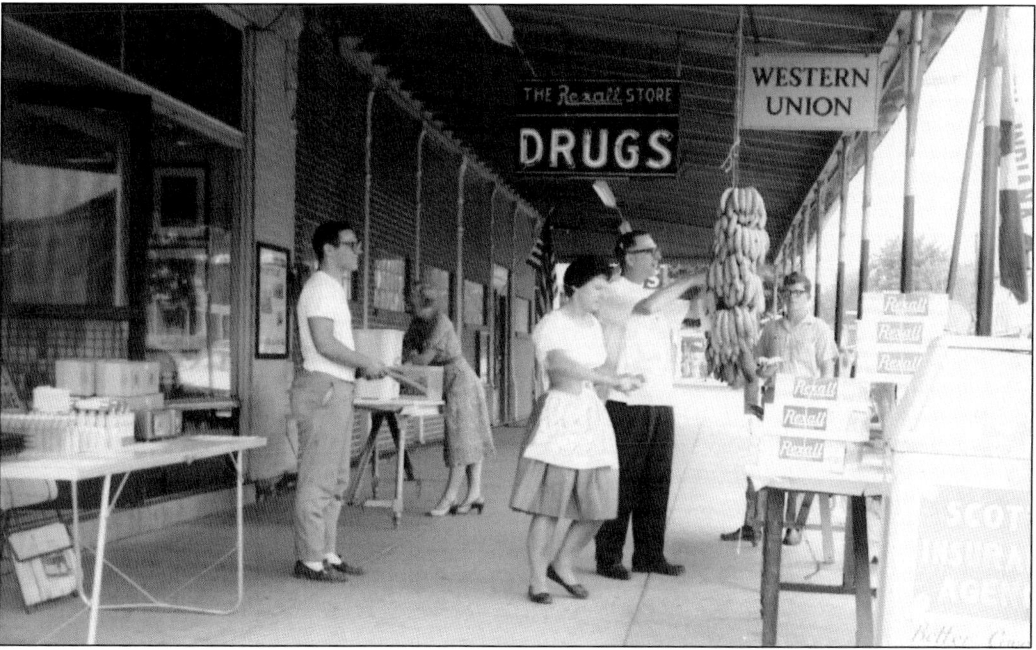

Old Fashioned Bargain Days was started in 1961 during the Schweizer Fest. This photograph was taken at Schreiber's Drug Store. Charles A. Schreiber is cutting bananas off a bunch. Pictured are, from left to right, Edward Dickman; unidentified; Edward's mother, Margaret Dickman; Schreiber; and Wayne Smith. (Courtesy of Tell City Historical Society.)

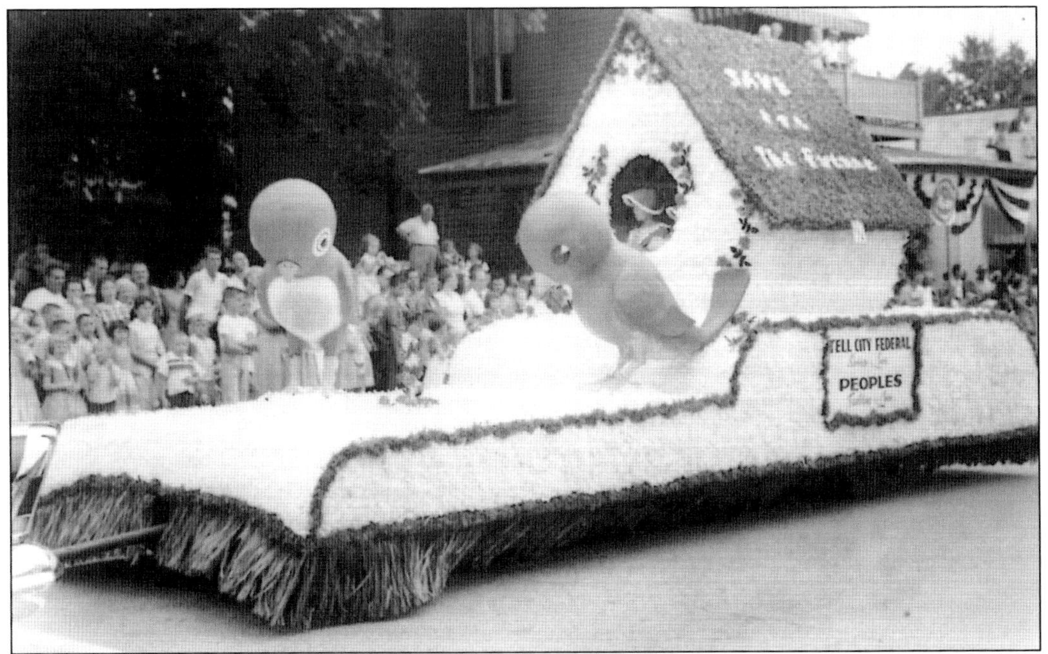

Tell City Federal Savings and Peoples Building & Loan combined forces to offer this float featuring two lovebirds; it won second place for most novel or original entry. Janet and Sally Rippy are the girls inside the birdhouse. (Courtesy of Tell City Historical Society.)

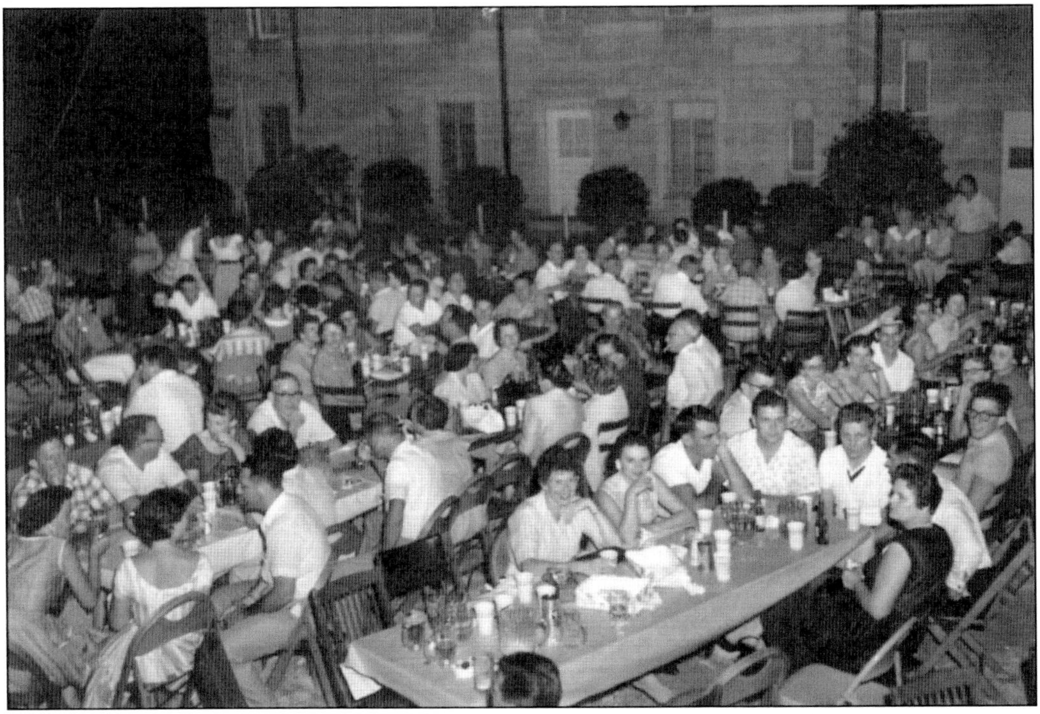

Each year during the Schweizer Fest, there is a beer garden along Main Street. Originally, the beer garden was in the empty lot next to the Moose Lodge on Jefferson Street. (Courtesy of Tell City Historical Society.)

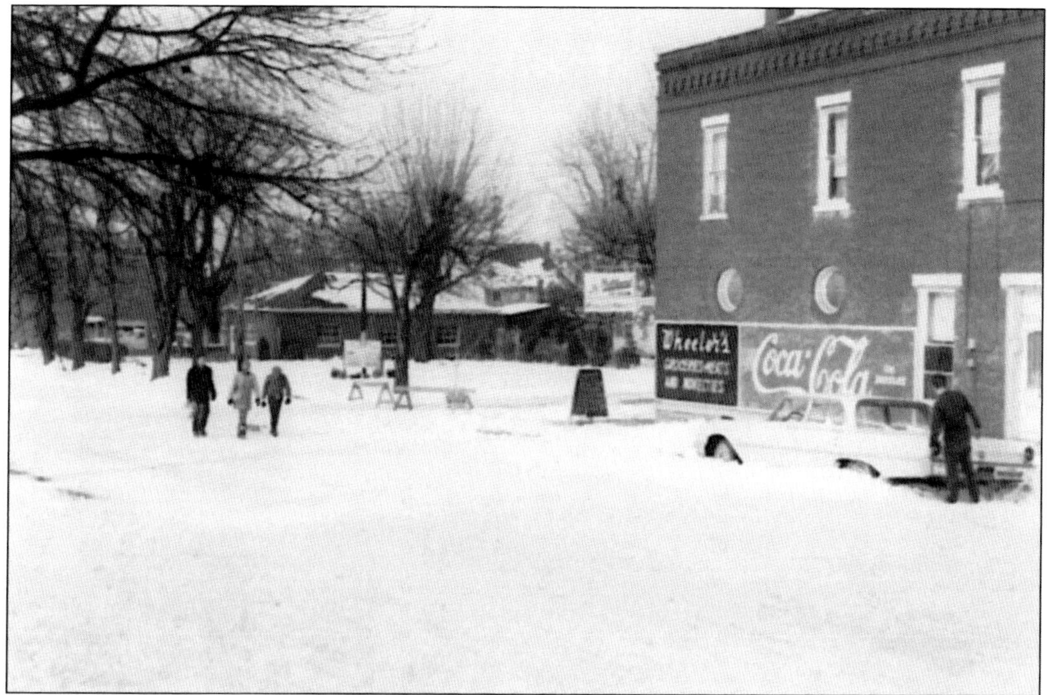

Wheelers Grocery and Meats, located on Washington Hill, was next to a favorite sledding slope. Usually, sledders coasted from Eleventh Street to Ninth Street, but in good coasting weather, some could go all the way to Seventh Street. During these times, the street was roped off and closed to traffic. (Courtesy of Charles and Janet Wheeler.)

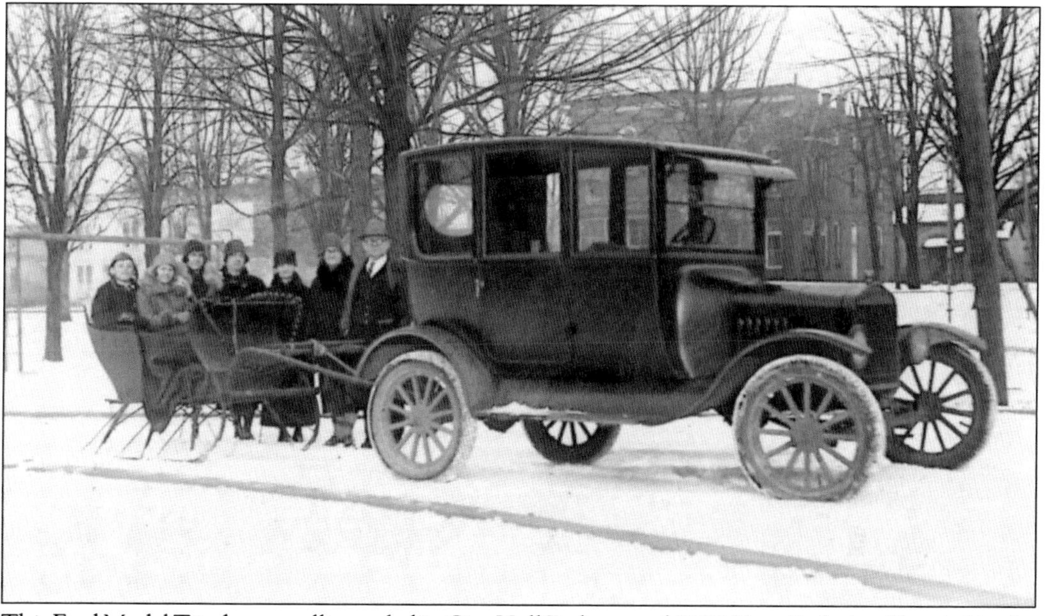

This Ford Model T is shown pulling a sled in City Hall Park around 1920. Note Parkview Hospital in the background, as well as the playground equipment. (Courtesy of Tell City Historical Society.)

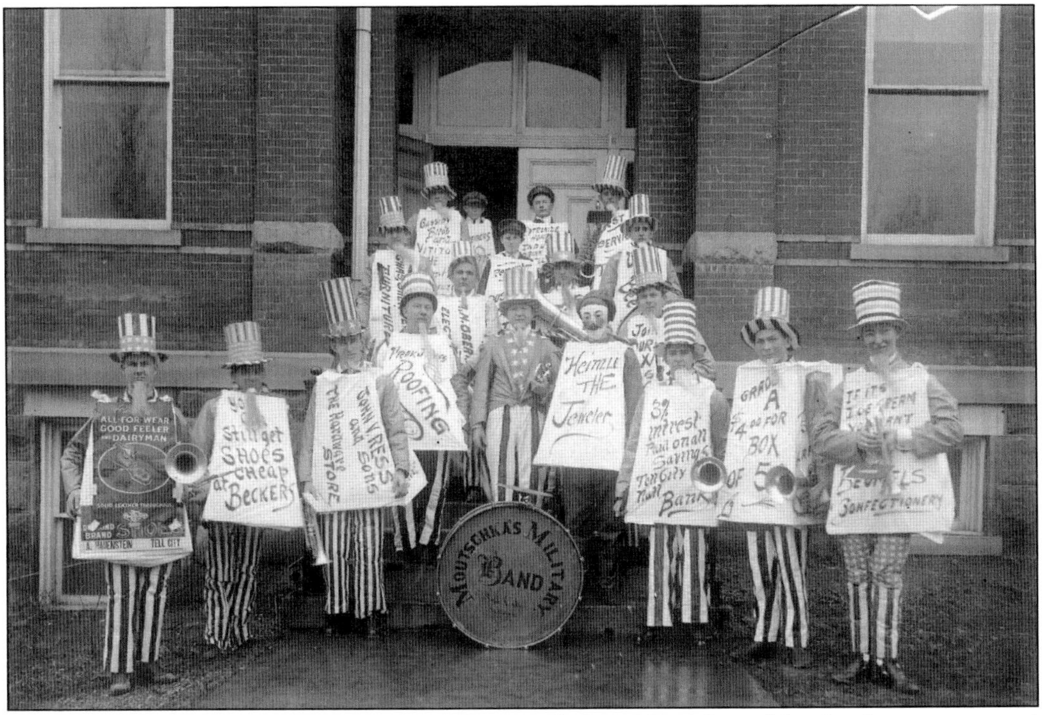

Moutschka's Military Band was very popular in Tell City. The Moutschka family was a musical family who lived in Tell City and played at many events in the community. Joseph Moutschka was the director. Band members pictured include Bill Nuetzel, Cleve Gelarden, John Gelarden, Louis Schneider, Irvin Brenner, Max Paulin, Clifford Siebert, Alex Kessler, Dr. Curtiz Clark, Walter Hanser, Volmer Franz, Al Birchler, Oscar Basedow, Otto Poehlein, Floyd Lamar, Fred Stueber, Carl Holtzman, Frank Ziegelgruber, Joseph Moutschka, William Moutschka, John Holpp, Ferd Becker, Clarence Goffinet, Albert Baumgart, and George Gibbs.

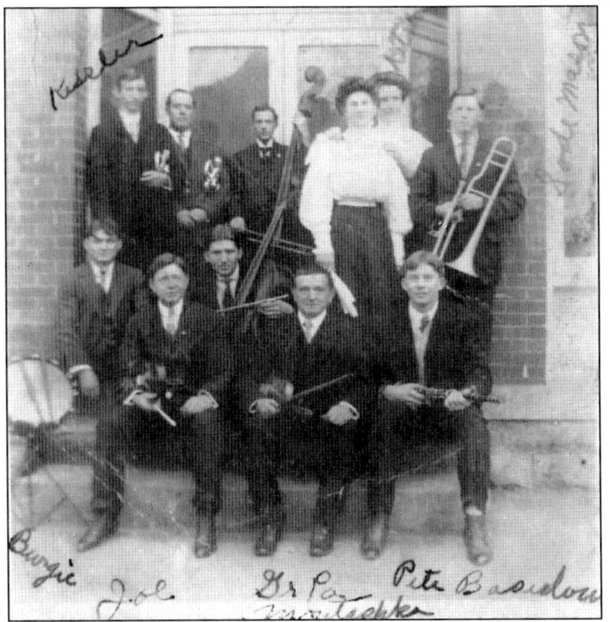

Moutschka Military Band is pictured here on the front porch of Oscar Basedow's business at the corner of Ninth and Washington Streets. With the original front doors and storefront still intact, this is one of very few buildings in town with its original features.

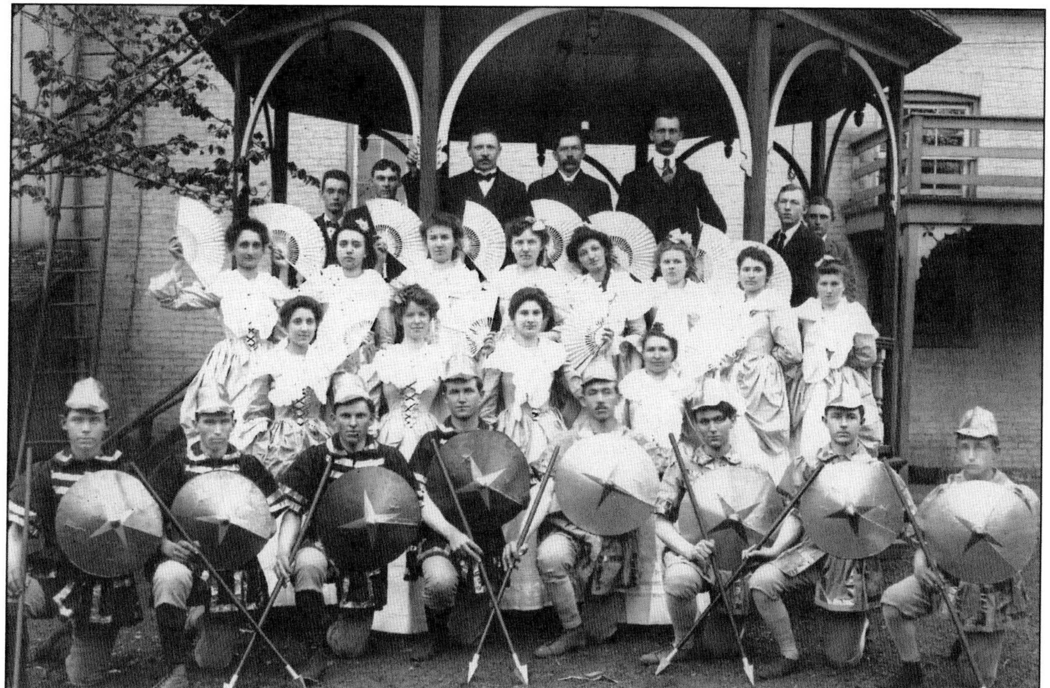

The cast of a play performed by the Turners poses in the bandstand in Hoffman Gardens around the 1890s. From left to right are (first row) Roland Keck, Charles Marchand, Louis Stamp, Henry Schroeder, Fred Ress, John Haerle, Otto Baumgart, and Harry ?; (second row) Florina Schauberger Adam, Carrie Schroeder, unidentified, Amelia Basedow Hart, and Nettie Muelchi Ress; (third row) Minnie Kuhn Fischer, Gustie Hauenstein, Ella Ahlf, Katie Ahlf Hauenstein, Hedwig Bott, Lizzie Koch, Tillie Muelchi Schroeder, and Maggie Braun; (fourth row) Ernst Stuehrk (teacher), Harry Sandleben, Henry Fuchs, a Mr. Jones (teacher), Otto Bott, Will Dreyling, and Joe Adam.

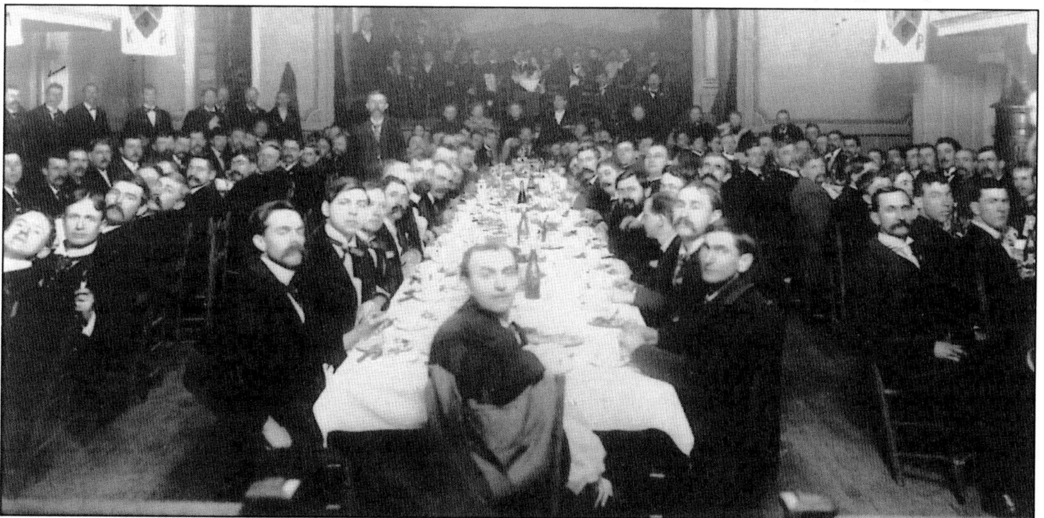

This view shows the interior of the Tell City Opera House. A district meeting of the Knights of Pythias Lodge is taking place. In this image, the floor has not been elevated yet and balconies are on each side of the room. The one on the right was set aside for use by people in the black community. (Courtesy of Tell City Historical Society.)

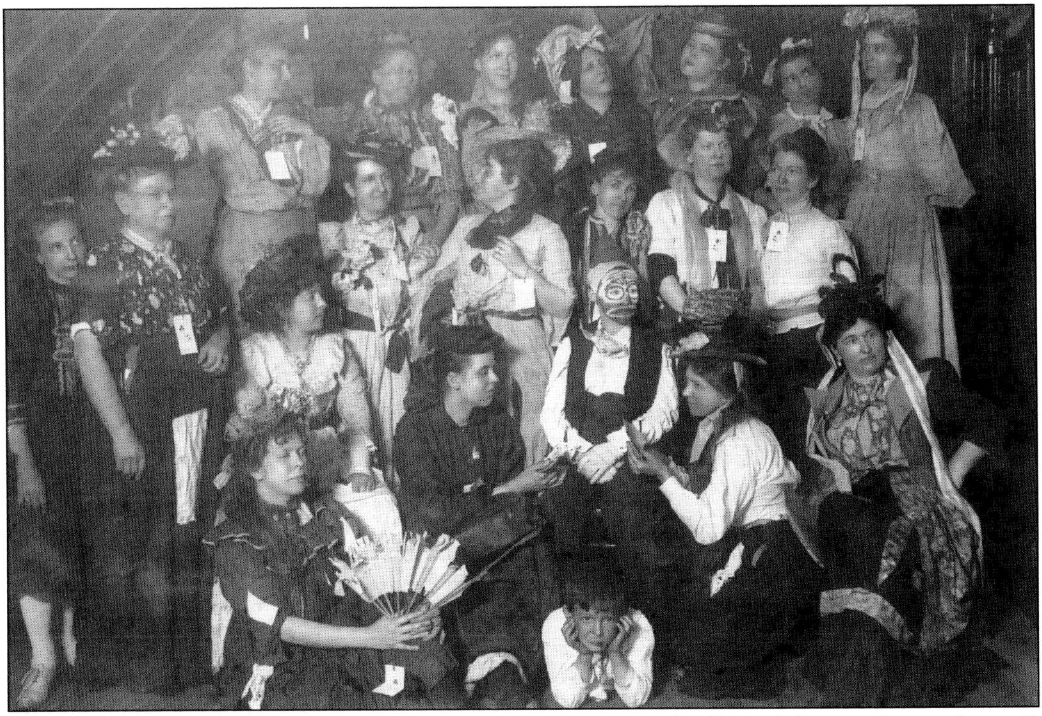

Pictured is a Halloween party at the home of Sophie Obrecht. From left to right are (seated) Mrs. Ed Harrer, two unidentified, Mrs. Stanly Obrecht, Sophia Obrecht, and a Mrs. Kniesche; (second row) unidentified, Rosie Baur, Anna Oberle, Edna Huthsteiner, and Mrs. Cad (William) Bettinger; (third row) Mrs. R.P. Carr, a Mrs. Ebach, unidentified, Anna Zoercher, Alice Zoercher, Mrs. Ola Stalder, and Katie Herr.

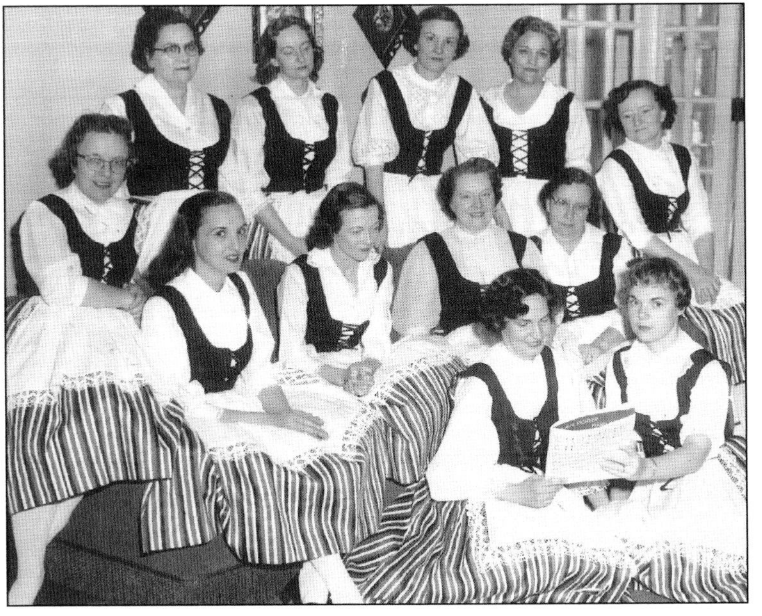

The Tell City String Ensemble in 1958 consists of Georgia Neifert, cello; Marilyn Kreisle, first violin; Hazel Oberhausen, second violin; Starr Scherholzer, first violin; Ona Mae Schauberger, second violin, Louise Becker, bass; Roberta Dauby, first violin; Evelyn Busam, second violin; Verna Hay, second violin; Betty Bender, vocalist; Nelda Lawrence, cello and second violin; and Mary M. Goffinet, piano.

Members of a "gang" are pictured with their first shack on Pestalozzi Hill around 1900. From left to right are (seated) Otto Fruehwald, Charles Fischer, Ed Ruckly, and Fritz Burkoff; (standing) George Kreisle, Henry Fruehwald, Ed Euer, Charles Becker, Gus Basedow, and Robert Ahlf. The second shack was built a year or so later. The Calathumpian Band took over the second shack around 1906. (Courtesy of Tell City Historical Society.)

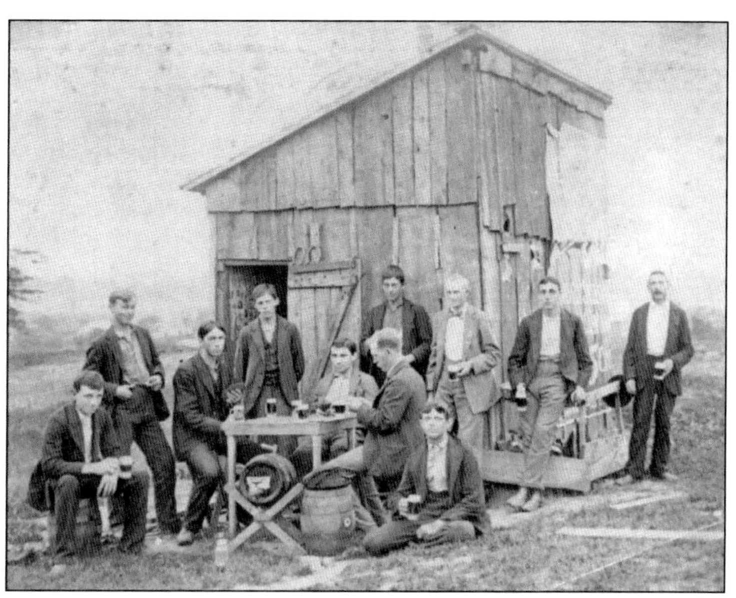

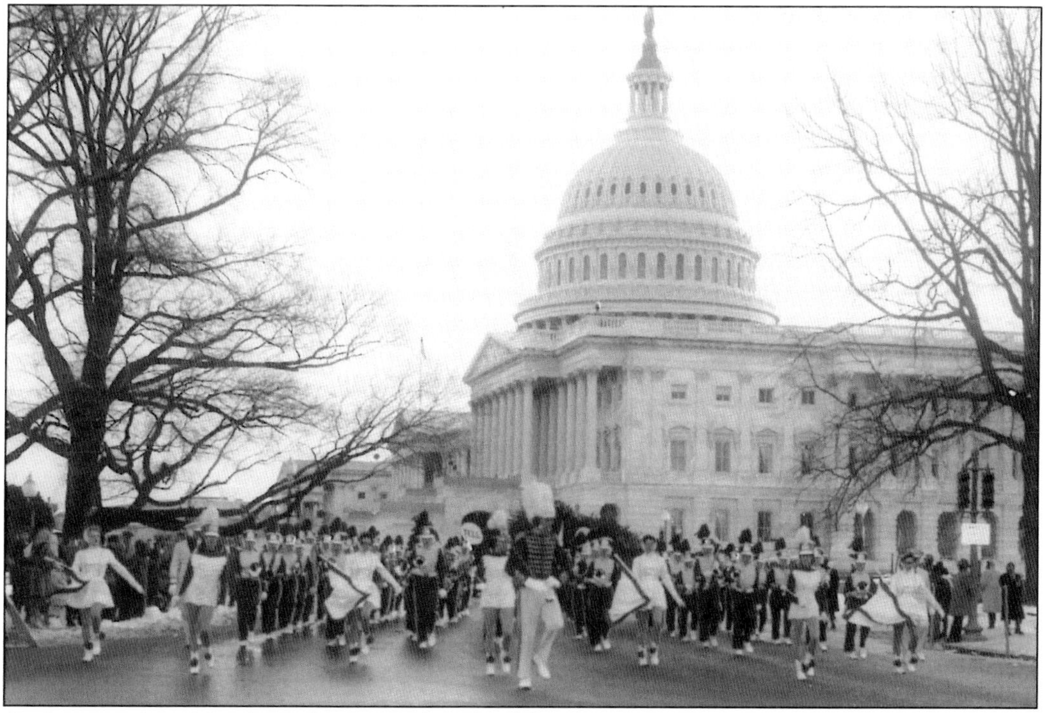

On January 20, 1961, the Tell City High School band marched in the inaugural parade for Pres. John F. Kennedy. (Courtesy of Tell City Historical Society.)

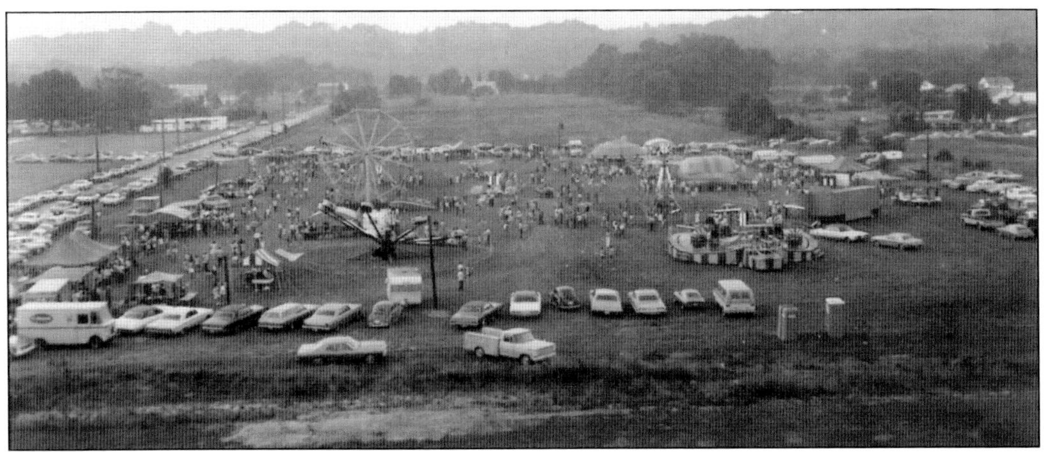

The Jaycees Fourth of July picnic was an annual event held every year in Zoercher Bettinger Park. Various carnival games and rides entertained families throughout the event. On the Fourth, a firework display would light up the sky. (Courtesy of Tell City Historical Society.)

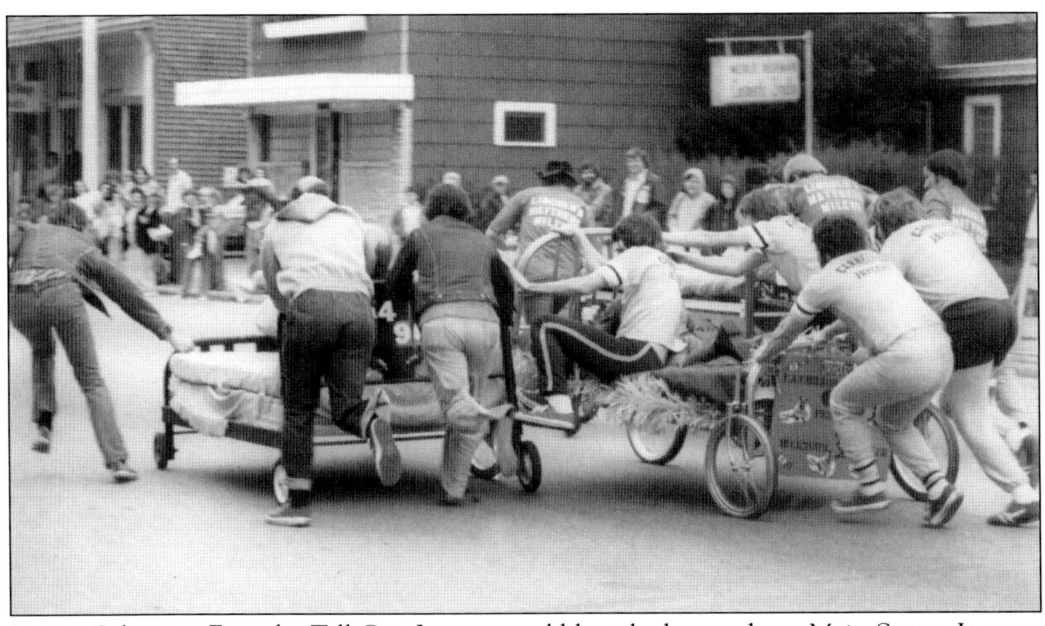

During Schweizer Fest, the Tell City Jaycees would host bed races down Main Street. It was a fun-filled contest.

Seven

People and Homes

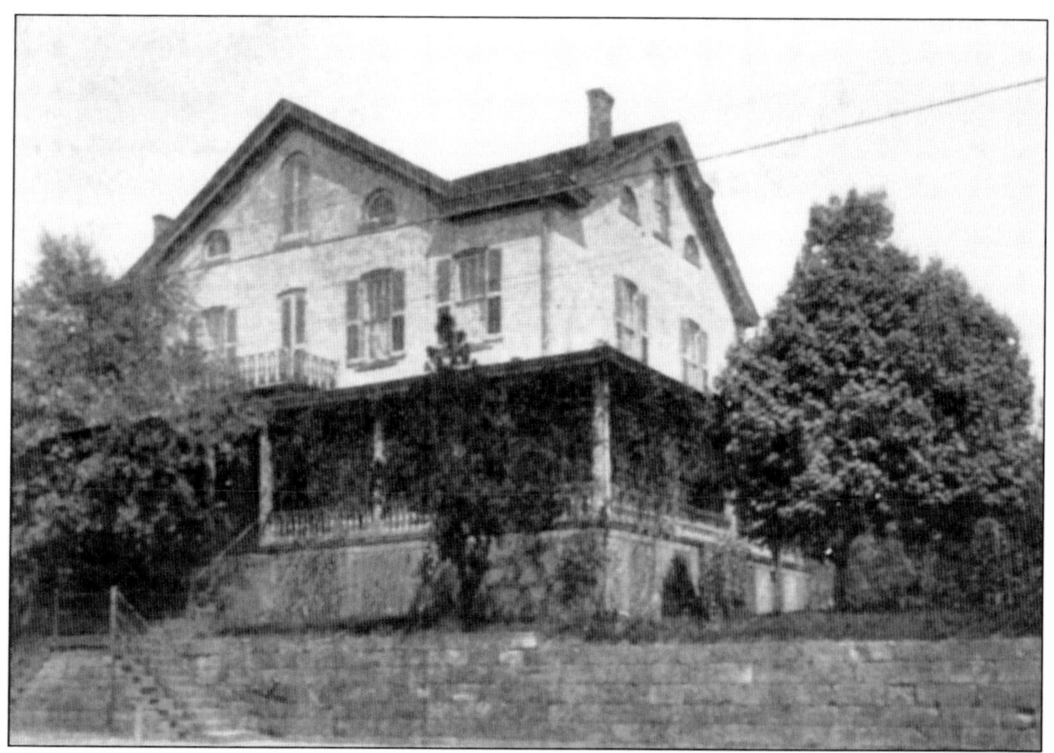

The Fred Voelke residence was located at Jefferson and Main Streets. It was later sold to the William Krogman family. A priest then resided there. Later, this site became St. Paul Catholic Church's parking lot.

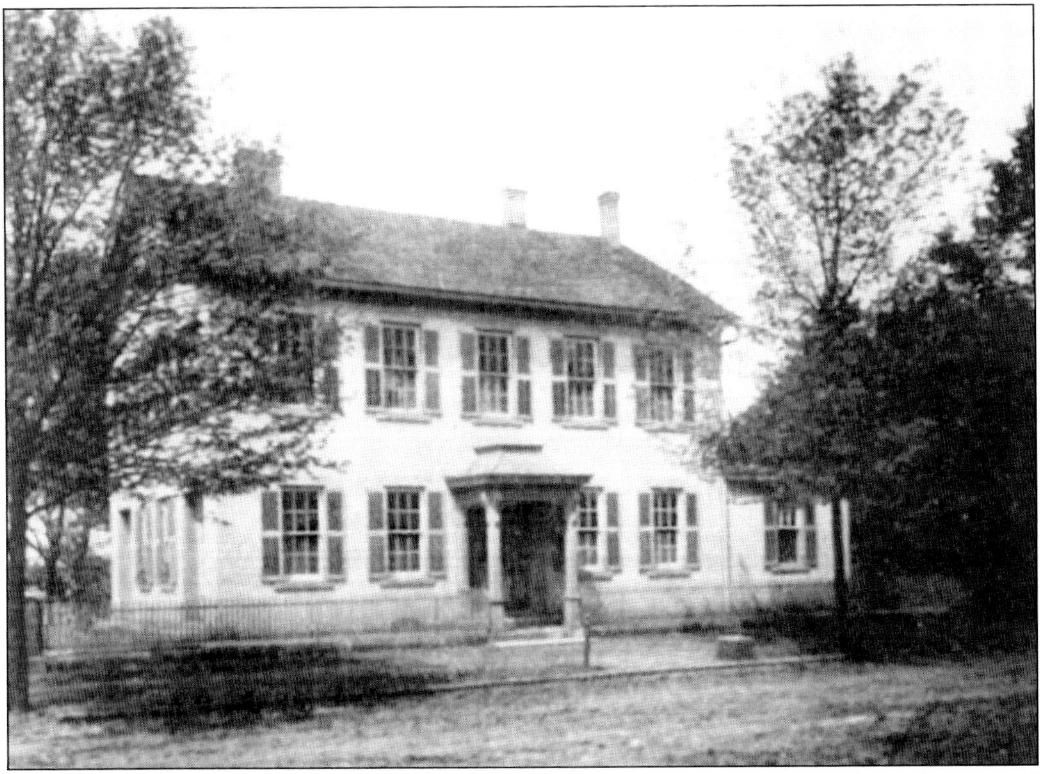

The Andy Steinhauer residence was in the 300 block of Seventh Street. This residence later served as an office for Southern in Resources Solutions (SIRS). Years later, the house was demolished.

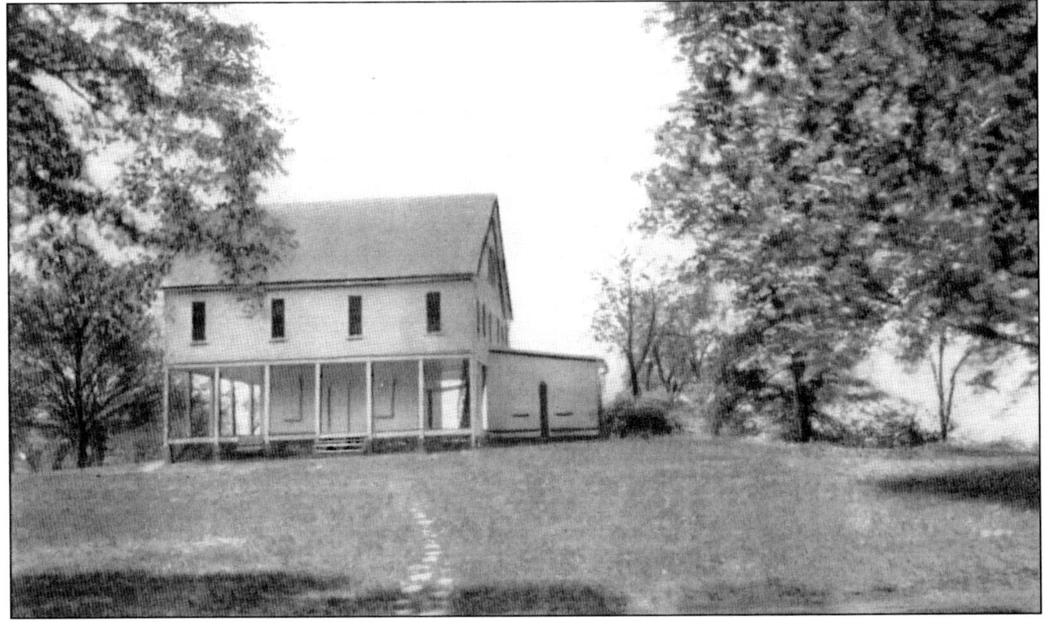

A.P. Fenn's summer residence was a popular place for gatherings. It was also known as Camp Sherman. This residence was torn down and replaced with homes for the Fenn family. (Courtesy of Tell City Historical Society.)

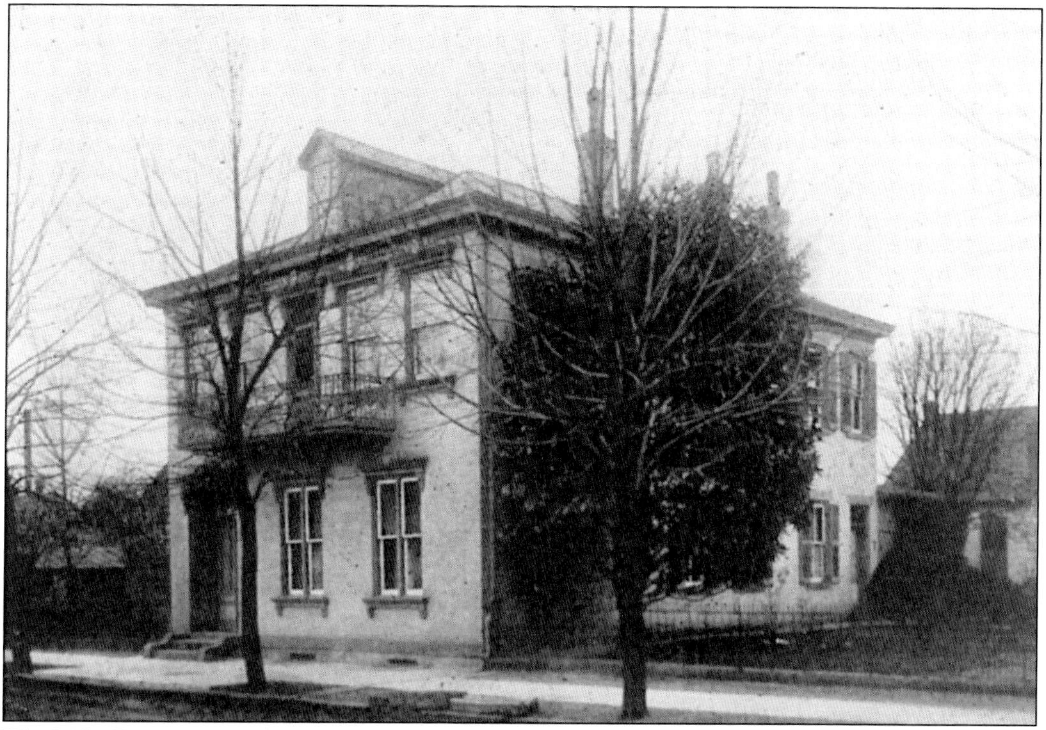

The Mike Bettinger residence was located on Pestalozzi Street between Main and Seventh Streets. This house was torn down in 1959. At the time of demolition, it was said to be one of the finest and most well-built homes the demolition crew had ever demolished.

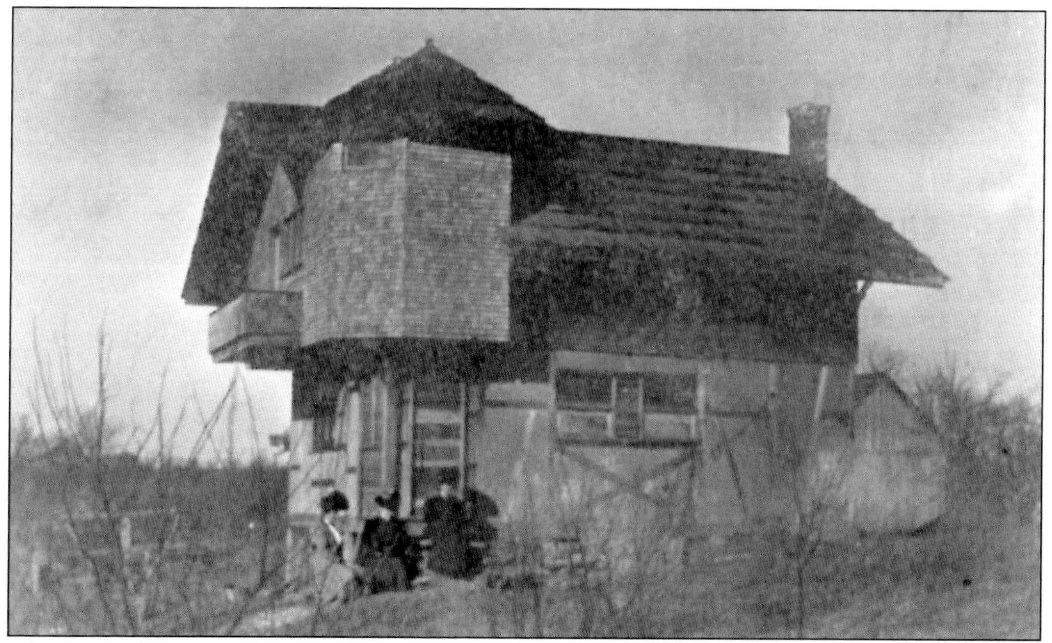

John Meyenberg's Swiss chalet stood on the hill between Tenth and Eleventh Streets near Blum Street. Meyenberg was a sculptor and painter and made the famous lion statues for the park. He later moved to Cincinnati. (Courtesy of Tell City Historical Society.)

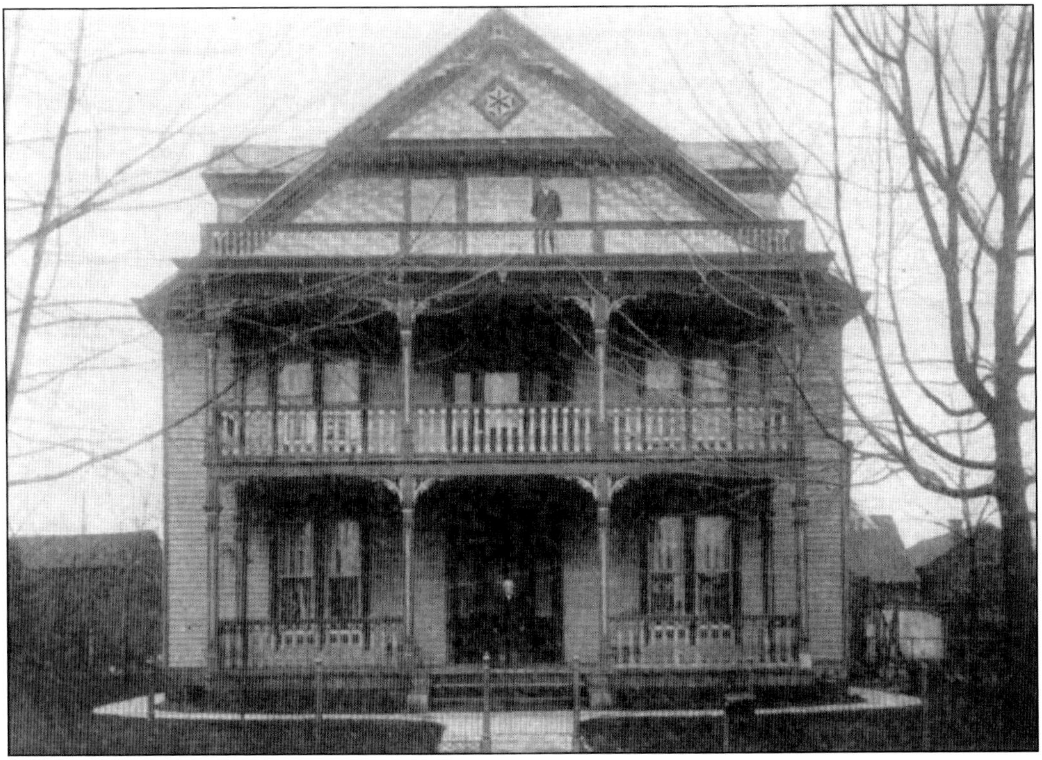

The A.P. Fenn residence was located in the 400 block of Seventh Street. This residence was razed to make room for expansion of the Tell City Chair Company.

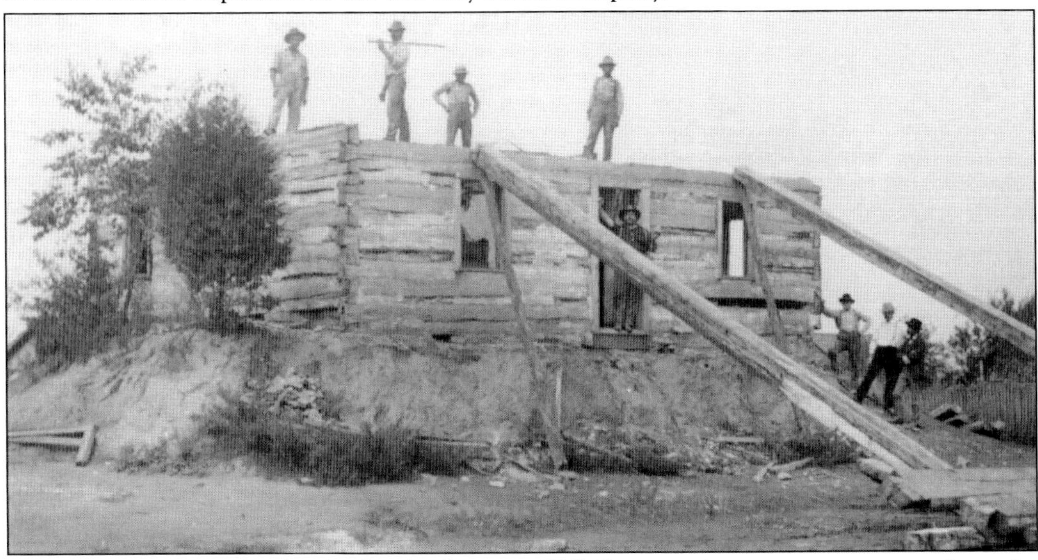

Pictured is what is said to be the first log house in Tell City; another report states it predates the city. Thomas De La Hunt notes, "Frank Herm erected the first house after the town site was platted, a log edifice, southwest corner Main and Tell." The log home stood on the southwest corner of Main and Tell Streets and was the residence of William Kampschaefer. Pictured are, from left to right, Frank Olberding, Jack Sims, Jack Lowry, Albert Rossman, Kampschaefer (in doorway), Peter Rossman, a Dr. Evans, and unidentified. (Courtesy of Tell City Historical Society.)

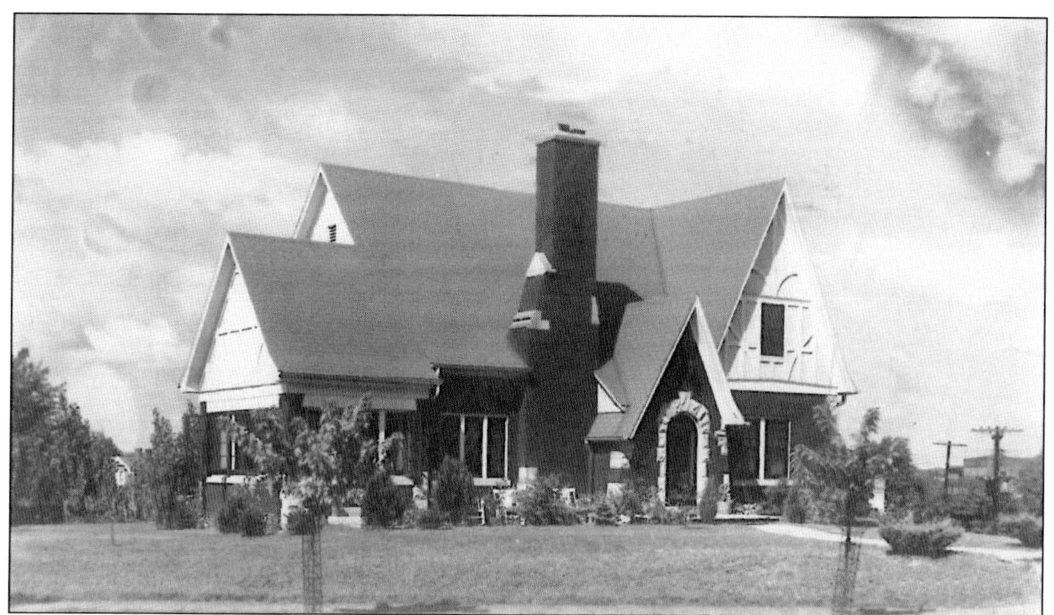

Located at 547 Ninth Street, the Vitoe residence was built in the 1930s.

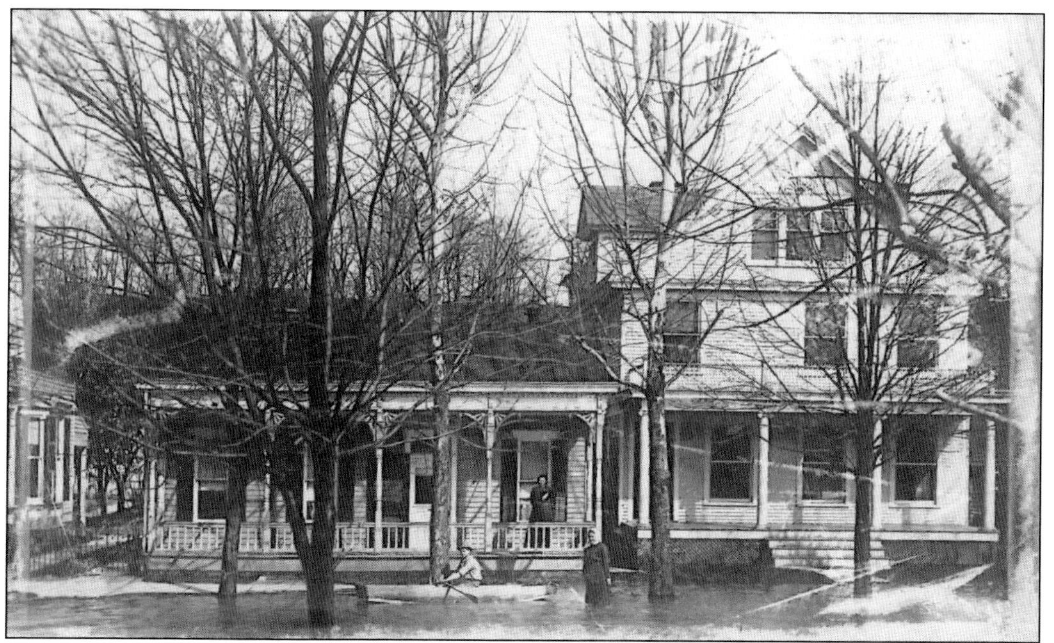

The Fred J. Herrman residence (at right) was located in the 200 block of Ninth Street. This house still stands today and looks the same as in this photograph.

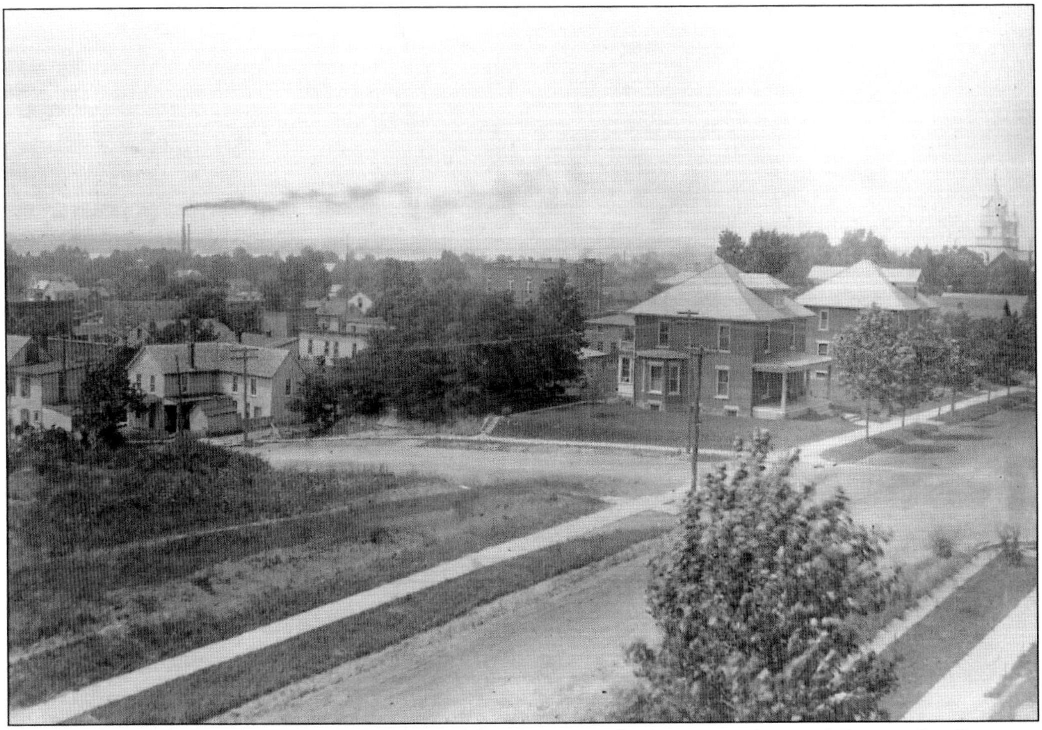

This view from the hill at Ninth and Franklin Streets is looking northwest. That is the Reiman home in foreground; it was the former Finch Funeral home. Next house on Ninth Street belonged to Robert Eith. (Courtesy of Tell City Historical Society.)

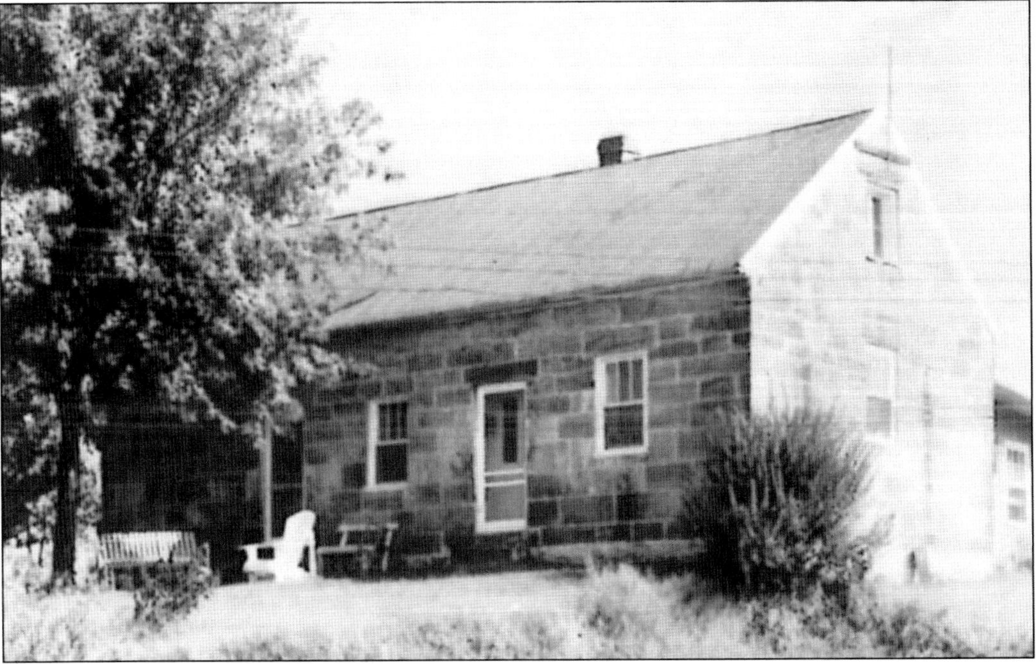

This old stone house is located in the 1239 Block of Thirteenth Street. It is the only house that still stands today that predates Tell City. It was used as a residence for the surveyor for the city.

The Obrecht house is located at 344 Seventh Street. This house has been raised twice due to flooding. However, the 1937 flood still got into the structure.

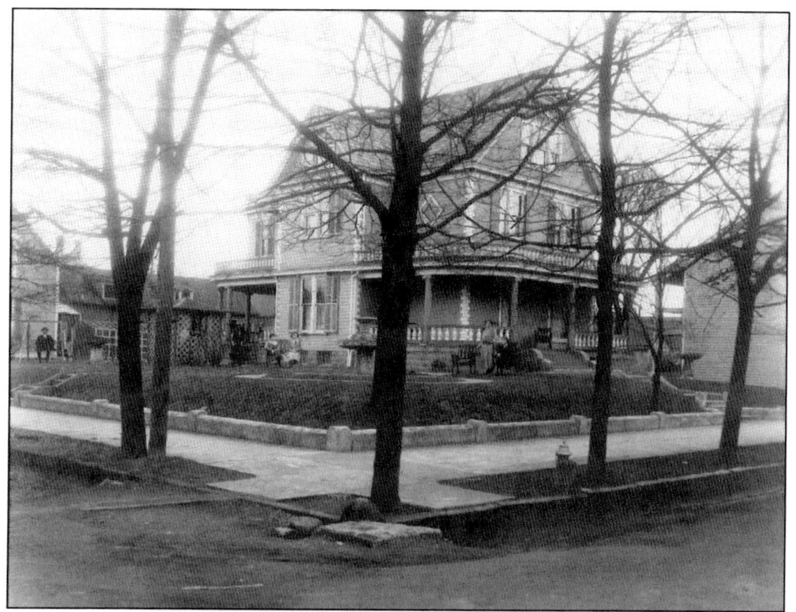

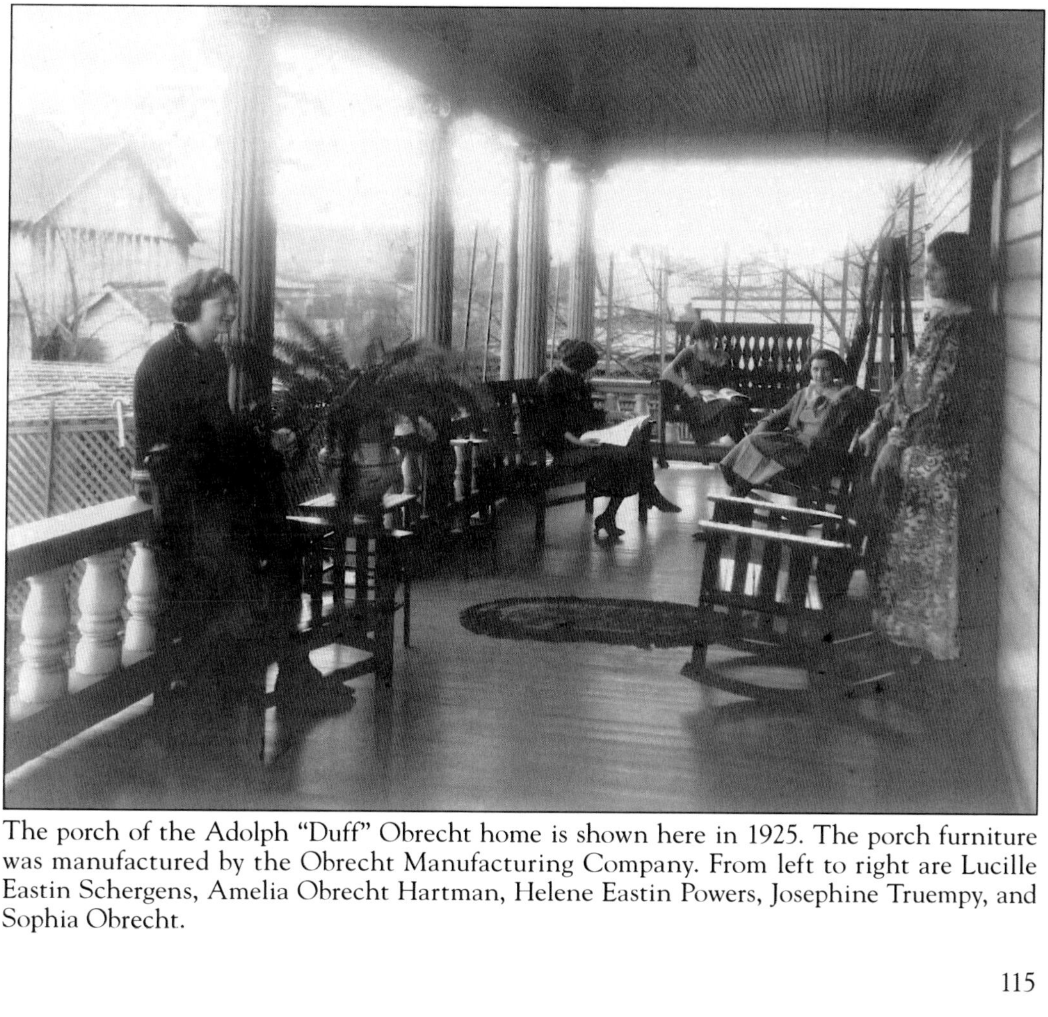

The porch of the Adolph "Duff" Obrecht home is shown here in 1925. The porch furniture was manufactured by the Obrecht Manufacturing Company. From left to right are Lucille Eastin Schergens, Amelia Obrecht Hartman, Helene Eastin Powers, Josephine Truempy, and Sophia Obrecht.

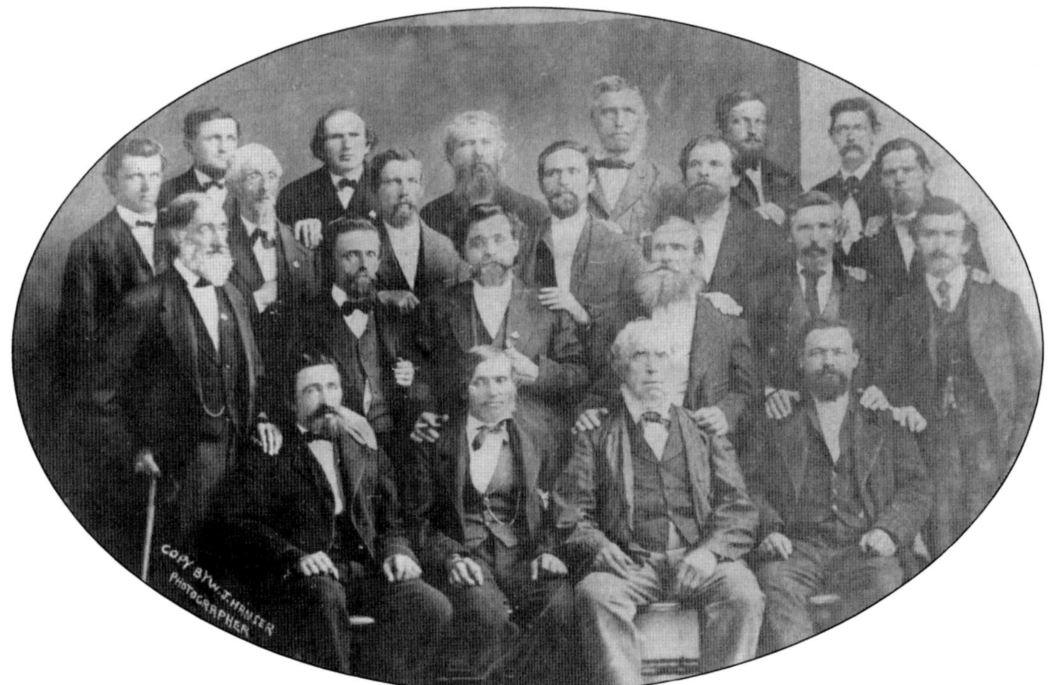

The First Swiss Society in Tell City is pictured above. From left to right are (first row) B. Herrmann, J. Weiss Jr., A. Strub, and ? Landold; (second row) D. Schweizer, J. Weiss Sr., T. Muller, C. Schmidt, H. Schuler, and J. Meisner; (third row) H. Froehlich, ? Buhler, ? Hefler, ? Euer, ? Dreir, and ? Kuntzler; (fourth row) J. Froehlich, C. Schweizer, ? Nedecker, Jacob Hirschbrunner, G. Phister, and ? Mangold. (Courtesy of Tell City Historical Society.)

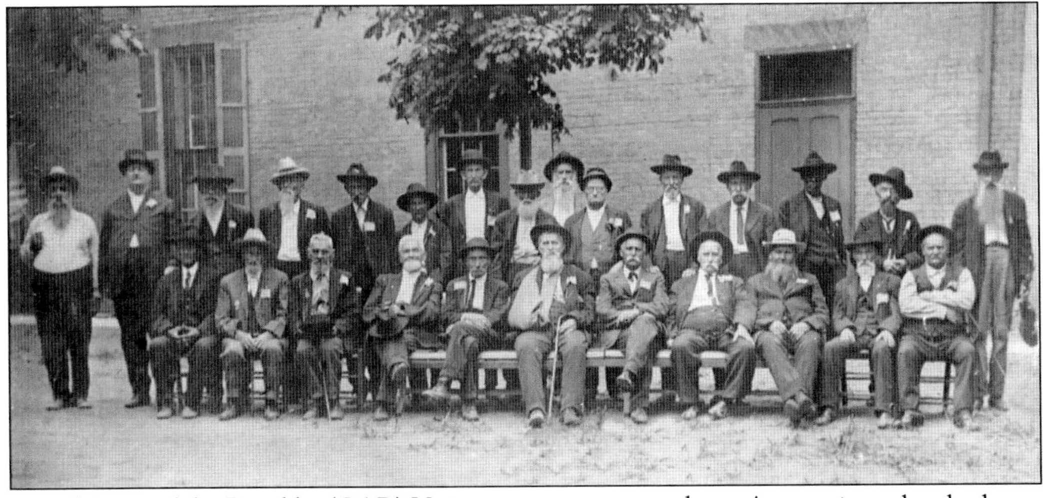

Grand Army of the Republic (GAR) Union veterans are seen here. At one time, they had over 400,000 members nationwide, including Pres. Ulysses S. Grant. The GAR was the forerunner of modern-day veterans' groups like the VFW and American Legion. Pictured are, from left to right, (seated) three unidentified, Charles Hess, unidentified, Auk Hemphill, three unidentified, Jim Lillipop, and Bob Boltinghouse; (standing) Anderson Preacher Bolin, Tobe Sprinkle, three unidentified, Bob McMann, three unidentified, Bill Johnson, Ben Hemphill, unidentified, W.M. Sanders, Larry Hicks, and Squire Robinson. (Courtesy of Tell City Historical Society.)

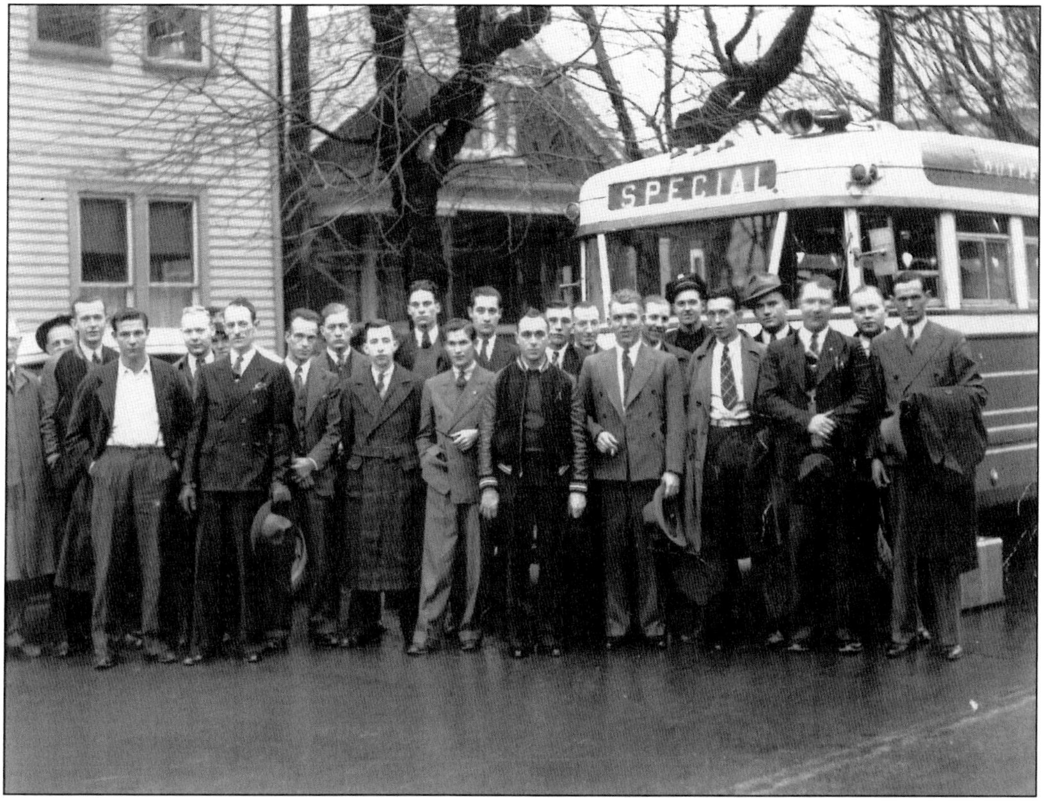

Draftees leave Tell City for training with the US Army on January 15, 1941. Pictured are, from left to right, Dr. P.J. Coultas, Volmar Franz (chairman of Perry County Selective Service Board), Walter F. Leimgruber, William David Alvey, Adolph Voelker, Carl Holtzman (barely visible), Earl Clements, Glen F. Sweat, Marshie Sprinkle, Lynn Hall, Gervase Dauby, Charles Adams, Charles Harding, Phedale McKim, John J. Berger, Phillip O. Hess, Fred Gaynor, Gilbert G. Parker, Herman Dickman, Ralph Plock, Raymond Schaefer, John E. Parrot, Clarence E. Kress, and Glenward "Jack" Briggeman. (Courtesy of Tell City Historical Society.)

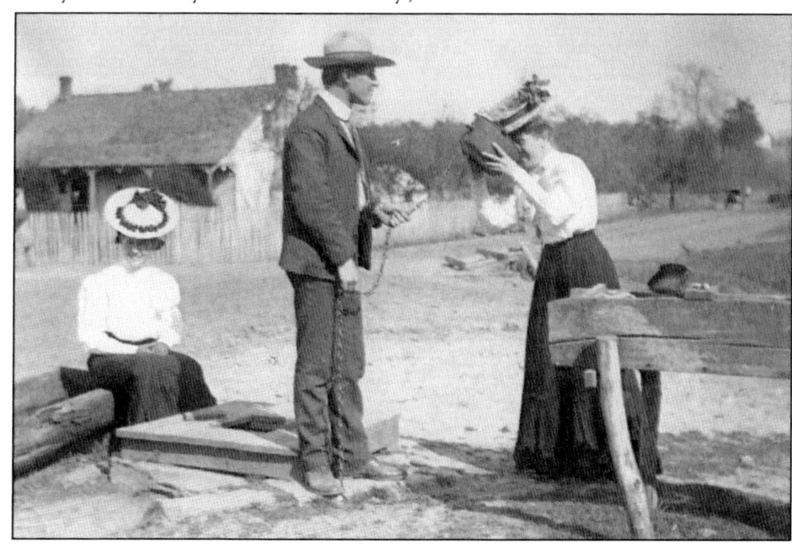

The Brazee well was located on the Tell City–Cannelton Road. This scene, taken from the Tell City side, shows, from left to right, Tillie Zuelly, Emil Kroessman, and Molly Gloor. The house in the background is the Merril Brazee home. (Courtesy of Tell City Historical Society.)

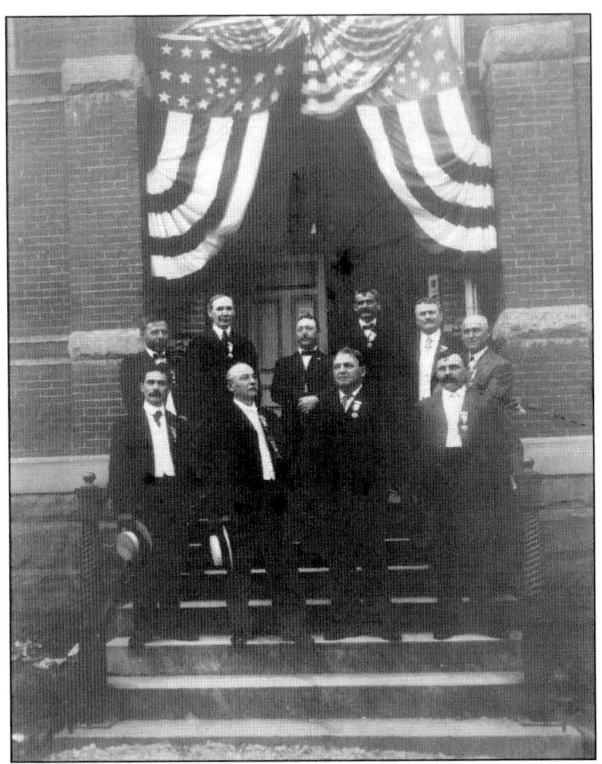

This group of notables at the 1916 Tell City Homecoming includes, from left to right, (first row) Rev. Theodore Schundt, Albert Bettinger, Eugene Huthsteiner, and Jacob Zoercher; (second row) Phillip Zoercher, unidentified, Fred Herrmann, Frank Ress, unidentified, and William Bettinger. (Courtesy of Tell City Historical Society.)

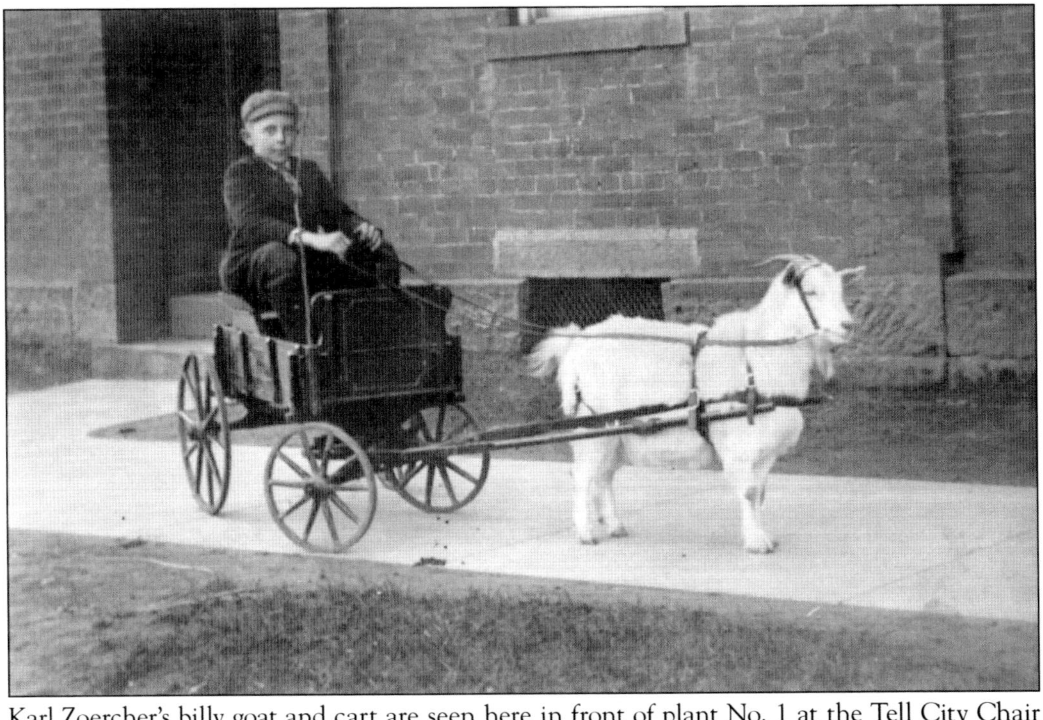

Karl Zoercher's billy goat and cart are seen here in front of plant No. 1 at the Tell City Chair Company, in the 400 block of Seventh Street. Zoercher's father was Jacob Zoercher, a partner in the chair company with A.P. Fenn. (Courtesy of Tell City Historical Society.)

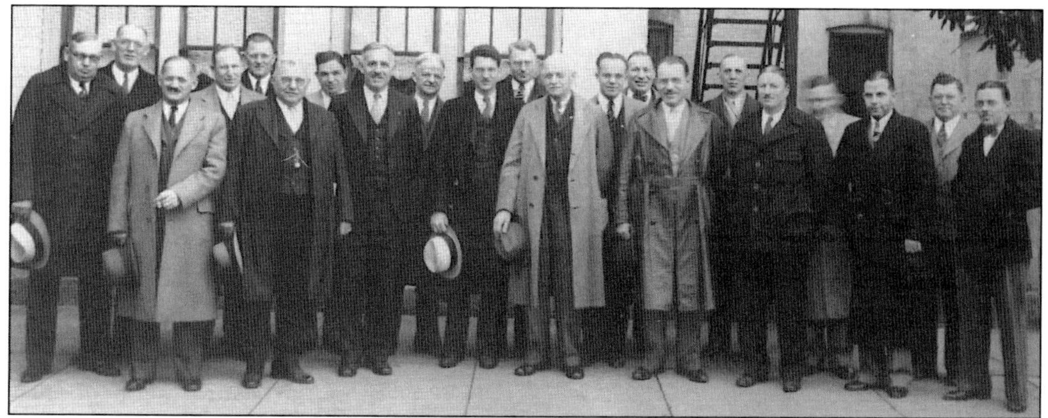

During the Depression in the 1930s, the Tell City Kiwanis Club sponsored a mustache-growing contest. This picture, taken outside the William Tell Hotel in 1936, shows Kiwanis members who participated. From left to right are Lawrence Carr, Dr. Thomas Mulholland, Magnus Kreisle, Glen Traw, Rev. H.H. Peters, Jacob Zoercher, Eugene Huthsteiner, Emil Kroessman, Walter Huthsteiner, Charles Schreiber, Ralph U. Imel, Maurice Carr, William Gerber, Chris Fenn, Roy Fenn, unidentified, Harold Heins, unidentified, Dr. L.C. Becher, Ed Engelbrecht, and Karl Zoercher. Several of the old-timers have been questioned as to who won the contest, but no one seems to remember. Certainly, Kreisle, Kroessman, and Fenn were top contenders. (Courtesy of Tell City Historical Society.)

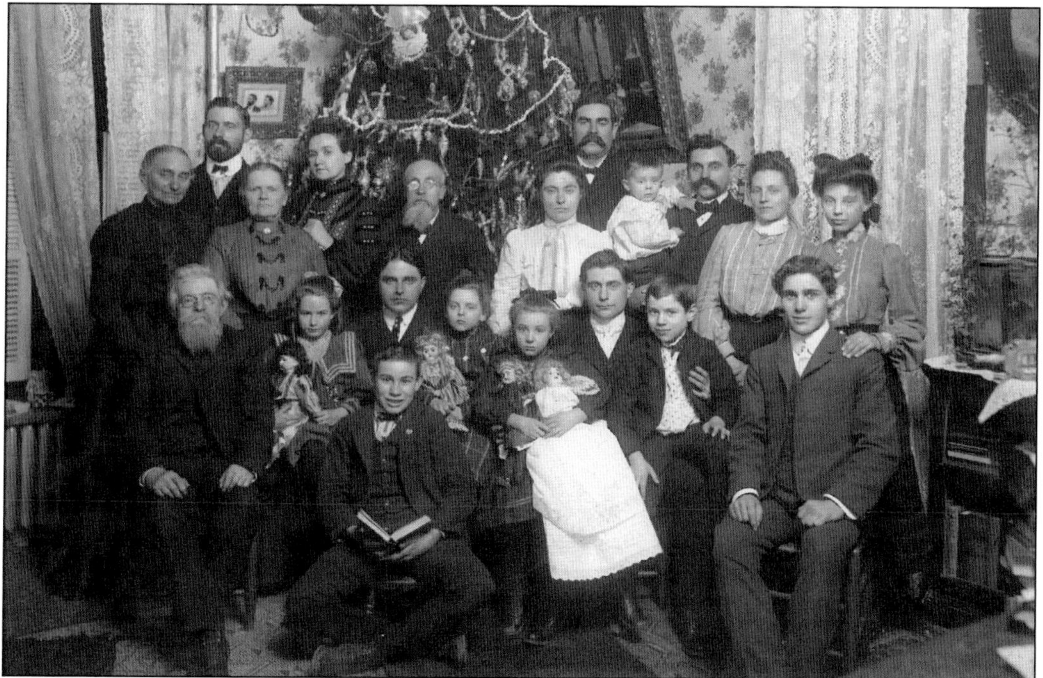

The Fenns are celebrating Christmas 1902 at the family residence. Identified in this photograph are (first row) Chris Fenn (in front holding book); (second row) Christian Fenn (grandpa), Mary Zoercher, Louis Zoercher, Anna Zoercher, and Bert Fenn; (third row) Mrs. Christian Zoercher (grandma), Phillip Zoercher, a Mrs. Ebach, "Mattie" (Martha) Zoercher, a Mr. Ebach, Anna and Albert Fenn, Jacob Zoercher holding Karl, Anna "Jake" Zoercher, and Emma Zoercher. (Courtesy of Tell City Historical Society.)

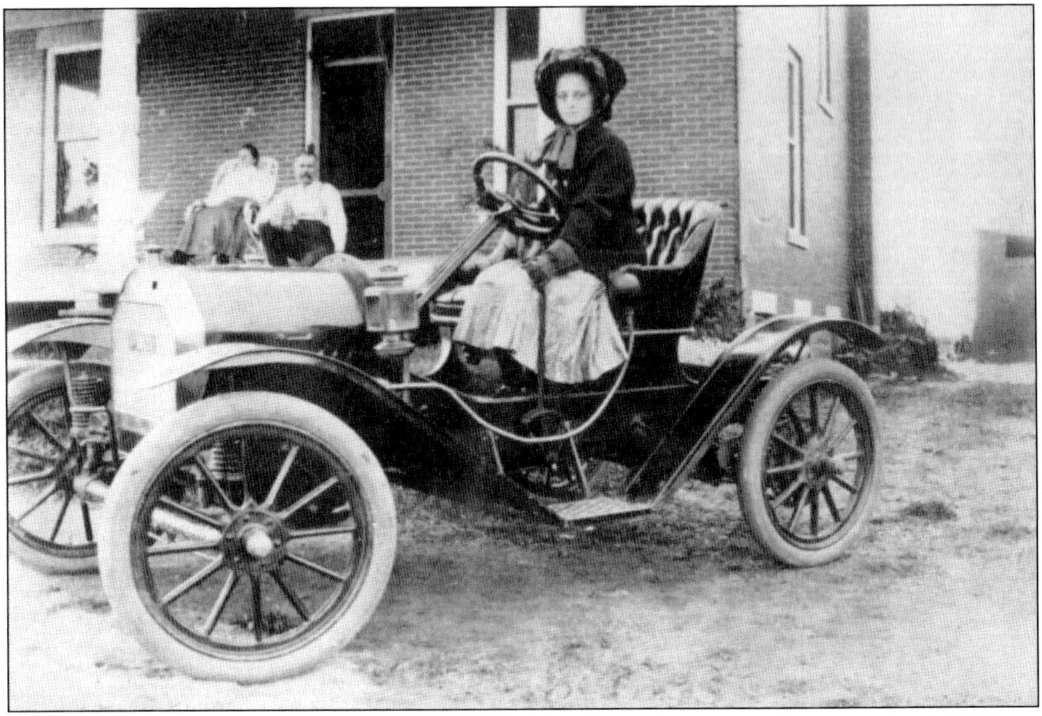

Elizabeth Eith sits in an old Brush car. On porch of their home, located on the west side of 600 block on Ninth Street, are Robert and Mary Eith. Elizabeth died at an early age from tuberculosis. She was said to be one of the first lady drivers in the city. (Courtesy of Tell City Historical Society.)

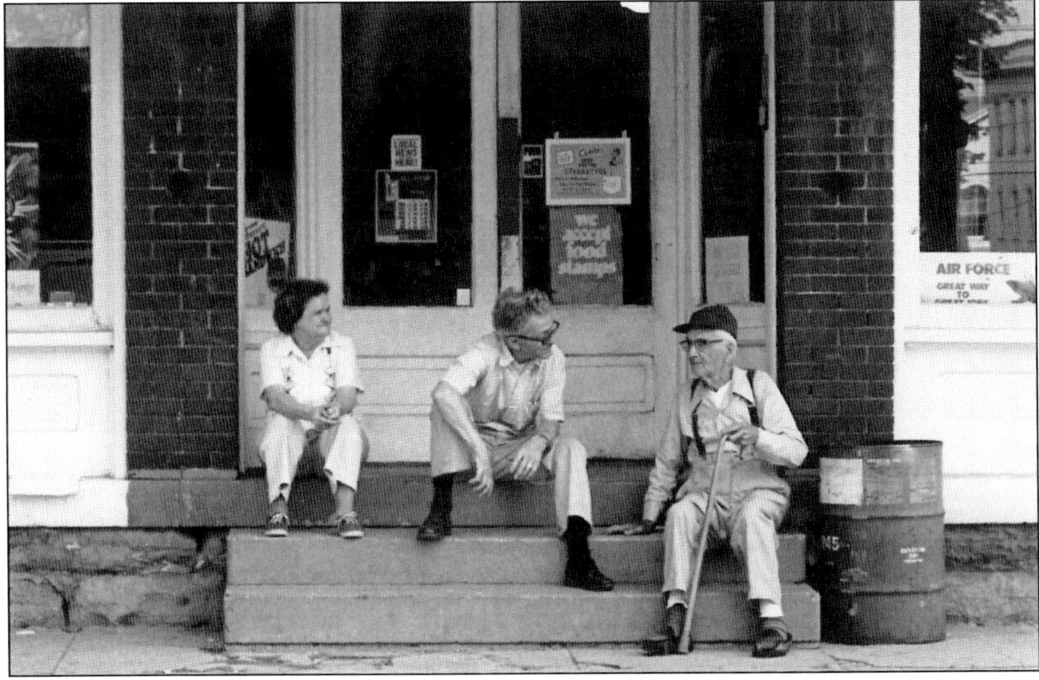

Alma Wheeler, Bill Wheeler, and Pete Lampkin (88 years old) sit out front of Wheelers Grocery and Meats, located at 302 Ninth Street, around 1979. (Courtesy of Curt and Sheila Wheeler.)

Eight

Around Town

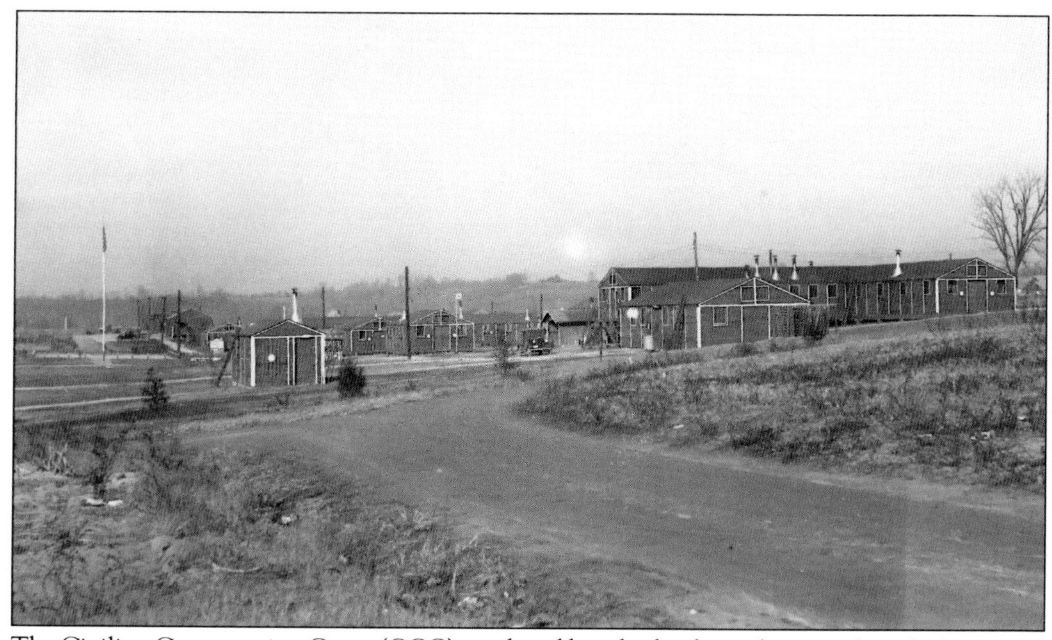

The Civilian Conservation Corps (CCC) employed hundreds of men from southern Indiana, and they worked on such projects as digging German Ridge Lake and building the shelter house there, repairing telephone lines, and erosion control in Perry County. Tell City's Camp William Tell originated in Crawford County and relocated to Tell City in 1936. The barracks were located in the 1300 block of Ninth and Tenth Streets close to the location of the old Tell City Pool (now the Senior Citizens Center) and Dennis Kress Park. The camp closed around 1943. After its closing, the barracks were reworked to provide apartments. Many returning veterans of World War II lived in these apartments until they were able to obtain permanent housing. The structures were razed in the early 1950s. (Courtesy of Tell City Historical Society.)

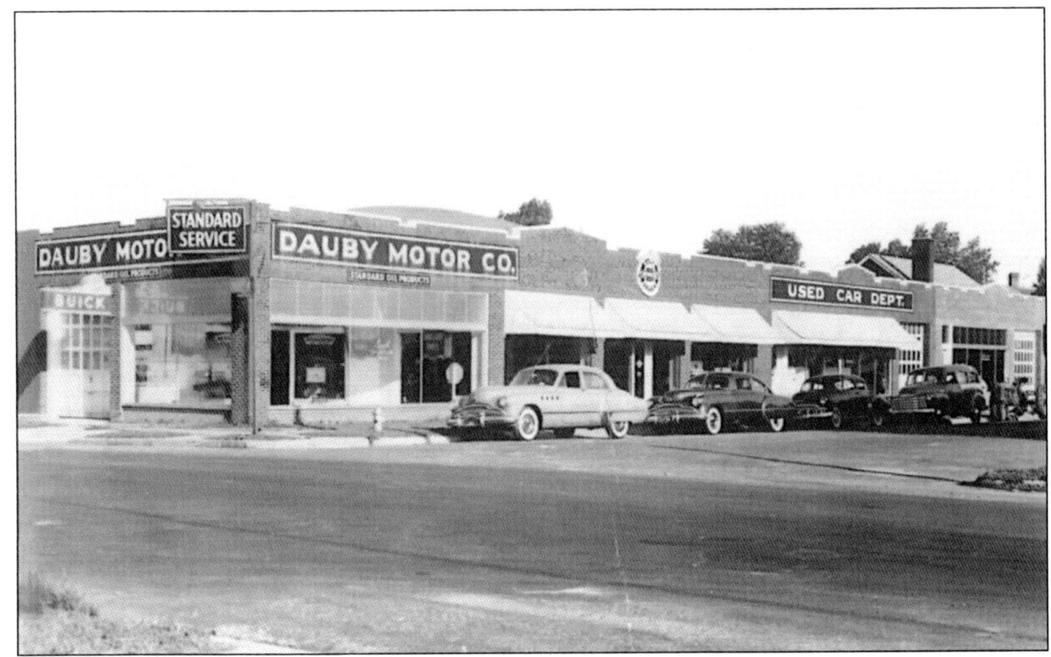

Dauby Motor Company was started in 1927 at Main and Tell Streets before moving to this location in the 900 block of Eleventh Street. The company also had a lot at the corner of Tell and Twelfth Streets. This building is still used by several businesses.

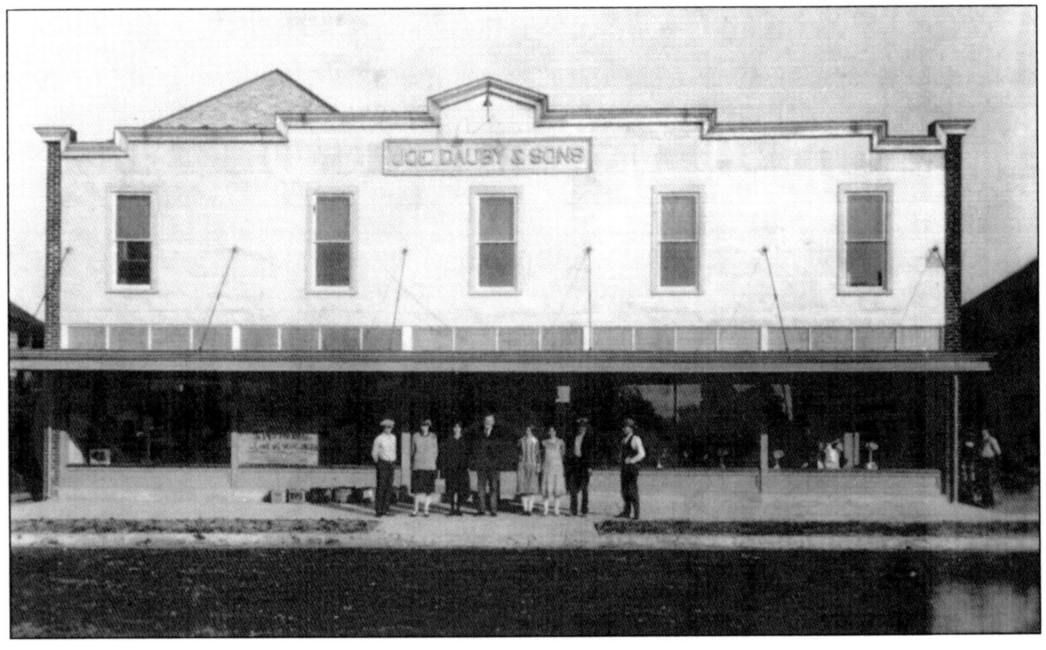

Daubys Department Store is seen here around 1928. Pictured are, from left to right, Dewey Dauby, Hettie Lauer, Anna Dauby, Frank Bruggenschmidt, Agenes Glenn, Teresa Gaesser, Joe Dauby, and Clarence Dauby. (Courtesy of Tell City Historical Society.)

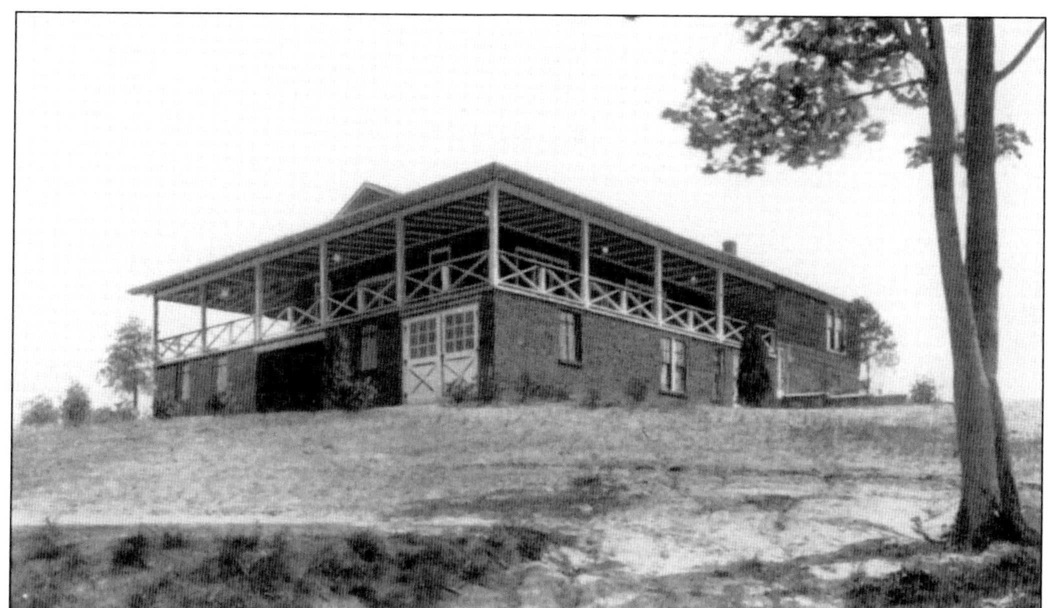
The Hoosier Height Country Club is located at 3822 Mozart Street. This structure burned in August 1996. A new clubhouse was built shortly after and is still in use today.

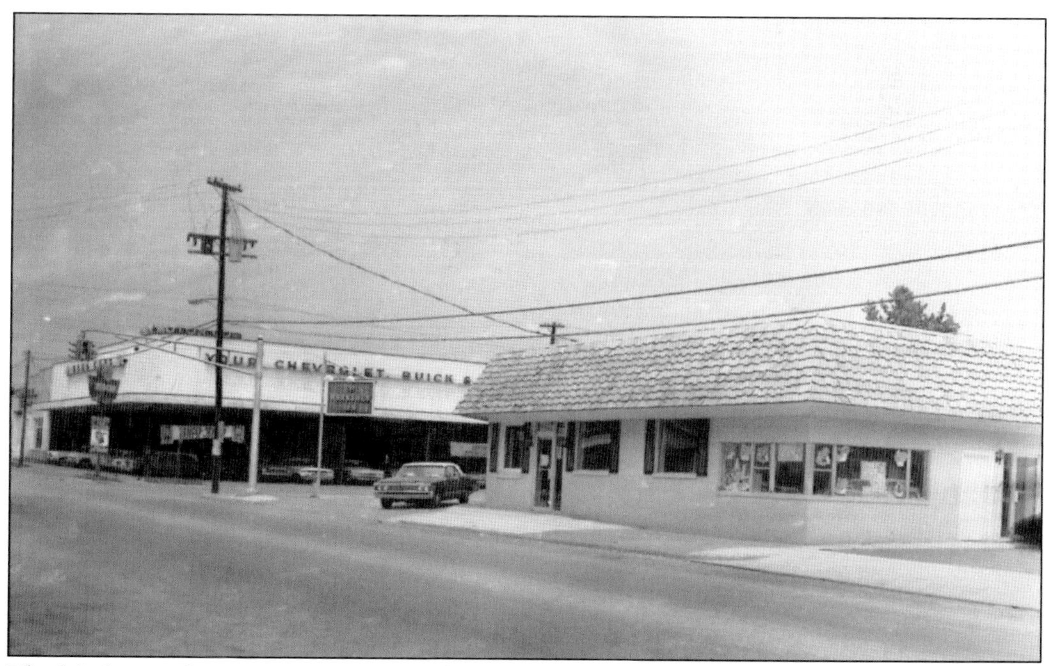

The Marksmen Inn was a very popular hangout for high schoolers in the 1960s and 1970s and was located across from Tell City High School on Tell Street.

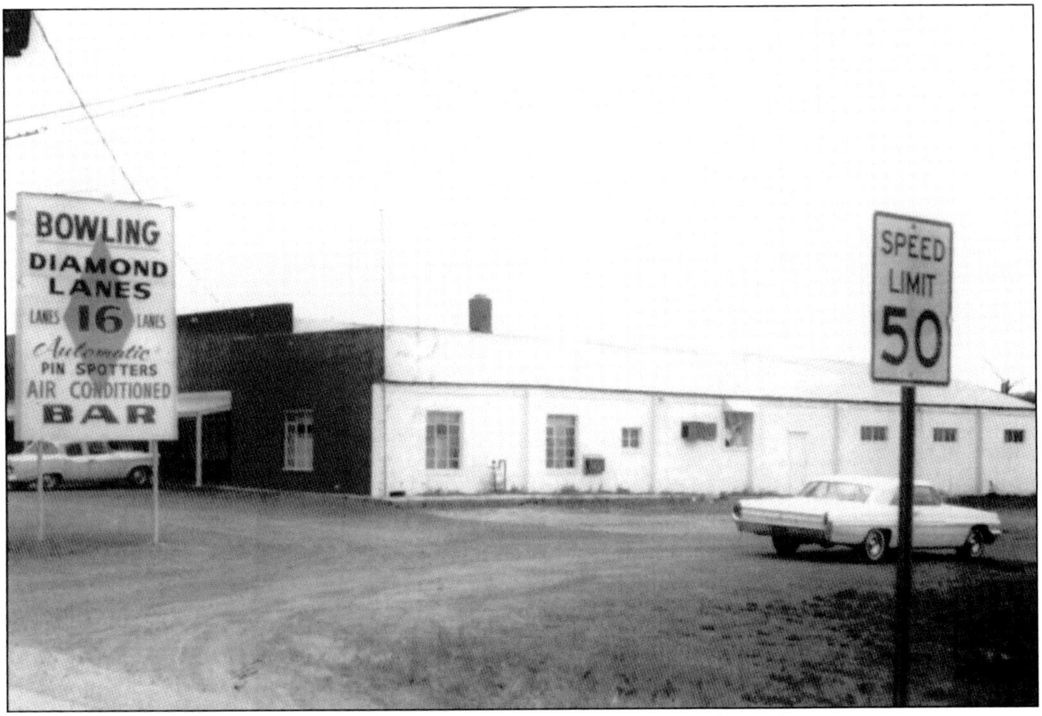

The Diamond Bowling Lanes were located on Indiana 37, on the north side of Tell City. (Courtesy of Tell City Historical Society.)

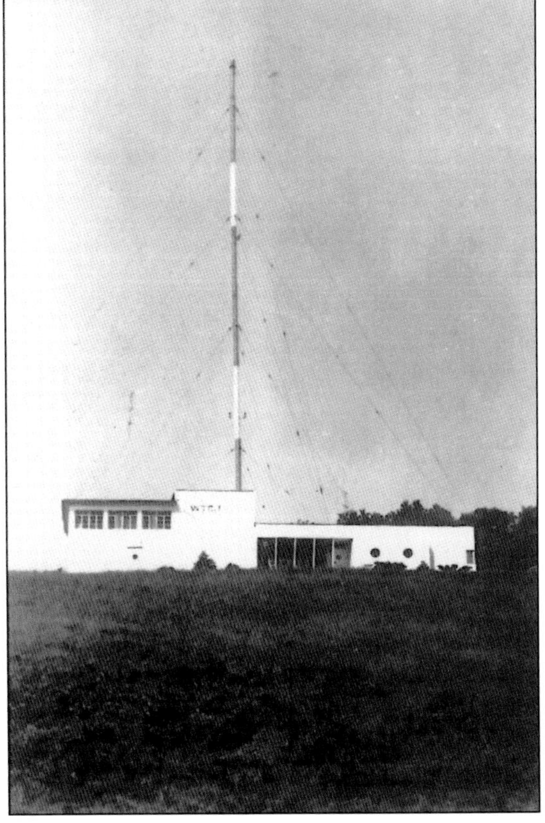

WTCJ started broadcasting at this location on February 6, 1948, at 7:00 a.m. This was located on Highway 66 towards Cannelton.

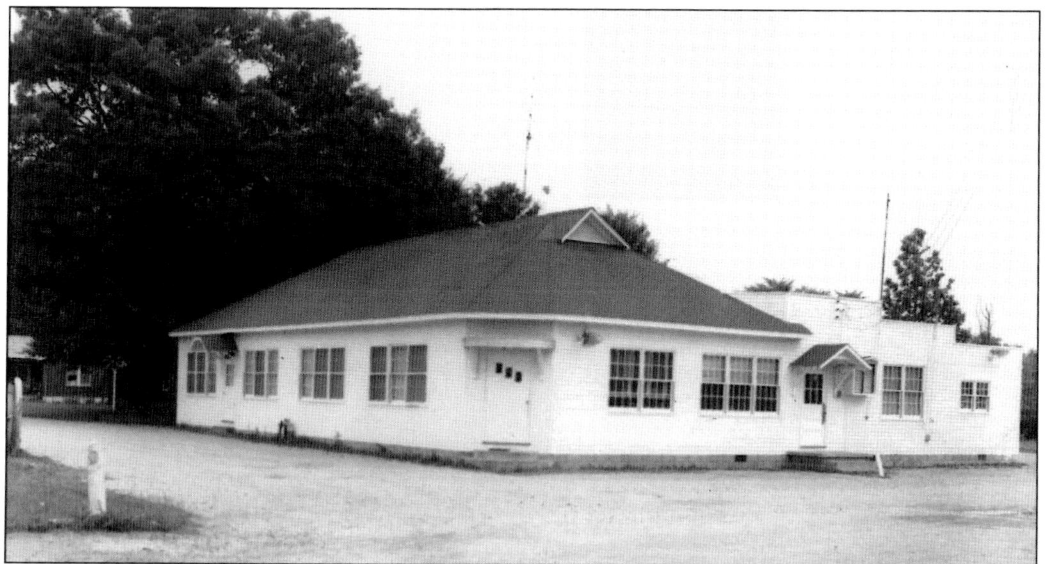

The American Legion Post No. 213 is located on State Road 66. The post had headquarters in city hall and in the Hartman Building at 344 Main Street before locating in this structure. After a fire, this building was replaced with the current structure. (Courtesy of Tell City Historical Society.)

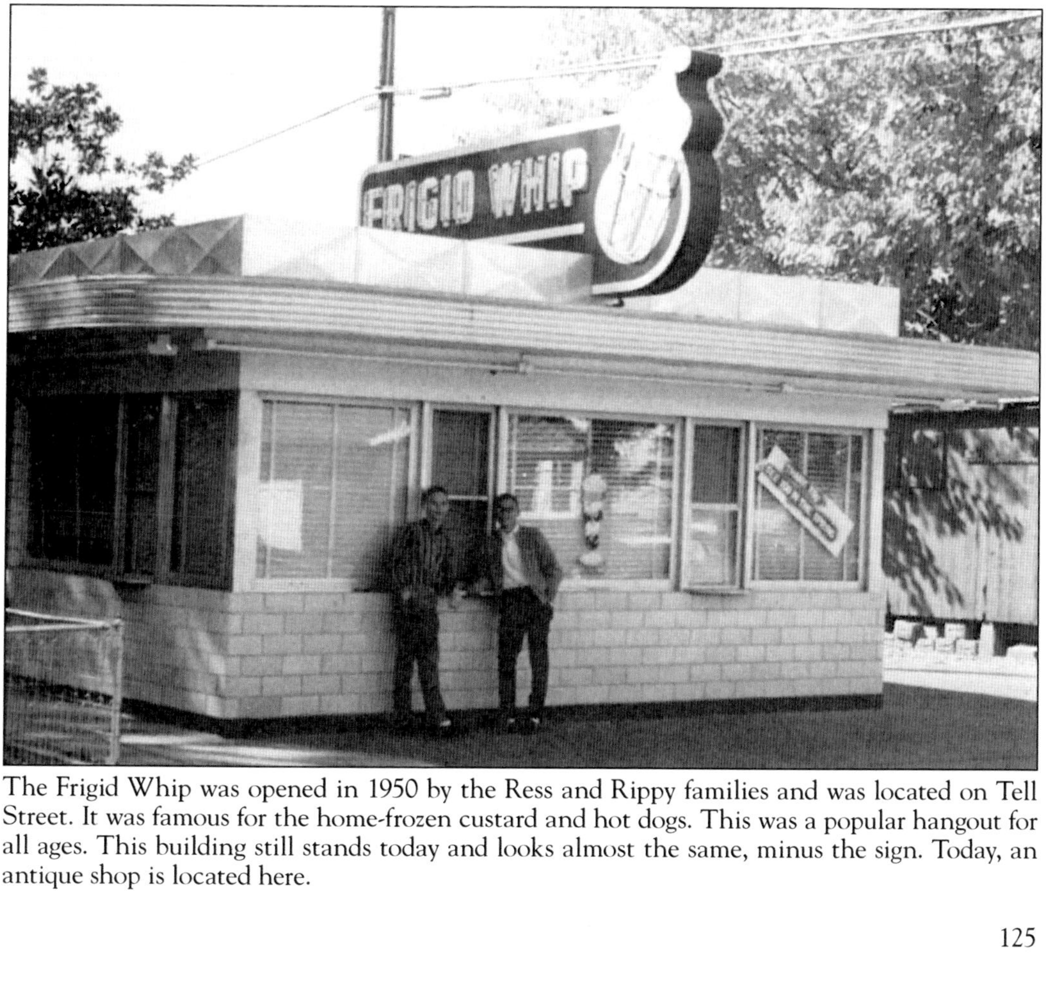

The Frigid Whip was opened in 1950 by the Ress and Rippy families and was located on Tell Street. It was famous for the home-frozen custard and hot dogs. This was a popular hangout for all ages. This building still stands today and looks almost the same, minus the sign. Today, an antique shop is located here.

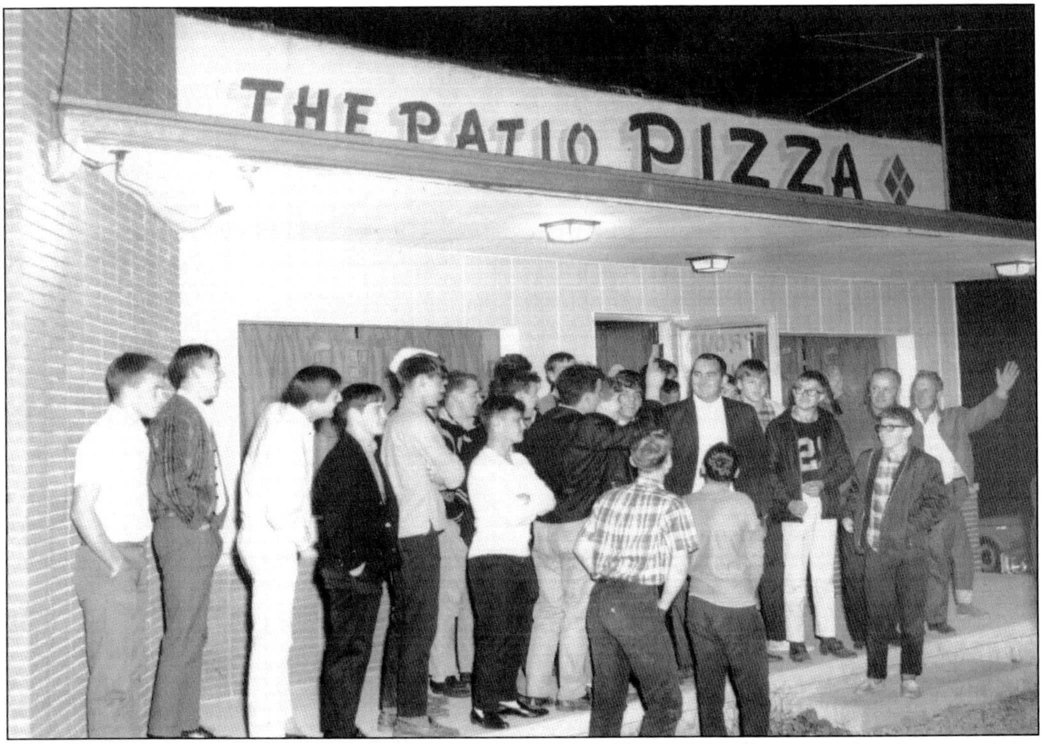

The Patio Pizza was a very popular place for teenagers to hangout. The Daum family owned the business and had mouthwatering pizza. Many remember playing pinball machines and Pong here. Sadly, this building burned down, but it was replaced by the Daum family with a new restaurant, the Patio. (Courtesy of Perry County Museum.)

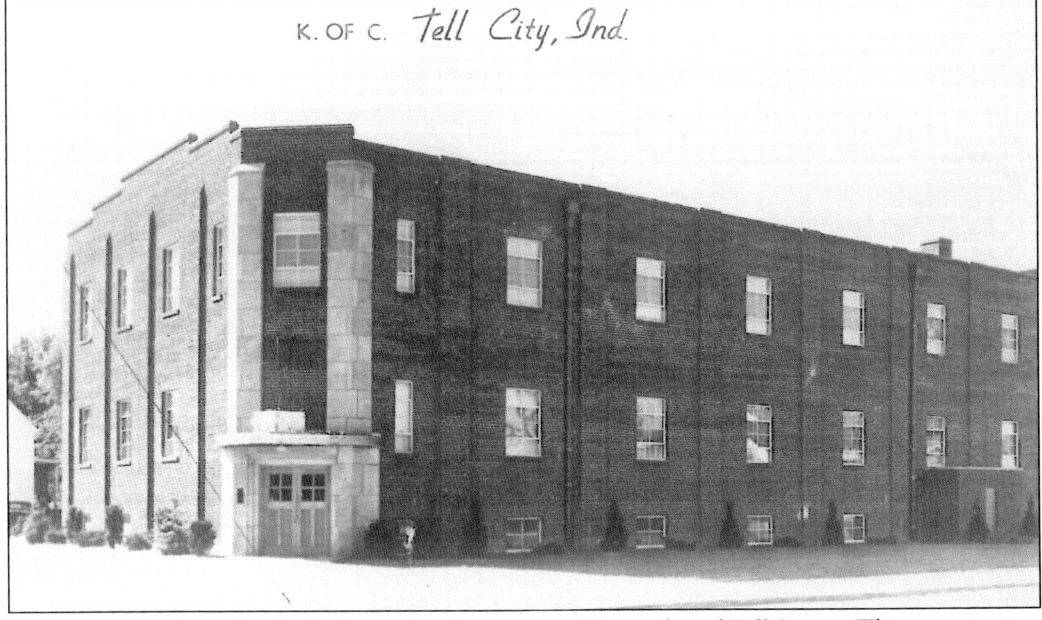

The Knights of Columbus hall is located at the corner of Eleventh and Tell Streets. This organization is still very active today.

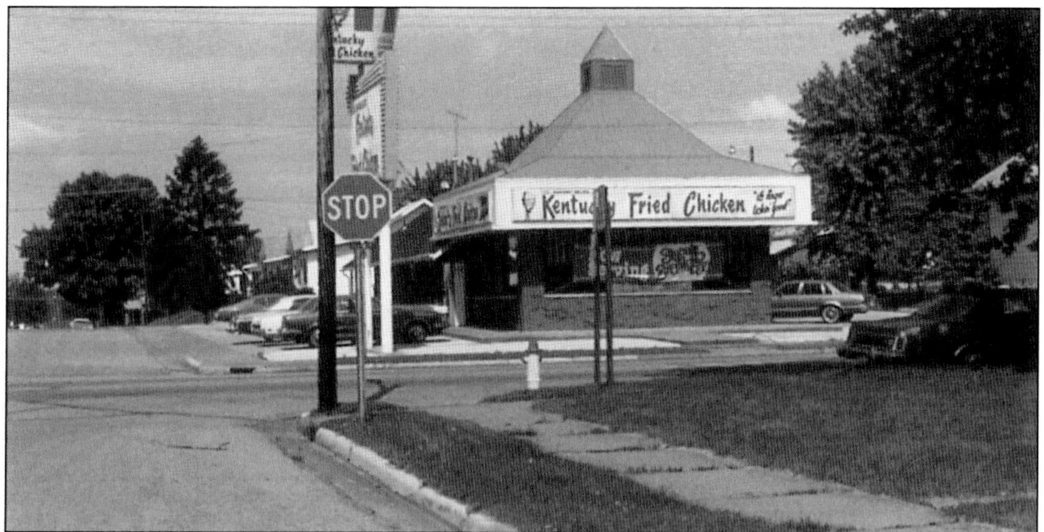

One of Tell City's earliest fast-food chains in Tell City was Kentucky Fried Chicken, located at 1101 Twelfth Street in the former Billy Briar Restaurant. The building was remodeled after this photograph was taken. This Kentucky Fried Chicken closed in the 1990s. (Courtesy of Tell City Historical Society.)

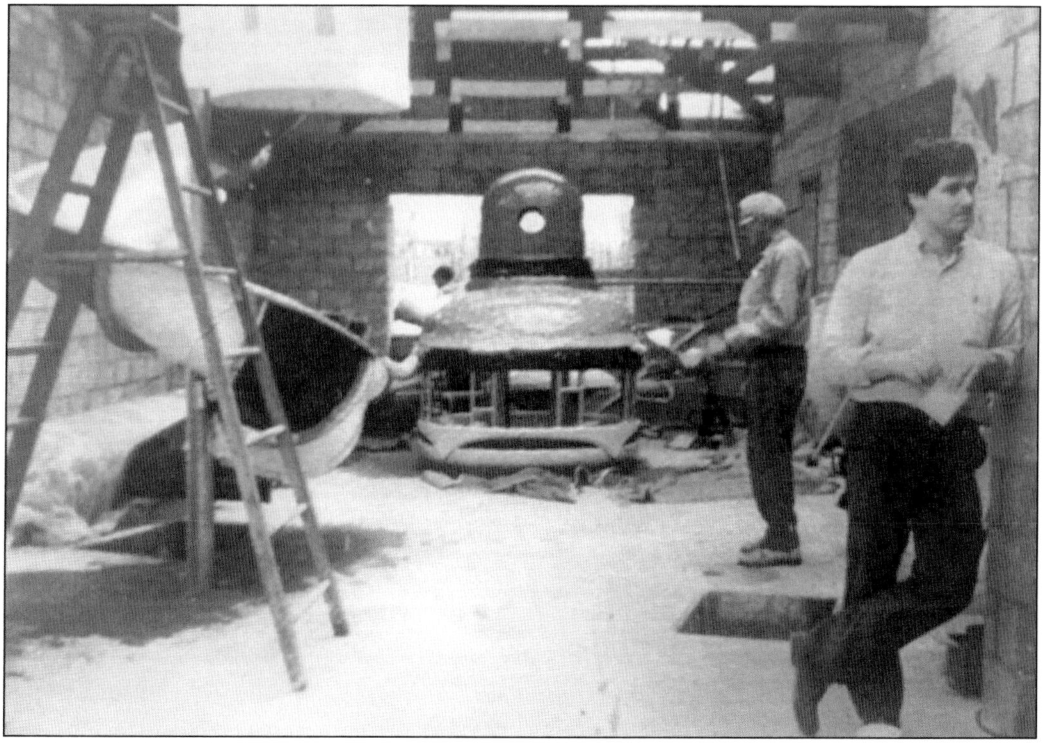

Tell City's McDonald's had one of the first indoor McDonaldland playgrounds in the country—only three existed before Tell City's was built. The Kramer family knew the importance of kids and their establishment, so it was an easy decision when the McDonald's Corporation proposed the playground idea to the Kramers. The building was demolished in 2015 and replaced with a new, modern McDonald's with an indoor PlayPlace. (Courtesy of Tom and Susan Kramer.)

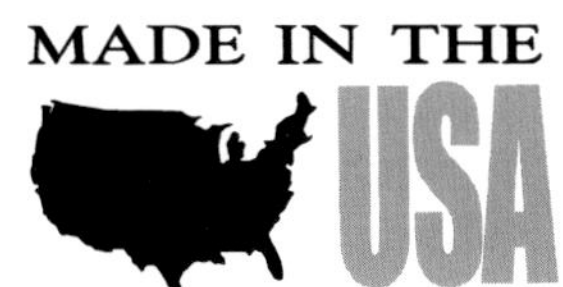
MADE IN THE
USA